Just The facts101

Textbook Key Facts

The Theory of Christian Psychology

by Cram101

Texbook NOT Included

Table of Contents

Just The Facts101

Exam Prep for

The Theory of Christian Psychology

Just The Facts101 Exam Prep is your link from
the textbook and lecture to your exams.

Just The Facts101 Exam Preps are unauthorized and comprehensive reviews of your textbooks.

Textbook publishers and textbook authors do not participate in or contribute to these reviews.

Just The Facts101 Exam Prep

eAIN 439818

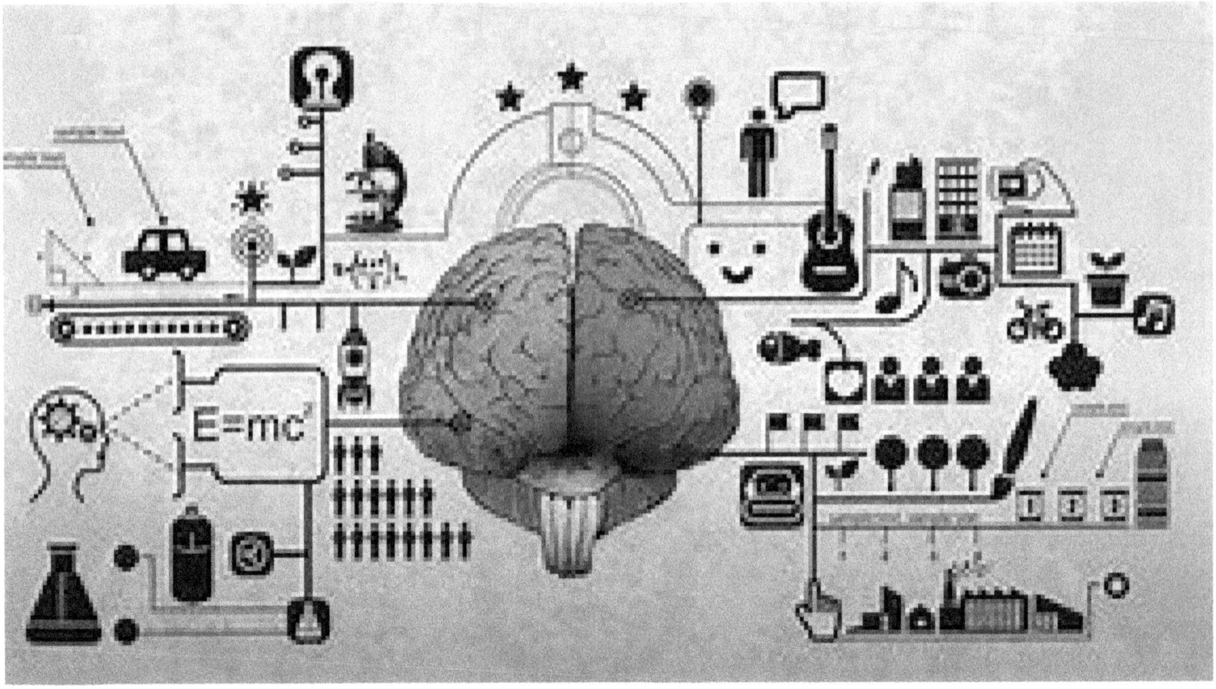

Foundations of Psychology

Psychology is the study of behavior and mind, embracing all aspects of human experience. It is an academic discipline and an applied science which seeks to understand individuals and groups by establishing general principles and researching specific cases.

:: Mood disorders ::

_________, also known as mood affective disorders, is a group of conditions where a disturbance in the person's mood is the main underlying feature. The classification is in the Diagnostic and Statistical Manual of Mental Disorders and International Classification of Diseases .

Exam Probability: **High**

1. *Answer choices:*

(see index for correct answer)

- a. Mood disorder
- b. Hypomania
- c. Inositol monophosphatase
- d. Blunted affect

Guidance: level 1

:: Motivation ::

_________ is an individual`s subjective evaluation of their own worth. _________ encompasses beliefs about oneself as well as emotional states, such as triumph, despair, pride, and shame. Smith and Mackie defined it by saying "The self-concept is what we think about the self; _________ , is the positive or negative evaluations of the self, as in how we feel about it."

Exam Probability: **High**

2. *Answer choices:*

(see index for correct answer)

- a. Business fable
- b. Effort optimism
- c. Reinforcing success
- d. Self-esteem

Guidance: level 1

:: Discrimination ::

In human social behavior, _________ is treatment or consideration of, or making a distinction towards, a person based on the group, class, or category to which the person is perceived to belong. These include age, colour, criminal record, height, disability, ethnicity, family status, gender identity, generation, genetic characteristics, marital status, nationality, race, religion, sex, and sexual orientation. _________ consists of treatment of an individual or group, based on their actual or perceived membership in a certain group or social category, "in a way that is worse than the way people are usually treated". It involves the group`s initial reaction or interaction going on to influence the individual`s actual behavior towards the group leader or the group, restricting members of one group from opportunities or privileges that are available to another group, leading to the exclusion of the individual or entities based on illogical or irrational decision making.

Exam Probability: **Low**

3. *Answer choices:*

(see index for correct answer)

- a. Dalit
- b. Days of Remembrance of the Victims of the Holocaust
- c. The Price of Admission
- d. Discrimination

Guidance: level 1

:: Neuropsychology ::

_________ is the physiological and psychological state of being awoken or of sense organs stimulated to a point of perception. It involves activation of the ascending reticular activating system in the brain, which mediates wakefulness, the autonomic nervous system, and the endocrine system, leading to increased heart rate and blood pressure and a condition of sensory alertness, mobility, and readiness to respond.

Exam Probability: **Low**

4. *Answer choices:*

(see index for correct answer)

- a. Psychological refractory period
- b. Neurological reparative therapy
- c. Arousal
- d. Salience

Guidance: level 1

:: Devices to alter consciousness ::

__________ is the process of gaining greater awareness of many physiological functions primarily using instruments that provide information on the activity of those same systems, with a goal of being able to manipulate them at will. Some of the processes that can be controlled include brainwaves, muscle tone, skin conductance, heart rate and pain perception. In __________, you are connected to electrical sensors that help you receive information about your body .

Exam Probability: **High**

5. *Answer choices:*

(see index for correct answer)

- a. I-Doser
- b. Hemi-Sync
- c. God helmet
- d. Biofeedback

Guidance: level 1

:: Applied psychology ::

_________ is the use of psychological methods and findings of scientific psychology to solve practical problems of human and animal behavior and experience. Mental health, organizational psychology, business management, education, health, product design, ergonomics, and law are just a few of the areas that have been influenced by the application of psychological principles and findings. Some of the areas of _________ include clinical psychology, counseling psychology, evolutionary psychology, industrial and organizational psychology, legal psychology, neuropsychology, occupational health psychology, human factors, forensic psychology, engineering psychology, school psychology, sports psychology, traffic psychology, community psychology, medical psychology. In addition, a number of specialized areas in the general field of psychology have applied branches . However, the lines between sub-branch specializations and major _________ categories are often blurred. For example, a human factors psychologist might use a cognitive psychology theory. This could be described as human factor psychology or as applied cognitive psychology.

Exam Probability: **Low**

6. *Answer choices:*

(see index for correct answer)

- a. Social marketing
- b. Applied psychology
- c. Educational psychologist
- d. Sport psychology

Guidance: level 1

:: History of psychology ::

The _________ is a psychological principle advanced by Edward Thorndike in 1898 on the matter of behavioral conditioning which states that "responses that produce a satisfying effect in a particular situation become more likely to occur again in that situation, and responses that produce a discomforting effect become less likely to occur again in thatsituation."

Exam Probability: **Medium**

7. *Answer choices:*

(see index for correct answer)

- a. Classical conditioning
- b. The Expression of the Emotions in Man and Animals
- c. Radical behaviorism
- d. Law of effect

Guidance: level 1

:: Social psychology ::

_________ , or intent to benefit others, is a social behavior that "benefit[s] other people or society as a whole", "such as helping, sharing, donating, co-operating, and volunteering". Obeying the rules and conforming to socially accepted behaviors are also regarded as _________ s. These actions may be motivated by empathy and by concern about the welfare and rights of others, as well as for egoistic or practical concerns, such as one`s social status or reputation, hope for direct or indirect reciprocity, or adherence to one`s perceived system of fairness. It may also be motivated by altruism, though the existence of pure altruism is somewhat disputed, and some have argued that this falls into philosophical rather than psychological realm of debate. Evidence suggests that pro sociality is central to the well-being of social groups across a range of scales, including schools. _________ in the classroom can have a significant impact on a student`s motivation for learning and contributions to the classroom and larger community. Empathy is a strong motive in eliciting _________ , and has deep evolutionary roots.

Exam Probability: **High**

8. *Answer choices:*

(see index for correct answer)

- a. Greater Good Science Center
- b. Closing time effect
- c. Role set
- d. Prosocial behavior

Guidance: level 1

:: Child care ::

_________ , otherwise known as day care, is the care and supervision of a child or multiple children at a time, whose ages range from six weeks to thirteen years. _________ is the action or skill of looking after children by a day-care center, nannies, babysitter, teachers or other providers. _________ is a broad topic that covers a wide spectrum of professionals, institutions, contexts, activities, and social and cultural conventions. Early _________ is an equally important and often overlooked component of child development. _________ providers can be children`s first teachers, and therefore play an integral role in systems of early childhood education. Quality care from a young age can have a substantial impact on the future successes of children. The main focus of childcare is on the development of the child, whether that be mental, social, or psychological.

Exam Probability: **High**

9. *Answer choices:*

(see index for correct answer)

- a. Nursery school
- b. Child care
- c. Childcare voucher scheme
- d. Anganwadi

Guidance: level 1

:: Psychiatry ::

_________ is the scientific study of mental disorders, including efforts to understand their genetic, biological, psychological, and social causes; develop classification schemes which can improve treatment planning and treatment outcomes; understand the course of psychiatric illnesses across all stages of development; more fully understand the manifestations of mental disorders; and investigate potentially effective treatments.

Exam Probability: **Low**

10. *Answer choices:*

(see index for correct answer)

- a. Shell shock
- b. Psychosis
- c. Psychopathology
- d. A Stranger in The Family: Culture, Families, and Therapy

Guidance: level 1

:: Cognitive disorders ::

_________ is a broad category of brain diseases that cause a long-term and often gradual decrease in the ability to think and remember that is great enough to affect a person's daily functioning. Other common symptoms include emotional problems, difficulties with language, and a decrease in motivation. A person's consciousness is usually not affected. A _________ diagnosis requires a change from a person's usual mental functioning and a greater decline than one would expect due to aging. These diseases also have a significant effect on a person's caregivers.

Exam Probability: **Low**

11. *Answer choices:*

(see index for correct answer)

- a. HIV-associated neurocognitive disorder
- b. Progressive nonfluent aphasia
- c. Dementia
- d. Postoperative cognitive dysfunction

Guidance: level 1

:: Phenomenology ::

_________ is the state or quality of awareness or of being aware of an external object or something within oneself. It has been defined variously in terms of sentience, awareness, qualia, subjectivity, the ability to experience or to feel, wakefulness, having a sense of selfhood or soul, the fact that there is something "that it is like" to "have" or "be" it, and the executive control system of the mind. Despite the difficulty in definition, many philosophers believe that there is a broadly shared underlying intuition about what _________ is. As Max Velmans and Susan Schneider wrote in The Blackwell Companion to _________ : "Anything that we are aware of at a given moment forms part of our _________ , making conscious experience at once the most familiar and most mysterious aspect of our lives."

Exam Probability: **Low**

12. *Answer choices:*

(see index for correct answer)

- a. Consciousness
- b. Munich phenomenology
- c. Phenomenon
- d. Fundamental ontology

Guidance: level 1

:: Stress ::

_________ is a wide spectrum of techniques and psychotherapies aimed at controlling a person`s level of stress, especially chronic stress, usually for the purpose of and for the motive of improving everyday functioning. In this context, the term `stress` refers only to a stress with significant negative consequences, or distress in the terminology advocated by Hans Selye, rather than what he calls eustress, a stress whose consequences are helpful or otherwise.

Exam Probability: **Low**

13. *Answer choices:*

(see index for correct answer)

- a. Chronic stress
- b. Life Events and Difficulties Schedule
- c. Stress ball
- d. Occupational burnout

Guidance: level 1

:: Cerebrum ::

The vertebrate cerebrum is formed by two __________ s that are separated by a groove, the longitudinal fissure. The brain can thus be described as being divided into left and right __________ s. Each of these hemispheres has an outer layer of grey matter, the cerebral cortex, that is supported by an inner layer of white matter. In eutherian mammals, the hemispheres are linked by the corpus callosum, a very large bundle of nerve fibers. Smaller commissures, including the anterior commissure, the posterior commissure and the fornix, also join the hemispheres and these are also present in other vertebrates. These commissures transfer information between the two hemispheres to coordinate localized functions.

Exam Probability: **High**

14. *Answer choices:*

(see index for correct answer)

- a. Globus pallidus
- b. Interior of the cerebral hemispheres
- c. Lingual gyrus
- d. Precuneus

Guidance: level 1

:: Reasoning ::

_________ s are steps in reasoning, moving from premises to logical consequences; etymologically, the word infer means to "carry forward". _________ is theoretically traditionally divided into deduction and induction, a distinction that in Europe dates at least to Aristotle . Deduction is _________ deriving logical conclusions from premises known or assumed to be true, with the laws of valid _________ being studied in logic. Induction is _________ from particular premises to a universal conclusion. A third type of _________ is sometimes distinguished, notably by Charles Sanders Peirce, distinguishing abduction from induction, where abduction is _________ to the best explanation.

Exam Probability: **Medium**

15. *Answer choices:*

(see index for correct answer)

- a. Qualitative reasoning
- b. Visual reasoning
- c. Akrasia
- d. Inference

Guidance: level 1

:: Phenomenology ::

_________ is any of several aspects of perception and consciousness in such fields as psychology, philosophy and epistemology.

Exam Probability: **High**

16. *Answer choices:*

(see index for correct answer)

- a. Eidetic reduction
- b. Central European Institute of Philosophy
- c. Psychosophy
- d. Phenomenological quantum gravity

Guidance: level 1

:: Toilet training ::

The _________ is the second stage in Sigmund Freud`s theory of psychosexual development, lasting from age 18 months to three years. According to Freud, the anus is the primary erogenous zone and pleasure is derived from controlling bladder and bowel movement. The major conflict issue during this stage is toilet training. A fixation at this stage can result in a personality that is too rigid or one that is too disordered.

Exam Probability: **Medium**

17. *Answer choices:*

(see index for correct answer)

- a. Anal stage
- b. Diurnal enuresis

- c. Wendy Sweeney
- d. UnderJams

Guidance: level 1

:: Heuristic algorithms ::

A _________ technique , often called simply a _________ , is any approach to problem solving or self-discovery that employs a practical method, not guaranteed to be optimal, perfect, logical, or rational, but instead sufficient for reaching an immediate goal. Where finding an optimal solution is impossible or impractical, _________ methods can be used to speed up the process of finding a satisfactory solution. _________ s can be mental shortcuts that ease the cognitive load of making a decision. Examples that employ _________ s include using a rule of thumb, an educated guess, an intuitive judgment, a guesstimate, profiling, or common sense.

Exam Probability: **Medium**

18. *Answer choices:*

(see index for correct answer)

- a. HeuristicLab
- b. Thompson sampling
- c. Nearest neighbour algorithm
- d. 3-opt

Guidance: level 1

:: Psychosis ::

__________ is a mental disorder characterized by abnormal behavior, strange speech, and a decreased ability to understand reality. Other symptoms include false beliefs, unclear or confused thinking, hearing voices that do not exist, reduced social engagement and emotional expression, and lack of motivation. People with __________ often have additional mental health problems such as anxiety, depression, or substance-use disorders. Symptoms typically come on gradually, begin in young adulthood, and, in many cases, never resolve.

Exam Probability: **Low**

19. *Answer choices:*

(see index for correct answer)

- a. Schizophrenia
- b. Americus Dotter
- c. Unitary psychosis
- d. Ghost sickness

Guidance: level 1

:: Communication disorders ::

__________ is an inability to comprehend or formulate language because of damage to specific brain regions. This damage is typically caused by a cerebral vascular accident , or head trauma; however, these are not the only possible causes. To be diagnosed with __________ , a person's speech or language must be significantly impaired in one of the four communication modalities following acquired brain injury or have significant decline over a short time period . The four communication modalities are auditory comprehension, verbal expression, reading and writing, and functional communication.

Exam Probability: **High**

20. *Answer choices:*

(see index for correct answer)

- a. Aphasia
- b. International Stuttering Association
- c. Deafness
- d. Scanning speech

Guidance: level 1

:: Cognitive science ::

_________ is the process of acquiring new, or modifying existing, knowledge, behaviors, skills, values, or preferences. The ability to learn is possessed by humans, animals, and some machines; there is also evidence for some kind of _________ in some plants. Some _________ is immediate, induced by a single event , but much skill and knowledge accumulates from repeated experiences. The changes induced by _________ often last a lifetime, and it is hard to distinguish learned material that seems to be "lost" from that which cannot be retrieved.

Exam Probability: **Low**

21. *Answer choices:*

(see index for correct answer)

- a. Language and Communication Technologies
- b. Learning sciences
- c. Simplicity theory
- d. Learning

Guidance: level 1

:: Philosophers of mind ::

_________ was an American philosopher and psychologist, and the first educator to offer a psychology course in the United States. James was a leading thinker of the late nineteenth century, one of the most influential U.S. philosophers, and has been labelled the "Father of American psychology".

Exam Probability: **High**

22. *Answer choices:*

(see index for correct answer)

- a. William James
- b. Alexius Meinong
- c. Friedrich Kambartel
- d. Georg Henrik von Wright

Guidance: level 1

:: Consciousness ::

_________ is the capacity for introspection and the ability to recognize oneself as an individual separate from the environment and other individuals. It is not to be confused with consciousness in the sense of qualia. While consciousness is being aware of one`s environment and body and lifestyle, _________ is the recognition of that awareness. _________ is how an individual consciously knows and understands their own character, feelings, motives, and desires. There are two broad categories of _________ : internal _________ and external _________ .

Exam Probability: **High**

23. *Answer choices:*

(see index for correct answer)

- a. Mental substance
- b. Chaitanya
- c. Animal consciousness
- d. Self-awareness

Guidance: level 1

:: Mental health ::

__________ is defined as the level of psychological well-being or an absence of mental illness. It is the state of someone who is "functioning at a satisfactory level of emotional and behavioural adjustment". From the perspectives of positive psychology or of holism, __________ may include an individual`s ability to enjoy life, and to create a balance between life activities and efforts to achieve psychological resilience.According to the World Health Organization , __________ includes "subjective well-being, perceived self-efficacy, autonomy, competence, inter-generational dependence, and self-actualization of one`s intellectual and emotional potential, among others." The WHO further states that the well-being of an individual is encompassed in the realization of their abilities, coping with normal stresses of life, productive work and contribution to their community.Cultural differences, subjective assessments, and competing professional theories all affect how one defines " __________ ".

Exam Probability: **Medium**

24. *Answer choices:*

(see index for correct answer)

- a. Person-centred planning

- b. Child and Youth Worker
- c. Mental health
- d. Care programme approach

Guidance: level 1

:: Behavioural sciences ::

_________ is the scientific study of how people`s thoughts, feelings and behaviors are influenced by the actual, imagined or implied presence of others. In this definition, scientific refers to the empirical investigation using the scientific method. The terms thoughts, feelings and behavior refer to psychological variables that can be measured in humans. The statement that others` presence may be imagined or implied suggests that humans are malleable to social influences even when alone, such as when watching television looking at reality shows,music videos and movies they can be influenced to follow the behaviour in the visual setting or following internalized cultural norms. Social psychologists typically explain human behavior as a result of the interaction of mental states and social situations.

Exam Probability: **Low**

25. *Answer choices:*

(see index for correct answer)

- a. Future Orientation Index
- b. Necrophoresis
- c. Level of analysis
- d. Social psychology

Guidance: level 1

:: Cognitive science ::

_________ is the scientific field that is concerned with the study of the biological processes and aspects that underlie cognition, with a specific focus on the neural connections in the brain which are involved in mental processes. It addresses the questions of how cognitive activities are affected or controlled by neural circuits in the brain. _________ is a branch of both neuroscience and psychology, overlapping with disciplines such as behavioral neuroscience, cognitive psychology, physiological psychology and affective neuroscience. _________ relies upon theories in cognitive science coupled with evidence from neurobiology, and computational modeling.

Exam Probability: **Medium**

26. *Answer choices:*

(see index for correct answer)

- a. Cognitive Systems Research
- b. Narrative inquiry
- c. Learning sciences
- d. Cognitive neuroscience

Guidance: level 1

:: Cognitive science ::

_________ s are mental representations, abstract objects or abilities that make up the fundamental building blocks of thoughts and beliefs. They play an important role in all aspects of cognition.

Exam Probability: **High**

27. *Answer choices:*

(see index for correct answer)

- a. Learning sciences
- b. Concept
- c. Conceptual metaphor
- d. Situated cognition

Guidance: level 1

:: Cybernetics ::

A _________ is a group of interacting or interrelated entities that form a unified whole. A _________ is delineated by its spatial and temporal boundaries, surrounded and influenced by its environment, described by its structure and purpose and expressed in its functioning.

Exam Probability: **Low**

28. *Answer choices:*

(see index for correct answer)

- a. LIFO
- b. Systems science
- c. Good Regulator
- d. Principia Cybernetica

Guidance: level 1

:: Alcohol abuse ::

__________ is a mental disorder that can develop after a person is exposed to a traumatic event, such as sexual assault, warfare, traffic collisions, or other threats on a person`s life. Symptoms may include disturbing thoughts, feelings, or dreams related to the events, mental or physical distress to trauma-related cues, attempts to avoid trauma-related cues, alterations in how a person thinks and feels, and an increase in the fight-or-flight response. These symptoms last for more than a month after the event. Young children are less likely to show distress, but instead may express their memories through play. A person with PTSD is at a higher risk for suicide and intentional self-harm.

Exam Probability: **Medium**

29. *Answer choices:*

(see index for correct answer)

- a. Seeing pink elephants
- b. Severity of Alcohol Dependence Questionnaire
- c. Cirrhosis

- d. Calcium carbimide

Guidance: level 1

:: Signal transduction ::

A _________ is any member of a class of signaling molecules produced by glands in multicellular organisms that are transported by the circulatory system to target distant organs to regulate physiology and behavior. _________ s have diverse chemical structures, mainly of three classes: eicosanoids, steroids, and amino acid/protein derivatives . The glands that secrete _________ s comprise the endocrine signaling system. The term _________ is sometimes extended to include chemicals produced by cells that affect the same cell or nearby cells .

Exam Probability: **Medium**

30. *Answer choices:*

(see index for correct answer)

- a. Retinal
- b. CHEK2
- c. Histamine receptor
- d. Adhesion G protein-coupled receptors

Guidance: level 1

:: Psychology ::

A _________ is the formulation of general concepts from specific instances by abstracting common properties. _________ s posit the existence of a domain or set of elements, as well as one or more common characteristics shared by those elements . As such, they are the essential basis of all valid deductive inferences. The process of verification is necessary to determine whether a _________ holds true for any given situation.

Exam Probability: **Medium**

31. *Answer choices:*

(see index for correct answer)

- a. O. Carl Simonton
- b. Diverspection
- c. Psychic numbing
- d. Macabre constant

Guidance: level 1

:: Motivation ::

_________ involves the development of an action plan designed to motivate and guide a person or group toward a goal. _________ can be guided by goal-setting criteria such as SMART criteria. _________ is a major component of personal-development and management literature.

Exam Probability: **Medium**

32. *Answer choices:*

(see index for correct answer)

- a. Locus of control
- b. Dopamine
- c. Business fable
- d. Motivational interviewing

Guidance: level 1

:: Behavioral concepts ::

_________ is a form of non-associative learning in which an innate response to a stimulus decreases after repeated or prolonged presentations of that stimulus. Responses that habituate include those that involve the intact organism or those that involve only components of the organism . The broad ubiquity of _________ across all biologic phyla has resulted in it being called "the simplest, most universal form of learning...as fundamental a characteristic of life as DNA." Functionally-speaking, by diminishing the response to an inconsequential stimulus, _________ is thought to free-up cognitive resources to other stimuli that are associated with biologically important events . For example, organisms may habituate to repeated sudden loud noises when they learn these have no consequences. A progressive decline of a behavior in a _________ procedure may also reflect nonspecific effects such as fatigue, which must be ruled out when the interest is in _________ . _________ may also be clinically relevant, as a number of neuropsychiatric conditions, including autism, schizophrenia, migraine, and Tourette`s, show reductions in _________ to a variety of stimulus-types both simple and complex .

Exam Probability: **Medium**

33. *Answer choices:*

(see index for correct answer)

- a. Attention restoration theory
- b. Latent inhibition
- c. Habituation
- d. Imitative learning

Guidance: level 1

:: Memory ::

_________ is the stage of the Atkinson–Shiffrin memory model where informative knowledge is held indefinitely. It is defined in contrast to short-term and working memory, which persist for only about 18 to 30 seconds. _________ is commonly labelled as explicit memory , as well as episodic memory, semantic memory, autobiographical memory, and implicit memory .

Exam Probability: **High**

34. *Answer choices:*

(see index for correct answer)

- a. Now Print!
- b. Hyperthymesia

- c. Folk memory
- d. Long-term memory

Guidance: level 1

:: Misogyny ::

_________ is a type of harassment technique that relates to a sexual nature and the unwelcome or inappropriate promise of rewards in exchange for sexual favors. _________ includes a range of actions from mild transgressions to sexual abuse or assault. Harassment can occur in many different social settings such as the workplace, the home, school, churches, etc. Harassers or victims may be of any gender.

Exam Probability: **Low**

35. *Answer choices:*

(see index for correct answer)

- a. Finkbeiner test
- b. Problem Solved
- c. Misogyny
- d. Violence against women

Guidance: level 1

:: Cerebrum ::

The _________ , also callosal commissure, is a wide, thick, nerve tract consisting of a flat bundle of commissural fibers, beneath the cerebral cortex in the brain. The _________ is only found in placental mammals. It spans part of the longitudinal fissure, connecting the left and right cerebral hemispheres, enabling communication between them. It is the largest white matter structure in the human brain, about ten centimetres in length and consisting of 200300 million axonal projections.

Exam Probability: **High**

36. *Answer choices:*

(see index for correct answer)

- a. Pontocerebellar fibers
- b. Corpus callosum
- c. Telencephalon
- d. Posterior parahippocampal gyrus

Guidance: level 1

:: Rhetorical techniques ::

_________ is the pattern of narrative development that aims to make vivid a place, object, character, or group. _________ is one of four rhetorical modes , along with exposition, argumentation, and narration. In practice it would be difficult to write literature that drew on just one of the four basic modes.

Exam Probability: **Low**

37. *Answer choices:*

(see index for correct answer)

- a. Tautophrase
- b. Hyperbaton
- c. Description
- d. Antonomasia

Guidance: level 1

:: Memory ::

_________ is one of the two main types of long-term human memory. It is acquired and used unconsciously, and can affect thoughts and behaviours. One of its most common forms is procedural memory, which helps people performing certain tasks without conscious awareness of these previous experiences.

Exam Probability: **High**

38. *Answer choices:*

(see index for correct answer)

- a. Memory work
- b. Subconscious Password
- c. Autobiographical memory
- d. Implicit memory

Guidance: level 1

:: Personality ::

The first personality assessment measures were developed in the 1920s and were intended to ease the process of personnel selection, particularly in the armed forces. Since these early efforts, a wide variety of personality scales and questionnaires have been developed, including the Minnesota Multiphasic Personality Inventory , the Sixteen Personality Factor Questionnaire , the Comrey Personality Scales , among many others. Although popular especially among personnel consultants, the Myers–Briggs Type Indicator has numerous psychometric deficiencies. More recently, a number of instruments based on the Five Factor Model of personality have been constructed such as the Revised NEO Personality Inventory. However, the Big Five and related Five Factor Model have been challenged for accounting for less than two-thirds of the known trait variance in the normal personality sphere alone.

Exam Probability: **High**

39. *Answer choices:*

(see index for correct answer)

- a. Personality development
- b. Kingdomality
- c. Personality test
- d. Positive affectivity

Guidance: level 1

:: Consciousness ::

_________ is the knowledge or mastery of an event or subject gained through involvement in or exposure to it. Terms in philosophy such as "empirical knowledge" or "a posteriori knowledge" are used to refer to knowledge based on _________ . A person with considerable _________ in a specific field can gain a reputation as an expert. The concept of _________ generally refers to know-how or procedural knowledge, rather than propositional knowledge: on-the-job training rather than book-learning.

Exam Probability: **Low**

40. *Answer choices:*

(see index for correct answer)

- a. Experience
- b. Consciousness Industry
- c. Self-conscious
- d. Functional approach

Guidance: level 1

:: Psychology ::

A _________ studies normal and abnormal mental states, cognitive, emotional, and social processes and behavior by observing, interpreting, and recording how individuals relate to one another and to their environments. To become a _________ , a person often completes a graduate university degree in psychology, but in most jurisdictions, members of other behavioral professions can also evaluate, diagnose, treat, and study mental processes.

Exam Probability: **Medium**

41. *Answer choices:*

(see index for correct answer)

- a. Trans-species psychology
- b. Kappa effect
- c. Icarus complex
- d. Psychologist

Guidance: level 1

:: Neuroanatomy ::

A _________ is an enclosed, cable-like bundle of _________ fibres called axons, in the peripheral nervous system. A _________ provides a common pathway for the electrochemical _________ impulses called action potentials that are transmitted along each of the axons to peripheral organs or, in the case of sensory _________ s, from the periphery back to the central nervous system. Each axon within the _________ is an extension of an individual neuron, along with other supportive cells such as Schwann cells that coat the axons in myelin.

Exam Probability: **High**

42. *Answer choices:*

(see index for correct answer)

- a. Catecholaminergic cell groups
- b. Lunate sulcus
- c. Supratentorial region
- d. Nerve

Guidance: level 1

:: Educational psychology ::

_________ is a statistical method used to describe variability among observed, correlated variables in terms of a potentially lower number of unobserved variables called factors. For example, it is possible that variations in six observed variables mainly reflect the variations in two unobserved variables. _________ searches for such joint variations in response to unobserved latent variables. The observed variables are modelled as linear combinations of the potential factors, plus "error" terms. _________ aims to find independent latent variables.

Exam Probability: **Medium**

43. *Answer choices:*

(see index for correct answer)

- a. Educational technology
- b. Cognitive tutor
- c. Institutional pedagogy
- d. Factor analysis

Guidance: level 1

:: Psychological schools ::

_________ is a type of psychotherapy developed by American psychiatrist Aaron T. Beck. CT is one of the therapeutic approaches within the larger group of cognitive behavioral therapies and was first expounded by Beck in the 1960s. _________ is based on the cognitive model, which states that thoughts, feelings and behavior are all connected, and that individuals can move toward overcoming difficulties and meeting their goals by identifying and changing unhelpful or inaccurate thinking, problematic behavior, and distressing emotional responses. This involves the individual working collaboratively with the therapist to develop skills for testing and modifying beliefs, identifying distorted thinking, relating to others in different ways, and changing behaviors. A tailored cognitive case conceptualization is developed by the cognitive therapist as a roadmap to understand the individual`s internal reality, select appropriate interventions and identify areas of distress.

Exam Probability: **Low**

44. *Answer choices:*

(see index for correct answer)

- a. Psychical school
- b. Positive psychology

- c. Gestalt psychology
- d. Post-cognitivist psychology

Guidance: level 1

:: Autonomic nervous system ::

The _________ , formerly the vegetative nervous system, is a division of the peripheral nervous system that supplies smooth muscle and glands, and thus influences the function of internal organs. The _________ is a control system that acts largely unconsciously and regulates bodily functions such as the heart rate, digestion, respiratory rate, pupillary response, urination, and sexual arousal. This system is the primary mechanism in control of the fight-or-flight response.

Exam Probability: **Medium**

45. *Answer choices:*

(see index for correct answer)

- a. Vagus nerve
- b. Sympathetic trunk
- c. Non-noradrenergic, non-cholinergic transmitter
- d. San Francisco Syncope Rule

Guidance: level 1

:: Behavioural sciences ::

_________ is an integration of science, theory, and clinical knowledge for the purpose of understanding, preventing, and relieving psychologically-based distress or dysfunction and to promote subjective well-being and personal development. Central to its practice are psychological assessment, clinical formulation, and psychotherapy, although clinical psychologists also engage in research, teaching, consultation, forensic testimony, and program development and administration. In many countries, _________ is a regulated mental health profession.

Exam Probability: **High**

46. *Answer choices:*

(see index for correct answer)

- a. Abnormal psychology
- b. Clinical psychology
- c. Criminology
- d. Behavioral immune system

Guidance: level 1

:: Nonverbal communication ::

It includes the use of visual cues such as body language , distance and physical environments/appearance, of voice and of touch . It can also include the use of time and eye contact and the actions of looking while talking and listening, frequency of glances, patterns of fixation, pupil dilation, and blink rate .

Exam Probability: **High**

47. *Answer choices:*

(see index for correct answer)

- a. Facepalm
- b. Nonverbal communication
- c. Message stick
- d. Yellow flag

Guidance: level 1

:: Psychoanalytic theory ::

_________ is the theory of personality organization and the dynamics of personality development that guides psychoanalysis, a clinical method for treating psychopathology. First laid out by Sigmund Freud in the late 19th century, _________ has undergone many refinements since his work. _________ came to full prominence in the last third of the twentieth century as part of the flow of critical discourse regarding psychological treatments after the 1960s, long after Freud`s death in 1939, and its validity is now widely disputed or rejected. Freud had ceased his analysis of the brain and his physiological studies and shifted his focus to the study of the mind and the related psychological attributes making up the mind, and on treatment using free association and the phenomena of transference. His study emphasized the recognition of childhood events that could influence the mental functioning of adults. His examination of the genetic and then the developmental aspects gave the _________ its characteristics. Starting with his publication of The Interpretation of Dreams in 1899, his theories began to gain prominence.

Exam Probability: **Low**

48. *Answer choices:*

(see index for correct answer)

- a. Brain lesion theory
- b. Lene Auestad
- c. Victor Tausk
- d. Psychoanalytic theory

Guidance: level 1

:: Adolescence ::

A secondary school is both an organization that provides secondary education and the building where this takes place. Some secondary schools can provide both lower secondary education and upper secondary education , but these can also be provided in separate schools, as in the American middle and _______ system.

Exam Probability: **High**

49. *Answer choices:*

(see index for correct answer)

- a. National Longitudinal Study of Adolescent Health
- b. Off the derech
- c. High school
- d. Adolescent Mentalization-Based Integrative Treatment

Guidance: level 1

:: Social issues ::

_______ involves alteration of the social order of a society. It may include changes in social institutions, social behaviours or social relations.

Exam Probability: **Low**

50. *Answer choices:*

(see index for correct answer)

- a. Social change
- b. Social services
- c. Social rights
- d. The Globalized City

Guidance: level 1

:: Stereotypes ::

In social psychology, a _________ is an over-generalized belief about a particular category of people. _________ s are generalized because one assumes that the _________ is true for each individual person in the category. While such generalizations may be useful when making quick decisions, they may be erroneous when applied to particular individuals. _________ s encourage prejudice and may arise for a number of reasons.

Exam Probability: **High**

51. *Answer choices:*

(see index for correct answer)

- a. Stuff White People Like
- b. Malandragem
- c. Stereotype
- d. Ugly American

Guidance: level 1

:: Emotions ::

_________ is the feeling of apprehension, lack of comfort, or awkwardness especially when a person is around other people. This commonly occurs in new situations or with unfamiliar people. _________ can be a characteristic of people who have low self-esteem. Stronger forms of _________ are usually referred to as social anxiety or social phobia.The primary defining characteristic of _________ is a largely ego-driven fear of what other people will think of a person`s behavior. This results in a person becoming scared of doing or saying what they want to out of fear of negative reactions, being laughed at, humiliated or patronised, criticism or rejection. A shy person may simply opt to avoid social situations instead.

Exam Probability: **Medium**

52. *Answer choices:*

(see index for correct answer)

- a. Shyness
- b. Sadness
- c. Reverence
- d. Acedia

Guidance: level 1

:: Behaviorism ::

_________ is a broad term referring to clinical psychotherapy that uses techniques derived from behaviorism. Those who practice _________ tend to look at specific, learned behaviors and how the environment influences those behaviors. Those who practice _________ are called behaviourists, or behavior analysts. They tend to look for treatment outcomes that are objectively measurable. _________ does not involve one specific method but it has a wide range of techniques that can be used to treat a person`s psychological problems.

Exam Probability: **Low**

53. *Answer choices:*

(see index for correct answer)

- a. Matching law
- b. Operant conditioning
- c. Behavior therapy
- d. Counterconditioning

Guidance: level 1

:: Menopause ::

__________ , also known as the climacteric, is the time in most women`s lives when menstrual periods stop permanently, and they are no longer able to bear children. __________ typically occurs between 49 and 52 years of age. Medical professionals often define __________ as having occurred when a woman has not had any vaginal bleeding for a year. It may also be defined by a decrease in hormone production by the ovaries. In those who have had surgery to remove their uterus but still have ovaries, __________ may be considered to have occurred at the time of the surgery or when their hormone levels fell. Following the removal of the uterus, symptoms typically occur earlier, at an average of 45 years of age.

Exam Probability: **Low**

54. *Answer choices:*

(see index for correct answer)

- a. Menerba
- b. Grandmother hypothesis
- c. Andropause
- d. Hormone replacement therapy

Guidance: level 1

:: Intelligence ::

In psychology, fluid and __________ are factors of general intelligence, originally identified by Raymond Cattell. Concepts of fluid and __________ were further developed by Cattell`s student John L. Horn.

Exam Probability: **Medium**

55. *Answer choices:*

(see index for correct answer)

- a. Fluid intelligence
- b. Yves-Michel Marti
- c. Moral intelligence
- d. Evolution of human intelligence

Guidance: level 1

:: Neurological disorders in children ::

__________ is a group of neurological disorders characterized by epileptic seizures. Epileptic seizures are episodes that can vary from brief and nearly undetectable periods to long periods of vigorous shaking. These episodes can result in physical injuries, including occasionally broken bones. In __________, seizures tend to recur and, as a rule, have no immediate underlying cause. Isolated seizures that are provoked by a specific cause such as poisoning are not deemed to represent __________. People with __________ may be treated differently in various areas of the world and experience varying degrees of social stigma due to their condition.

Exam Probability: **Low**

56. *Answer choices:*

(see index for correct answer)

- a. Batten disease
- b. Myoclonic astatic epilepsy
- c. Metachromatic leukodystrophy
- d. Epilepsy

Guidance: level 1

:: Motivation ::

A _________ is an idea of the future or desired result that a person or a group of people envisions, plans and commits to achieve. People endeavor to reach _________ s within a finite time by setting deadlines.

Exam Probability: **Medium**

57. *Answer choices:*

(see index for correct answer)

- a. Goal
- b. Burnout
- c. Work motivation
- d. Keep Calm and Carry On

Guidance: level 1

:: Euphoriants ::

__________ is a central nervous system stimulant that is used in the treatment of attention deficit hyperactivity disorder , narcolepsy, and obesity. __________ was discovered in 1887 and exists as two enantiomers: levo __________ and dextro __________ . __________ properly refers to a specific chemical, the racemic free base, which is equal parts of the two enantiomers, levo __________ and dextro __________ , in their pure amine forms. The term is frequently used informally to refer to any combination of the enantiomers, or to either of them alone. Historically, it has been used to treat nasal congestion and depression. __________ is also used as an athletic performance enhancer and cognitive enhancer, and recreationally as an aphrodisiac and euphoriant. It is a prescription drug in many countries, and unauthorized possession and distribution of __________ are often tightly controlled due to the significant health risks associated with recreational use.

Exam Probability: **High**

58. *Answer choices:*

(see index for correct answer)

- a. Nitrous oxide
- b. Dextrorphan
- c. Acetylfentanyl
- d. Amfonelic acid

Guidance: level 1

:: Philosophy of psychology ::

_________ is a systematic approach to understanding the behavior of humans and other animals. It assumes that all behaviors are either reflexes produced by a response to certain stimuli in the environment, or a consequence of that individual`s history, including especially reinforcement and punishment, together with the individual`s current motivational state and controlling stimuli. Although behaviorists generally accept the important role of inheritance in determining behavior, they focus primarily on environmental factors.

Exam Probability: **Medium**

59. *Answer choices:*

(see index for correct answer)

- a. Behaviorism
- b. The Moral Philosopher and the Moral Life
- c. Mentalism
- d. The Philosophy of the Unconscious

Guidance: level 1

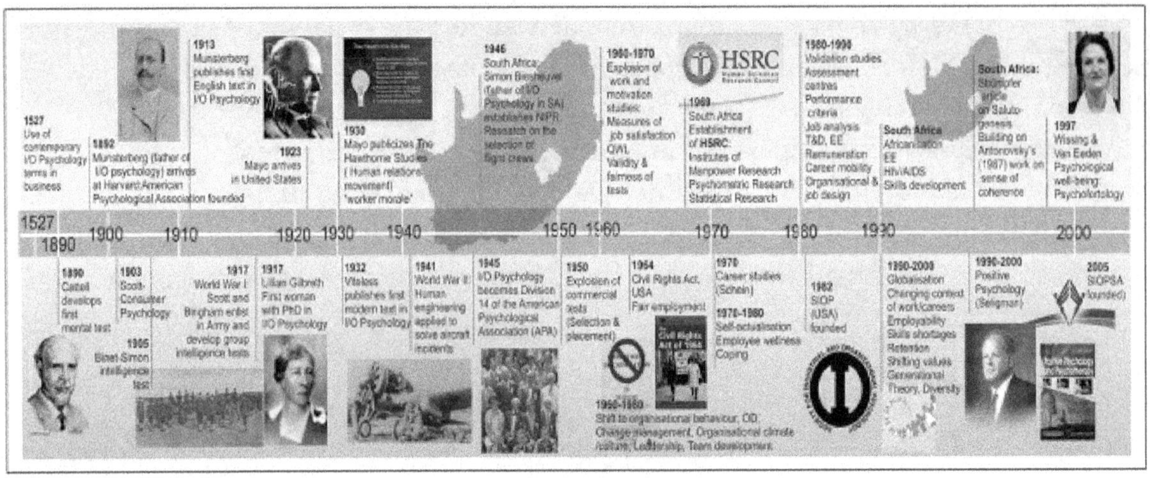

History of Psychology

Psychology was a branch of the domain of philosophy until the 1870s, when it developed as an independent scientific discipline in Germany and the United States. Psychology as a self-conscious field of experimental study began in 1879, in Leipzig Germany, when Wilhelm Wundt founded the first laboratory dedicated exclusively to psychological research in Germany. Wundt was also the first person to refer to himself as a psychologist. Other important early contributors to the field include Hermann Ebbinghaus (a pioneer in the study of memory), William James (the American father of pragmatism), and Ivan Pavlov (who developed the procedures associated with classical conditioning).

:: Scientific method ::

Progress is the movement towards a refined, improved, or otherwise desired state or, in the context of progressivism, the idea that advancements in technology, science, and social organization can result in an improved human condition; the latter may happen as a result of direct human action, as in social enterprise or through activism, or as a natural part of sociocultural evolution.

Exam Probability: **Low**

1. *Answer choices:*

(see index for correct answer)

- a. Scientific evidence
- b. Source criticism
- c. Scientific progress
- d. Double-blind

Guidance: level 1

:: Research methods ::

__________ is "creative and systematic work undertaken to increase the stock of knowledge, including knowledge of humans, culture and society, and the use of this stock of knowledge to devise new applications." It is used to establish or confirm facts, reaffirm the results of previous work, solve new or existing problems, support theorems, or develop new theories. A __________ project may also be an expansion on past work in the field. __________ projects can be used to develop further knowledge on a topic, or in the example of a school __________ project, they can be used to further a student`s __________ prowess to prepare them for future jobs or reports. To test the validity of instruments, procedures, or experiments, __________ may replicate elements of prior projects or the project as a whole. The primary purposes of basic __________ are documentation, discovery, interpretation, or the __________ and development of methods and systems for the advancement of human knowledge. Approaches to __________ depend on epistemologies, which vary considerably both within and between humanities and sciences. There are several forms of __________: scientific, humanities, artistic, economic, social, business, marketing, practitioner __________, life, technological, etc. The scientific study of __________ practices is known as metascience.

Exam Probability: **High**

2. *Answer choices:*

(see index for correct answer)

- a. Aquad
- b. Data storage tag
- c. Springer Protocols
- d. Research

Guidance: level 1

:: Psycholinguistics ::

________ or psychology of language is the study of the interrelation between linguistic factors and psychological aspects.

Exam Probability: **Medium**

3. *Answer choices:*

(see index for correct answer)

- a. Language and thought
- b. Competition model
- c. Psycholinguistics
- d. Heterosemy

Guidance: level 1

:: Emotions ::

_________ is an emotion characterized by an unpleasant state of inner turmoil, often accompanied by nervous behaviour such as pacing back and forth, somatic complaints, and rumination. It is the subjectively unpleasant feelings of dread over anticipated events, such as the feeling of imminent death. _________ is not the same as fear, which is a response to a real or perceived immediate threat, whereas _________ involves the expectation of future threat. _________ is a feeling of uneasiness and worry, usually generalized and unfocused as an overreaction to a situation that is only subjectively seen as menacing. It is often accompanied by muscular tension, restlessness, fatigue and problems in concentration. _________ can be appropriate, but when experienced regularly the individual may suffer from an _________ disorder.

Exam Probability: **High**

4. *Answer choices:*

(see index for correct answer)

- a. Melancholia
- b. Sadness
- c. Anxiety
- d. Nostalgia

Guidance: level 1

:: Motivation ::

An _________ is a contingent motivator. Traditional _________ s are extrinsic motivators which reward actions to yield a desired outcome. The effectiveness of traditional _________ s has changed as the needs of Western society have evolved. While the traditional _________ model is effective when there is a defined procedure and goal for a task, Western society started to require a higher volume of critical thinkers, so the traditional model became less effective. Institutions are now following a trend in implementing strategies that rely on intrinsic motivations rather than the extrinsic motivations that the traditional _________ s foster.

Exam Probability: **High**

5. *Answer choices:*

(see index for correct answer)

- a. Incentive
- b. Superordinate goals
- c. The Winning Edge
- d. Drive reduction theory

Guidance: level 1

:: History of psychology ::

_________ is a book by Sigmund Freud, the founder of psychoanalysis. It was written in 1929 and first published in German in 1930 as Das Unbehagen in der Kultur . Exploring what Freud sees as the important clash between the desire for individuality and the expectations of society, the book is considered one of Freud`s most important and widely read works, and one of the most influential and studied books in the field of modern psychology.

Exam Probability: **Medium**

6. *Answer choices:*

(see index for correct answer)

- a. Archives of the History of American Psychology
- b. Civilization and Its Discontents
- c. Gustave Le Bon
- d. Phrenology

Guidance: level 1

:: Behaviorism ::

A _________ is a routine of behavior that is repeated regularly and tends to occur subconsciously.

Exam Probability: **Medium**

7. *Answer choices:*

(see index for correct answer)

- a. Habit
- b. Behavioral activation
- c. Flooding
- d. Curriculum-based measurement

Guidance: level 1

:: History of psychology ::

The ________ is an 1890 book about psychology by William James, an American philosopher and psychologist who trained to be a physician before going into psychology. There are four methods from James` book: stream of consciousness ; emotion ; habit ; and will .

Exam Probability: **High**

8. *Answer choices:*

(see index for correct answer)

- a. Principles of Psychology
- b. Archives of the History of American Psychology
- c. Extraordinary Popular Delusions and the Madness of Crowds
- d. The Pursuit of the Millennium

Guidance: level 1

:: Women and psychology ::

_________ is a stage theorized by Sigmund Freud regarding female psychosexual development, in which young girls experience anxiety upon realization that they do not have a penis. Freud considered this realization a defining moment in a series of transitions toward a mature female sexuality and gender identity. In Freudian theory, the _________ stage begins the transition from an attachment to the mother to competition with the mother for the attention, recognition and affection of the father. The parallel reaction of a boy`s realization that women do not have a penis is castration anxiety.

Exam Probability: **Low**

9. *Answer choices:*

(see index for correct answer)

- a. Histrionic personality
- b. Marianismo
- c. Jacqueline Rose
- d. Cassandra

Guidance: level 1

:: Educational psychology ::

A _________ is a statistical analysis that combines the results of multiple scientific studies. _________ can be performed when there are multiple scientific studies addressing the same question, with each individual study reporting measurements that are expected to have some degree of error. The aim then is to use approaches from statistics to derive a pooled estimate closest to the unknown common truth based on how this error is perceived. Existing methods for _________ yield a weighted average from the results of the individual studies, and what differs is the manner in which these weights are allocated and also the manner in which the uncertainty is computed around the point estimate thus generated. In addition to providing an estimate of the unknown common truth, _________ has the capacity to contrast results from different studies and identify patterns among study results, sources of disagreement among those results, or other interesting relationships that may come to light in the context of multiple studies.

Exam Probability: **High**

10. *Answer choices:*

(see index for correct answer)

- a. Meta-analysis
- b. Testing effect
- c. Oswego Movement
- d. Formal education

Guidance: level 1

:: Learning ::

_________ is a phenomenon of learning and memory that was first named and described by Ivan Pavlov in his studies of classical conditioning. In that context, it refers to the re-emergence of a previously extinguished conditioned response after a delay. Such a recovery of "lost" behaviors can be observed within a variety of domains, and the recovery of lost human memories is often of particular interest. For a mathematical model for _________ see Further Reading.

Exam Probability: **High**

11. *Answer choices:*

(see index for correct answer)

- a. Phonics
- b. Elkonin boxes
- c. Spontaneous recovery
- d. Networked learning

Guidance: level 1

:: Theories of mind ::

Although the term " _________ " is derived from Western philosophy to typify positions in the mind–body problem, it has also been used to typify religious traditions. In modern Hinduism, the term "absolute _________ " is being used for Advaita Vedanta.

Exam Probability: **Low**

12. *Answer choices:*

(see index for correct answer)

- a. Psychological nominalism
- b. Type physicalism
- c. Anomalous monism
- d. Psychological egoism

Guidance: level 1

:: Educational psychology ::

_________ is a field of study concerned with the theory and technique of psychological measurement. As defined by the National Council on Measurement in Education , _________ refers to psychological measurement. Generally, it refers to the field in psychology and education that is devoted to testing, measurement, assessment, and related activities.

Exam Probability: **Low**

13. *Answer choices:*

(see index for correct answer)

- a. Inquiry education
- b. Summer Enrichment Program
- c. Psychometrics
- d. Thesis circle

Guidance: level 1

:: Psychological schools ::

__________ is a psychological perspective that rose to prominence in the mid-20th century in answer to the limitations of Sigmund Freud`s psychoanalytic theory and B. F. Skinner`s behaviorism. With its roots running from Socrates through the Renaissance, this approach emphasizes individuals` inherent drive towards self-actualization, the process of realizing and expressing one`s own capabilities and creativity.

Exam Probability: **Low**

14. *Answer choices:*

(see index for correct answer)

- a. Humanistic psychology
- b. Individual psychology
- c. Institute for International and Cross-Cultural Psychology
- d. Archetypal psychology

Guidance: level 1

:: Hypothesis testing ::

_________ is the magnitude or dimensions of a thing. _________ can be measured as length, width, height, diameter, perimeter, area, volume, or mass.

Exam Probability: **High**

15. *Answer choices:*

(see index for correct answer)

- a. P-value
- b. Familywise error rate
- c. Generalized p-value
- d. Size

Guidance: level 1

:: Branches of psychology ::

_________ is an approach to psychological research that is based on mathematical modeling of perceptual, thought, cognitive and motor processes, and on the establishment of law-like rules that relate quantifiable stimulus characteristics with quantifiable behavior. The mathematical approach is used with the goal of deriving hypotheses that are more exact and thus yield stricter empirical validations. Quantifiable behavior is in practice often constituted by task performance.

Exam Probability: **Low**

16. *Answer choices:*

(see index for correct answer)

- a. Critical psychology
- b. Mathematical psychology
- c. Integral psychology
- d. Photo psychology

Guidance: level 1

:: Learning ::

_________ is defined in psychology as the ability to respond differently to different stimuli. This type of learning is used in studies regarding operant and classical conditioning. Operant conditioning involves the modification of a behavior by means of reinforcement or punishment. In this way, a discriminative stimulus will act as an indicator to when a behavior will persist and when it will not. Classical conditioning involves learning through association when two stimuli are paired together repeatedly. This conditioning demonstrates discrimination through specific micro-instances of reinforcement and non-reinforcement. This phenomenon is considered to be more advanced than learning styles such as generalization and yet simultaneously acts as a basic unit to learning as a whole. The complex and fundamental nature of _________ allows for psychologists and researchers to perform more in-depth research that supports psychological advancements. Research on the basic principles underlying this learning style has their roots in neuropsychology sub-processes.

Exam Probability: **High**

17. *Answer choices:*

(see index for correct answer)

- a. Discrimination learning
- b. Mate choice copying
- c. Conditioned place preference
- d. Errorless learning

Guidance: level 1

:: Causality ::

_________ is a philosophical theory about causation which says that created substances cannot be efficient causes of events. Instead, all events are taken to be caused directly by God. The theory states that the illusion of efficient causation between mundane events arises out of God`s causing of one event after another. However, there is no necessary connection between the two: it is not that the first event causes God to cause the second event: rather, God first causes one and then causes the other.

Exam Probability: **Medium**

18. *Answer choices:*

(see index for correct answer)

- a. Occasionalism
- b. Butterfly effect
- c. Fatalism

- d. Physical determinism

Guidance: level 1

:: Behaviorism ::

_________ is, in contrast to analog observation, a research tool in which a subject is observed in its natural habitat without any manipulation by the observer. During _________ , researchers take great care to avoid interfering with the behavior they are observing by using unobtrusive methods. _________ involves two main differences that set it apart from other forms of data gathering. In the context of a _________ , the environment is in no way being manipulated by the observer nor was it created by the observer.

Exam Probability: **Medium**

19. *Answer choices:*

(see index for correct answer)

- a. Teaching-family model
- b. Pair by association
- c. Social competence
- d. Naturalistic observation

Guidance: level 1

:: Psychologists ::

Ibn Rushd , often Latinized as _________ , was a Muslim Andalusian philosopher and thinker who wrote about many subjects, including philosophy, theology, medicine, astronomy, physics, Islamic jurisprudence and law, and linguistics. His philosophical works include numerous commentaries on Aristotle, for which he was known in the West as The Commentator. He also served as a judge and a court physician for the Almohad caliphate.

Exam Probability: **Medium**

20. *Answer choices:*

(see index for correct answer)

- a. Max Friedrich Meyer
- b. David Budescu
- c. Dermot Barnes-Holmes
- d. Averroes

Guidance: level 1

:: Criticism ::

_________ is a method of disciplined, systematic study of a written or oral discourse. Although _________ is commonly understood as fault finding and negative judgment, it can also involve merit recognition, and in the philosophical tradition it also means a methodical practice of doubt. The contemporary sense of _________ has been largely influenced by the Enlightenment _________ of prejudice and authority, which championed the emancipation and autonomy from religious and political authorities.

Exam Probability: **Low**

21. *Answer choices:*

(see index for correct answer)

- a. Critique
- b. Critical Metrics
- c. Peer critique
- d. Pancritical rationalism

Guidance: level 1

:: Phenomenology ::

A _________ is any thing which manifests itself. Phenomena are often, but not always, understood as "things that appear" or "experiences" for a sentient being, or in principle may be so.

Exam Probability: **Medium**

22. *Answer choices:*

(see index for correct answer)

- a. Phenomenon
- b. Neurophenomenology
- c. Schismogenesis
- d. Categories

Guidance: level 1

:: Conceptions of self ::

True self and false self are psychological concepts often used in connection with narcissism.

Exam Probability: **Low**

23. *Answer choices:*

(see index for correct answer)

- a. self-identity
- b. Internarrative identity
- c. Real self
- d. True Will

Guidance: level 1

:: Psychodynamics ::

_________ is defined as redirection of a psychotherapist`s feelings toward a client – or, more generally, as a therapist`s emotional entanglement with a client.

Exam Probability: **High**

24. *Answer choices:*

(see index for correct answer)

- a. Mentalization-based treatment
- b. Enrico Borla
- c. Psychodynamics
- d. Countertransference

Guidance: level 1

:: Psychotherapy ::

The _________ was a French hypnosis-centered school of psychotherapy. The origins of the thoughts were brought about by Ambroise-Auguste Liébeault in 1866, in Nancy, France. Through his publications and therapy sessions he was able to gain the attention/support from Hippolyte Bernheim: another Nancy Doctor that further evolved Liébeault's thoughts and practices to form what is known as the _________ .

Exam Probability: **High**

25. *Answer choices:*

(see index for correct answer)

- a. Guided affective imagery
- b. Nancy School

- c. Metapsychiatry
- d. Rejection Therapy

Guidance: level 1

:: Freudian psychology ::

In Freudian psychoanalysis, the _________ is the third stage of psychosexual development, spanning the ages of three to six years, wherein the infant`s libido centers upon his or her genitalia as the erogenous zone. When children become aware of their bodies, the bodies of other children, and the bodies of their parents, they gratify physical curiosity by undressing and exploring each other and their genitals, the center of the _________, in course of which they learn the physical differences between "male" and "female", and the gender differences between "boy" and "girl", experiences which alter the psychologic dynamics of the parent and child relationship. The _________ is the third of five Freudian psychosexual development stages: the oral, the anal, the phallic, the latent, and the genital.

Exam Probability: **High**

26. *Answer choices:*

(see index for correct answer)

- a. Oral stage
- b. Afterwardsness
- c. Mortido
- d. Phallic stage

Guidance: level 1

:: Psychodynamics ::

__________ is a theoretical phenomenon characterized by unconscious redirection of the feelings a person has about their parents, as one example, on to the therapist. It usually concerns feelings from a primary relationship during childhood. At times, this projection can be considered inappropriate. __________ was first described by Sigmund Freud, the founder of psychoanalysis, who considered it an important part of psychoanalytic treatment.

Exam Probability: **High**

27. *Answer choices:*

(see index for correct answer)

- a. Psychodynamic psychotherapy
- b. Resistance
- c. Transference
- d. Enrico Borla

Guidance: level 1

:: Psychological schools ::

_________ or gestaltism is a philosophy of mind of the Berlin School of experimental psychology. _________ is an attempt to understand the laws behind the ability to acquire and maintain meaningful perceptions in an apparently chaotic world. The central principle of _________ is that the mind forms a global whole with self-organizing tendencies through the law of prägnanz

Exam Probability: **High**

28. *Answer choices:*

(see index for correct answer)

- a. Gestalt psychology
- b. Cognitive therapy
- c. Ecological systems theory
- d. Post-cognitivist psychology

Guidance: level 1

:: History of psychology ::

_________ was pioneered by B. F. Skinner and is his "philosophy of the science of behavior." It refers to the philosophy behind behavior analysis, and is to be distinguished from methodological behaviorismwhich has an intense emphasis on observable behaviorsby its inclusion of thinking, feeling, and other private events in the analysis of human and animal psychology. The research in behavior analysis is called the experimental analysis of behavior and the application of this field is called applied behavior analysis , which was originally termed "behavior modification."

Exam Probability: **High**

29. *Answer choices:*

(see index for correct answer)

- a. Radical behaviorism
- b. The Pursuit of the Millennium
- c. Functional psychology
- d. Little Albert experiment

Guidance: level 1

:: Metaphysics of mind ::

_________ is the philosophical idea that only one`s own mind is sure to exist. As an epistemological position, _________ holds that knowledge of anything outside one`s own mind is unsure; the external world and other minds cannot be known and might not exist outside the mind. As a metaphysical position, _________ goes further to the conclusion that the world and other minds do not exist. This extreme position is claimed to be irrefutable, as the solipsist believes himself to be the only true authority, all others being creations of their own mind.

Exam Probability: **Low**

30. *Answer choices:*

(see index for correct answer)

- a. World riddle
- b. Solipsism
- c. Supervenience
- d. Property dualism

Guidance: level 1

:: Information science ::

In scholarship, a _________ is a document or recording that relates or discusses information originally presented elsewhere. A _________ contrasts with a primary source, which is an original source of the information being discussed; a primary source can be a person with direct knowledge of a situation, or a document created by such a person.

Exam Probability: **Medium**

31. *Answer choices:*

(see index for correct answer)

- a. Document
- b. Secondary source
- c. Engineering informatics
- d. Informedia Digital Library

Guidance: level 1

:: Neuropsychology ::

_________ is the branch of psychology that is concerned with the physiological bases of psychological processes. While _________ was a general broad field of research in the 1960s and 1970s, it has now become quite specialized, and has branched into subspecializations such as social _________, cardiovascular _________, cognitive _________, and cognitive neuroscience.

Exam Probability: **Medium**

32. *Answer choices:*

(see index for correct answer)

- a. NEPSY
- b. Psychophysiology
- c. American Board of Professional Neuropsychology
- d. Neuropsychological assessment

Guidance: level 1

:: Philosophy of life ::

In philosophy, _________ means the existence of a thing. Anything that exists has _________ . Ontology is the branch of philosophy that studies _________ . _________ is a concept encompassing objective and subjective features of reality and existence. Anything that partakes in _________ is also called a " _________ ", though often this usage is limited to entities that have subjectivity . The notion of " _________ " has, inevitably, been elusive and controversial in the history of philosophy, beginning in Western philosophy with attempts among the pre-Socratics to deploy it intelligibly. The first effort to recognize and define the concept came from Parmenides, who famously said of it that "what is-is". Common words such as "is", "are", and "am" refer directly or indirectly to _________ .

Exam Probability: **High**

33. *Answer choices:*

(see index for correct answer)

- a. Moral responsibility
- b. Obligation
- c. Being
- d. Alternative lifestyle

Guidance: level 1

:: Perception ::

In neuroscience and psychophysics, an _________ was originally defined as the lowest level of a stimulus – light, sound, touch, etc. – that an organism could detect. Under the influence of signal detection theory, _________ has been redefined as the level at which a stimulus will be detected a specified percentage of the time. The _________ can be influenced by several different factors, such as the subject`s motivations and expectations, cognitive processes, and whether the subject is adapted to the stimulus.The _________ can be compared to the difference threshold, which is the measure of how different two stimuli must be for the subject to notice that they are not the same.

Exam Probability: **Medium**

34. *Answer choices:*

(see index for correct answer)

- a. Absolute threshold
- b. Perceptual system
- c. Chubb illusion
- d. Numerosity adaptation effect

Guidance: level 1

:: Perception ::

_________ is an ability of animals to perceive differences between light composed of different wavelengths independently of light intensity. The perception is a part of the larger vision system and is mediated by a complex process between neurons that begins with differential stimulation of different types of photoreceptors by light entering the eye. Those photoreceptors then emit outputs that are then propagated through many layers of neurons and then ultimately to the brain. _________ is found in many animals and is mediated by similar underlying mechanisms with common types of biological molecules and a complex history of evolution in different animal taxa. In primates, _________ may have evolved to under selective pressure for a variety of visual tasks including the foraging for nutritious young leaves, ripe fruit and flowers as well as detecting predator camouflage and emotional states in other primates.

Exam Probability: **High**

35. *Answer choices:*

(see index for correct answer)

- a. Geometrical-optical illusions
- b. Tactile discrimination
- c. Color vision
- d. Form perception

Guidance: level 1

:: Personality tests ::

The _________ , created by Aaron T. Beck and other colleagues, is a 21-question multiple-choice self-report inventory that is used for measuring the severity of anxiety in children and adults. The questions used in this measure ask about common symptoms of anxiety that the subject has had during the past week . It is designed for individuals who are of 17 years of age or older and takes 5 to 10 minutes to complete. Several studies have found the _________ to be an accurate measure of anxiety symptoms in children and adults.

Exam Probability: **High**

36. *Answer choices:*

(see index for correct answer)

- a. Oxford Capacity Analysis
- b. Animal Metaphor Test
- c. DISC assessment
- d. Holland Codes

Guidance: level 1

:: Causality ::

An _________ is a set of statements usually constructed to describe a set of facts which clarifies the causes, context, and consequences of those facts. This description of the facts et cetera may establish rules or laws, and may clarify the existing rules or laws in relation to any objects, or phenomena examined. The components of an _________ can be implicit, and interwoven with one another.

Exam Probability: **Medium**

37. *Answer choices:*

(see index for correct answer)

- a. Chain reaction
- b. Explanation
- c. etiological
- d. Causal loop diagram

Guidance: level 1

:: Research methods ::

_________ is a type of research which involves seeking out and extracting evidence from archival records. These records may be held either in collecting institutions, such as libraries and museums, or in the custody of the organization that originally generated or accumulated them, or in that of a successor body . _________ can be contrasted with secondary research , which involves identifying and consulting secondary sources relating to the topic of enquiry; and with other types of primary research and empirical investigation such as fieldwork and experiment.

Exam Probability: **High**

38. *Answer choices:*

(see index for correct answer)

- a. Mode effect
- b. Cooperative inquiry
- c. Archival research
- d. The Three Rs

Guidance: level 1

:: Theories of mind ::

_________ is a position on the mind–body problem which holds that physical and biochemical events within the human body are causal with respect to mental events . According to this view, subjective mental events are completely dependent for their existence on corresponding physical and biochemical events within the human body and themselves have no causal efficacy on physical events. The appearance that subjective mental states influence physical events is merely an illusion. For instance, fear seems to make the heart beat faster, but according to _________ the biochemical secretions of the brain and nervous system —not the experience of fear—is what raises the heartbeat. Because mental events are a kind of overflow that cannot cause anything physical, yet have non-physical properties, _________ is viewed as a form of property dualism.

Exam Probability: **Medium**

39. *Answer choices:*

(see index for correct answer)

- a. Methodological solipsism
- b. Psychological egoism

- c. Psychophysical parallelism
- d. Epiphenomenalism

Guidance: level 1

:: Emotions ::

_________ is a multifaceted response to loss, particularly to the loss of someone or something that has died, to which a bond or affection was formed. Although conventionally focused on the emotional response to loss, it also has physical, cognitive, behavioral, social, cultural, spiritual and philosophical dimensions. While the terms are often used interchangeably, bereavement refers to the state of loss, and _________ is the reaction to that loss.

Exam Probability: **High**

40. *Answer choices:*

(see index for correct answer)

- a. Calmness
- b. Grief
- c. Emotions in virtual communication
- d. Loneliness

Guidance: level 1

:: Behavioural sciences ::

__________ is the scientific study of how people`s thoughts, feelings and behaviors are influenced by the actual, imagined or implied presence of others. In this definition, scientific refers to the empirical investigation using the scientific method. The terms thoughts, feelings and behavior refer to psychological variables that can be measured in humans. The statement that others` presence may be imagined or implied suggests that humans are malleable to social influences even when alone, such as when watching television looking at reality shows,music videos and movies they can be influenced to follow the behaviour in the visual setting or following internalized cultural norms. Social psychologists typically explain human behavior as a result of the interaction of mental states and social situations.

Exam Probability: **Low**

41. *Answer choices:*

(see index for correct answer)

- a. Social psychology
- b. Occupational health psychology
- c. Future Orientation Index
- d. Implicit cognition

Guidance: level 1

:: Qualities of thought ::

_________ is the number of occurrences of a repeating event per unit of time. It is also referred to as temporal _________, which emphasizes the contrast to spatial _________ and angular _________. The period is the duration of time of one cycle in a repeating event, so the period is the reciprocal of the _________. For example: if a newborn baby's heart beats at a _________ of 120 times a minute, its period—the time interval between beats—is half a second. _________ is an important parameter used in science and engineering to specify the rate of oscillatory and vibratory phenomena, such as mechanical vibrations, audio signals, radio waves, and light.

Exam Probability: **Low**

42. *Answer choices:*

(see index for correct answer)

- a. Efficiency
- b. Efficacy

Guidance: level 1

:: Cybernetics ::

A _________ is a group of interacting or interrelated entities that form a unified whole. A _________ is delineated by its spatial and temporal boundaries, surrounded and influenced by its environment, described by its structure and purpose and expressed in its functioning.

Exam Probability: **Low**

43. *Answer choices:*

(see index for correct answer)

- a. Synergetics
- b. Cyborg Foundation
- c. T.O.T.E.
- d. System

Guidance: level 1

:: Philosophy of mind ::

In physics, _________ is the quantitative property that must be transferred to an object in order to perform work on, or to heat, the object. _________ is a conserved quantity; the law of conservation of _________ states that _________ can be converted in form, but not created or destroyed. The SI unit of _________ is the joule, which is the _________ transferred to an object by the work of moving it a distance of 1 metre against a force of 1 newton.

Exam Probability: **High**

44. *Answer choices:*

(see index for correct answer)

- a. Cognitive closure
- b. Brain dump
- c. Passive intellect
- d. Energy

Guidance: level 1

:: Perception ::

In physiology, psychology, or psychophysics, a _________ or a liminal point is a threshold of a physiological or psychological response. It is the boundary of perception. On one side of a _________ a stimulus is perceivable, on the other side it is not.

Exam Probability: **Medium**

45. *Answer choices:*

(see index for correct answer)

- a. Limen
- b. Ambient optic array
- c. Jamais vu
- d. Lip reading

Guidance: level 1

:: Philosophy of psychology ::

_________ is the examination of one`s own conscious thoughts and feelings. In psychology, the process of _________ relies exclusively on observation of one`s mental state, while in a spiritual context it may refer to the examination of one`s soul. _________ is closely related to human self-reflection and is contrasted with external observation.

Exam Probability: **High**

46. *Answer choices:*

(see index for correct answer)

- a. Freud and Philosophy
- b. Zettel
- c. Introspection
- d. Wilhelm Reich

Guidance: level 1

:: Validity (statistics) ::

_________ is the validity of applying the conclusions of a scientific study outside the context of that study. In other words, it is the extent to which the results of a study can be generalized to and across other situations, people, stimuli, and times. In contrast, internal validity is the validity of conclusions drawn within the context of a particular study. Because general conclusions are almost always a goal in research, _________ is an important property of any study. Mathematical analysis of _________ concerns a determination of whether generalization across heterogeneous populations is feasible, and devising statistical and computational methods that produce valid generalizations.

Exam Probability: **Medium**

47. *Answer choices:*

(see index for correct answer)

- a. Construct validity
- b. External validity
- c. Nomological validity
- d. Statistical conclusion validity

Guidance: level 1

:: Psychology ::

A _________ studies normal and abnormal mental states, cognitive, emotional, and social processes and behavior by observing, interpreting, and recording how individuals relate to one another and to their environments. To become a _________ , a person often completes a graduate university degree in psychology, but in most jurisdictions, members of other behavioral professions can also evaluate, diagnose, treat, and study mental processes.

Exam Probability: **High**

48. *Answer choices:*

(see index for correct answer)

- a. Psychologist
- b. Exemplar theory
- c. Approach/Inhibition Theory of Power
- d. Crime opportunity theory

Guidance: level 1

:: Psychological schools ::

_________ is the psychological method or science founded by the Viennese psychiatrist Alfred Adler . The English edition of Adler`s work on the subject is a collection of papers and lectures given mainly in 1912–1914, and covers the whole range of human psychology in a single survey, intended to mirror the indivisible unity of the personality.

Exam Probability: **High**

49. *Answer choices:*

(see index for correct answer)

- a. Filipino psychology
- b. Rational emotive behavior therapy
- c. Postmodern psychology
- d. Individual psychology

Guidance: level 1

:: Sleep ::

_________ is a naturally recurring state of mind and body, characterized by altered consciousness, relatively inhibited sensory activity, inhibition of nearly all voluntary muscles, and reduced interactions with surroundings. It is distinguished from wakefulness by a decreased ability to react to stimuli, but more reactive than coma or disorders of consciousness, _________ displaying very different and active brain patterns.

Exam Probability: **High**

50. *Answer choices:*

(see index for correct answer)

- a. Blindfold
- b. Sleep
- c. Biorhythm
- d. Seven Sleepers

Guidance: level 1

:: History of psychology ::

_________ was the first journal of experimental psychology founded by Wilhelm Wundt in 1881. Although its title referred to philosophy rather than psychology, it exclusively featured articles on psychological experiments of Wundt. The journal was succeeded by the Archiv für die gesamte Psychologie in 1903.

Exam Probability: **Low**

51. *Answer choices:*

(see index for correct answer)

- a. Hysteria
- b. History of the race and intelligence controversy
- c. Philosophische Studien
- d. Eastern philosophy in clinical psychology

Guidance: level 1

:: Psychotherapy ::

_________ is a form of training with the goal of making people more aware of their own goals as well as their prejudices, and more sensitive to others and to the dynamics of group interaction.

Exam Probability: **High**

52. *Answer choices:*

(see index for correct answer)

- a. Coherence therapy
- b. Emotional flooding
- c. Guided affective imagery
- d. Sensitivity training

Guidance: level 1

:: Analysis of variance ::

In the design of experiments and analysis of variance, a _________ is the effect of an independent variable on a dependent variable averaged across the levels of any other independent variables. The term is frequently used in the context of factorial designs and regression models to distinguish _________ s from interaction effects.

Exam Probability: **Low**

53. *Answer choices:*

(see index for correct answer)

- a. Main effect
- b. Covariate
- c. Pooled variance
- d. Mixed model

Guidance: level 1

:: Self ::

A _______ is a being that has certain capacities or attributes such as reason, morality, consciousness or self-consciousness, and being a part of a culturally established form of social relations such as kinship, ownership of property, or legal responsibility. The defining features of _______ hood and consequently what makes a _______ count as a _______ differ widely among cultures and contexts.

Exam Probability: **High**

54. *Answer choices:*

(see index for correct answer)

- a. Impression management
- b. Person
- c. The Self-Discrepancy Theory
- d. Self-compassion

Guidance: level 1

:: Problem solving ::

__________ is a cognitive bias that limits a person to use an object only in the way it is traditionally used. The concept of __________ originated in Gestalt psychology, a movement in psychology that emphasizes holistic processing. Karl Duncker defined __________ as being a "mental block against using an object in a new way that is required to solve a problem". This "block" limits the ability of an individual to use components given to them to complete a task, as they cannot move past the original purpose of those components. For example, if someone needs a paperweight, but they only have a hammer, they may not see how the hammer can be used as a paperweight. __________ is this inability to see a hammer`s use as anything other than for pounding nails; the person couldn`t think to use the hammer in a way other than in its conventional function.

Exam Probability: **High**

55. *Answer choices:*

(see index for correct answer)

- a. Dilemma
- b. How to Solve it by Computer
- c. Functional fixedness
- d. Lateral computing

Guidance: level 1

:: Communication ::

__________ is the act of conveying meanings from one entity or group to another through the use of mutually understood signs, symbols, and semiotic rules.

Exam Probability: **Medium**

56. *Answer choices:*

(see index for correct answer)

- a. Interpreter officer
- b. Communication
- c. Communication noise
- d. Information theory

Guidance: level 1

:: History of psychology ::

In sociology, anthropology, and linguistics, _________ is the methodology that implies elements of human culture must be understood by way of their relationship to a broader, overarching system or structure. It works to uncover the structures that underlie all the things that humans do, think, perceive, and feel. Alternatively, as summarized by philosopher Simon Blackburn, _________ is "the belief that phenomena of human life are not intelligible except through their interrelations. These relations constitute a structure, and behind local variations in the surface phenomena there are constant laws of abstract structure".

Exam Probability: **Low**

57. *Answer choices:*

(see index for correct answer)

- a. Structuralism
- b. Phrenology
- c. Variability hypothesis
- d. William James Lectures

Guidance: level 1

:: Behavioral concepts ::

__________ is the behavioral and cognitive process of selectively concentrating on a discrete aspect of information, whether deemed subjective or objective, while ignoring other perceivable information. It is a state of arousal. It is the taking possession by the mind in clear and vivid form of one out of what seem several simultaneous objects or trains of thought. Focalization, the concentration of consciousness, is of its essence. __________ has also been described as the allocation of limited cognitive processing resources.

Exam Probability: **Medium**

58. *Answer choices:*

(see index for correct answer)

- a. Barrier analysis
- b. Attention
- c. Social cognition
- d. Selective distortion

Guidance: level 1

:: Causality ::

_________ is efficacy, by which one process or state, a cause, contributes to the production of another process or state, an effect, where the cause is partly responsible for the effect, and the effect is partly dependent on the cause. In general, a process has many causes,which are also said to be causal factors for it, and all lie in its past. An effect can in turn be a cause of, or causal factor for, many other effects, which all lie in its future. Multiple philosophers have believed that _________ is metaphysically prior to notions of time and space.

Exam Probability: **Low**

59. *Answer choices:*

(see index for correct answer)

- a. Causality
- b. deterministic
- c. Dysteleology
- d. Four causes

Guidance: level 1

Educational Psychology

Educational psychology is the branch of psychology concerned with the scientific study of human learning. The study of learning processes, from both cognitive and behavioral perspectives, allows researchers to understand individual differences in intelligence, cognitive development, affect, motivation, self-regulation, and self-concept, as well as their role in learning. The field of educational psychology relies heavily on quantitative methods, including testing and measurement, to enhance educational activities related to instructional design, classroom management, and assessment, which serve to facilitate learning processes in various educational settings across the lifespan.

:: Misogyny ::

_________ is a type of harassment technique that relates to a sexual nature and the unwelcome or inappropriate promise of rewards in exchange for sexual favors. _________ includes a range of actions from mild transgressions to sexual abuse or assault. Harassment can occur in many different social settings such as the workplace, the home, school, churches, etc. Harassers or victims may be of any gender.

Exam Probability: **Low**

1. *Answer choices:*

(see index for correct answer)

- a. Sexual harassment
- b. Little Tales of Misogyny
- c. Albanian sworn virgins
- d. Besharmi Morcha

Guidance: level 1

:: Educational psychology ::

__________ or thinking style is a concept used in cognitive psychology to describe the way individuals think, perceive and remember information. __________ differs from cognitive ability , the latter being measured by aptitude tests or so-called intelligence tests. There is controversy over the exact meaning of the term " __________ " and whether it is a single or multiple dimension of human personality. However it remains a key concept in the areas of education and management. If a pupil has a __________ that is similar to that of his/her teacher, the chances are improved that the pupil will have a more positive learning experience. Likewise, team members with similar __________ s likely feel more positive about their participation with the team. While matching __________ s may make participants feel more comfortable when working with one another, this alone cannot guarantee the success of the outcome.

Exam Probability: **Low**

2. *Answer choices:*

(see index for correct answer)

- a. Cognitive style
- b. Hands On Learning Australia
- c. Reading
- d. Educational research

Guidance: level 1

:: Behaviorism ::

_________ is a general term for the explicit teaching of a skill-set using lectures or demonstrations of the material to students. A particular subset of _________ , denoted by capitalization as _________ , refers to a specific example of the approach developed by Siegfried Engelmann and Wesley C. Becker. DI teaches by explicit instruction, in contrast to exploratory models such as inquiry-based learning. DI includes tutorials, participatory laboratory classes, discussion, recitation, seminars, workshops, observation, active learning, practica, or internships.

Exam Probability: **High**

3. *Answer choices:*

(see index for correct answer)

- a. Logical behaviorism
- b. Social competence
- c. Rate of reinforcement
- d. Direct instruction

Guidance: level 1

:: Memory ::

_________ is a type of implicit memory and long-term memory which aids the performance of particular types of tasks without conscious awareness of these previous experiences.

Exam Probability: **Medium**

4. *Answer choices:*

(see index for correct answer)

- a. Procedural memory
- b. Arabian Memory Championship
- c. Effects of stress on memory
- d. Autobiographical memory

Guidance: level 1

:: Educational psychology ::

_________ is a student-centered pedagogy in which students learn about a subject through the experience of solving an open-ended problem found in trigger material. The PBL process does not focus on problem solving with a defined solution, but it allows for the development of other desirable skills and attributes. This includes knowledge acquisition, enhanced group collaboration and communication. The PBL process was developed for medical education and has since been broadened in applications for other programs of learning. The process allows for learners to develop skills used for their future practice. It enhances critical appraisal, literature retrieval and encourages ongoing learning within a team environment.

Exam Probability: **High**

5. *Answer choices:*

(see index for correct answer)

- a. Knowledge deficit

- b. Montessori sensorial materials
- c. Educational technology
- d. Dyslexia

Guidance: level 1

:: Educational psychology ::

_________ is a term teachers use to describe the process of ensuring that classroom lessons run smoothly without disruptive behavior from students compromising the delivery of instruction. The term also implies the prevention of disruptive behavior preemptively, as well as effectively responding to it after it happens.

Exam Probability: **High**

6. *Answer choices:*

(see index for correct answer)

- a. Strozzi Institute
- b. Classroom management
- c. Distributed scaffolding
- d. Inquiry education

Guidance: level 1

:: Child abuse ::

_________ or child maltreatment is physical, sexual, and/or psychological maltreatment or neglect of a child or children, especially by a parent or a caregiver. _________ may include any act or failure to act by a parent or a caregiver that results in actual or potential harm to a child, and can occur in a child`s home, or in the organizations, schools or communities the child interacts with.

Exam Probability: **High**

7. *Answer choices:*

(see index for correct answer)

- a. Verdingkinder
- b. Genie
- c. Child abuse
- d. Conflict tactics scale

Guidance: level 1

:: Research ::

Specifying the _________ is the methodological point of departure of scholarly research in both the natural and social sciences. The research will answer the question posed. At an undergraduate level, the answer to the _________ is the thesis statement. The answer to a _________ will help address a "research problem" which is a problem "readers think is worth solving".

Exam Probability: **High**

8. *Answer choices:*

(see index for correct answer)

- a. The Mammal Society
- b. Levels of evidence
- c. Research question
- d. Asian Banker Research

Guidance: level 1

:: Validity (statistics) ::

_________ is "the degree to which a test measures what it claims, or purports, to be measuring." In the classical model of test validity, _________ is one of three main types of validity evidence, alongside content validity and criterion validity. Modern validity theory defines _________ as the overarching concern of validity research, subsuming all other types of validity evidence.

Exam Probability: **Medium**

9. *Answer choices:*

(see index for correct answer)

- a. Concurrent validity
- b. Internal validity
- c. Face validity
- d. statistical conclusion

Guidance: level 1

:: Self ::

_________ is the avoidance of doing a task that needs to be accomplished by a certain deadline. It could be further stated as a habitual or intentional delay of starting or finishing a task despite knowing it might have negative consequences. It is a common human experience involving delay in everyday chores or even putting off salient tasks such as attending an appointment, submitting a job report or academic assignment, or broaching a stressful issue with a partner. Although typically perceived as a negative trait due to its hindering effect on one`s productivity often associated with depression, low self-esteem, guilt and inadequacy; it can also be considered a wise response to certain demands that could present risky or negative outcomes or require waiting for new information to arrive.

Exam Probability: **High**

10. *Answer choices:*

(see index for correct answer)

- a. Self-evaluation maintenance theory
- b. Impassibility
- c. Selfishness
- d. True self and false self

Guidance: level 1

:: Educational psychology ::

_________ is one of the domains of self-regulation, and is aligned most closely with educational aims. Broadly speaking, it refers to learning that is guided by metacognition , strategic action , and motivation to learn. "Self-regulated" describes a process of taking control of and evaluating one`s own learning and behavior.

Exam Probability: **Low**

11. *Answer choices:*

(see index for correct answer)

- a. Informal learning
- b. Achievement Orientation
- c. Cultural learning
- d. Cognitive strategy

Guidance: level 1

:: Razors (philosophy) ::

A __________ is a bladed tool primarily used in the removal of unwanted body hair through the act of shaving. Kinds of __________ s include straight __________ s, disposable __________ , and electric __________ s.

Exam Probability: **High**

12. *Answer choices:*

(see index for correct answer)

- a. Razor
- b. falsifiable
- c. Plenitude principle

Guidance: level 1

:: Scientific method ::

The _________ or method is a proposed description of scientific method. According to it, scientific inquiry proceeds by formulating a hypothesis in a form that can be falsifiable, using a test on observable data where the outcome is not yet known. A test outcome that could have and does run contrary to predictions of the hypothesis is taken as a falsification of the hypothesis. A test outcome that could have, but does not run contrary to the hypothesis corroborates the theory. It is then proposed to compare the explanatory value of competing hypotheses by testing how stringently they are corroborated by their predictions.

Exam Probability: **Low**

13. *Answer choices:*

(see index for correct answer)

- a. Visualized experimental biology
- b. OGHET
- c. Fringe science
- d. Hypothetico-deductive model

Guidance: level 1

:: Thought ::

__________ is the analysis of facts to form a judgment. The subject is complex, and several different definitions exist, which generally include the rational, skeptical, unbiased analysis, or evaluation of factual evidence. __________ is self-directed, self-disciplined, self-monitored, and self-corrective thinking. It presupposes assent to rigorous standards of excellence and mindful command of their use. It entails effective communication and problem-solving abilities as well as a commitment to overcome native egocentrism and sociocentrism.

Exam Probability: **Medium**

14. *Answer choices:*

(see index for correct answer)

- a. Bohm Dialogue
- b. Synectics
- c. Permanent brain
- d. Creative problem solving

Guidance: level 1

:: Educational psychology research methods ::

_________ is a systematic methodology in the social sciences involving the construction of theories through methodical gathering and analysis of data. _________ is a research methodology which operates inductively, in contrast to the hypothetico-deductive approach. A study using _________ is likely to begin with a question, or even just with the collection of qualitative data. As researchers review the data collected, repeated ideas, concepts or elements become apparent, and are tagged with codes, which have been extracted from the data. As more data is collected, and re-reviewed, codes can be grouped into concepts, and then into categories. These categories may become the basis for new theory. Thus, _________ is quite different from the traditional model of research, where the researcher chooses an existing theoretical framework, and only then collects data to show how the theory does or does not apply to the phenomenon under study.

Exam Probability: **Low**

15. *Answer choices:*

(see index for correct answer)

- a. Reliability
- b. Visual analogue scale
- c. Grounded theory
- d. Effect size

Guidance: level 1

:: Self ::

_________ is a macro theory of human motivation and personality that concerns people`s inherent growth tendencies and innate psychological needs. It is concerned with the motivation behind choices people make without external influence and interference. SDT focuses on the degree to which an individual`s behavior is self-motivated and self-determined.

Exam Probability: **High**

16. *Answer choices:*

(see index for correct answer)

- a. Gender identity
- b. Self-determination theory
- c. Self-actualization
- d. Self-complexity

Guidance: level 1

:: Evaluation ::

_________ is a systematic method for collecting, analyzing, and using information to answer questions about projects, policies and programs, particularly about their effectiveness and efficiency. In both the public and private sectors, stakeholders often want to know whether the programs they are funding, implementing, voting for, receiving or objecting to are producing the intended effect. While _________ first focuses around this definition, important considerations often include how much the program costs per participant, how the program could be improved, whether the program is worthwhile, whether there are better alternatives, if there are unintended outcomes, and whether the program goals are appropriate and useful. Evaluators help to answer these questions, but the best way to answer the questions is for the evaluation to be a joint project between evaluators and stakeholders.

Exam Probability: **Low**

17. *Answer choices:*

(see index for correct answer)

- a. Defence Evaluation and Research Agency
- b. International Association for the Evaluation of Educational Achievement
- c. Program evaluation
- d. Ecological indicator

Guidance: level 1

:: Behaviorism ::

CBM began in the mid 1970s with research headed by Stan Deno at the University of Minnesota. Over the course of 10 years, this work led to the establishment of measurement systems in reading, writing, and spelling that were: easy to construct, brief in administration and scoring, had technical adequacy , and provided alternate forms to allow time series data to be collected on student progress. This focus in the three language arts areas eventually was expanded to include mathematics, though the technical research in this area continues to lag that published in the language arts areas. An even later development was the application of CBM to middle-secondary areas: Espin and colleagues at the University of Minnesota developed a line of research addressing vocabulary and comprehension and by Tindal and colleagues at the University of Oregon developed a line of research on concept-based teaching and learning.

Exam Probability: **Medium**

18. *Answer choices:*

(see index for correct answer)

- a. Direct Instruction
- b. Mand
- c. Desensitization
- d. Sensitization

Guidance: level 1

:: Logical fallacies ::

An _________ is a formal fallacy in the interpretation of statistical data that occurs when inferences about the nature of individuals are deduced from inferences about the group to which those individuals belong. _________ sometimes refers to the fallacy of division, which is not a statistical issue. The four common statistical ecological fallacies are: confusion between ecological correlations and individual correlations, confusion between group average and total average, Simpson`s paradox, and confusion between higher average and higher likelihood.

Exam Probability: **High**

19. *Answer choices:*

(see index for correct answer)

- a. Ecological fallacy
- b. Idola specus
- c. Judgmental language
- d. Appeal to probability

Guidance: level 1

:: Educational psychology ::

_________ describes how newcomers become experienced members and eventually old timers of a community of practice or collaborative project . LPP identifies learning as a contextual social phenomenon, achieved through participation in a community practice. According to LPP, newcomers become members of a community initially by participating in simple and low-risk tasks that are nonetheless productive and necessary and further the goals of the community. Through peripheral activities, novices become acquainted with the tasks, vocabulary, and organizing principles of the community's practitioners.

Exam Probability: **Low**

20. *Answer choices:*

(see index for correct answer)

- a. Legitimate peripheral participation
- b. Project-based learning
- c. Active learning
- d. Generation effect

Guidance: level 1

:: Data analysis ::

In statistics, the _________ is a measure that is used to quantify the amount of variation or dispersion of a set of data values. A low _________ indicates that the data points tend to be close to the mean of the set, while a high _________ indicates that the data points are spread out over a wider range of values.

Exam Probability: **High**

21. *Answer choices:*

(see index for correct answer)

- a. Data reduction
- b. Quantile normalization
- c. Empirical distribution function
- d. Evolutionary data mining

Guidance: level 1

:: Sampling techniques ::

Sampling is the use of a subset of the population to represent the whole population or to inform about processes that are meaningful beyond the particular cases, individuals or sites studied. Probability sampling, or random sampling, is a sampling technique in which the probability of getting any particular sample may be calculated. _________ does not meet this criterion and, as any methodological decision, should adjust to the research question that one envisages to answer. _________ techniques are not intended to be used to infer from the sample to the general population in statistical terms. Instead, for example, grounded theory can be produced through iterative non-probability sampling until theoretical saturation is reached .

Exam Probability: **High**

22. *Answer choices:*

(see index for correct answer)

- a. Gradsect
- b. Survey sampling
- c. Cluster sampling
- d. Demon algorithm

Guidance: level 1

:: Behaviorism ::

In behavioral psychology, _________ is a consequence applied that will strengthen an organism`s future behavior whenever that behavior is preceded by a specific antecedent stimulus. This strengthening effect may be measured as a higher frequency of behavior , longer duration , greater magnitude , or shorter latency . There are two types of _________ , known as positive _________ and negative _________ ; positive is where by a reward is offered on expression of the wanted behaviour and negative is taking away an undesirable element in the persons environment whenever the desired behaviour is achieved.

Exam Probability: **Low**

23. *Answer choices:*

(see index for correct answer)

- a. Functional analytic psychotherapy
- b. Direct Instruction
- c. Reinforcing
- d. Reinforcement

Guidance: level 1

:: Mental health ::

_________ is the use of psychological methods, particularly when based on regular personal interaction, to help a person change behavior and overcome problems in desired ways. _________ aims to improve an individual`s well-being and mental health, to resolve or mitigate troublesome behaviors, beliefs, compulsions, thoughts, or emotions, and to improve relationships and social skills. Certain psychotherapies are considered evidence-based for treating some diagnosed mental disorders. Others have been criticized as pseudoscience.

Exam Probability: **High**

24. *Answer choices:*

(see index for correct answer)

- a. Mental health counselor
- b. FRIENDS program
- c. Psychiatric interview
- d. Psychotherapy

Guidance: level 1

:: Human behavior ::

_________ is a cognitive system with a limited capacity that is responsible for temporarily holding information available for processing. _________ is important for reasoning and the guidance of decision-making and behavior. _________ is often used synonymously with short-term memory, but some theorists consider the two forms of memory distinct, assuming that _________ allows for the manipulation of stored information, whereas short-term memory only refers to the short-term storage of information. _________ is a theoretical concept central to cognitive psychology, neuropsychology, and neuroscience.

Exam Probability: **High**

25. *Answer choices:*

(see index for correct answer)

- a. Working memory
- b. Accismus
- c. Troll
- d. Assertiveness

Guidance: level 1

:: Race and education in the United States ::

In the United States, _________ is a pejorative term, usually applied to black people, which refers to a person`s perceived betrayal of their culture by assuming the social expectations of white society. Success in education in particular can be seen as a form of "selling out" by being disloyal to one`s culture.

Exam Probability: **Medium**

26. *Answer choices:*

(see index for correct answer)

- a. Mission Hill School
- b. Hispanic-serving institution
- c. National Physical Science Consortium
- d. Racial achievement gap in the United States

Guidance: level 1

:: Discrimination ::

The term _________ has a range of meanings within the contexts of sociology, of political philosophy, and of colloquial use. In sociology and in everyday usage, it is a synonym for "ethnic pluralism", with the two terms often used interchangeably, for example, a cultural pluralism in which various ethnic groups collaborate and enter into a dialogue with one another without having to sacrifice their particular identities. It can describe a mixed ethnic community area where multiple cultural traditions exist or a single country within which they do . Groups associated with an aboriginal or autochthonous ethnic group and foreigner ethnic groups are often the focus.

Exam Probability: **High**

27. *Answer choices:*

(see index for correct answer)

- a. Multiculturalism
- b. Classicide
- c. Fundamental Rights Agency
- d. Days of Remembrance of the Victims of the Holocaust

Guidance: level 1

:: Behaviorism ::

_________ is the theory set forth by psychologist Albert Bandura which states that a person`s behavior both influences and is influenced by personal factors and the social environment. Bandura accepts the possibility that an individual`s behavior may be conditioned through the use of consequences. At the same time he asserts that a person`s behavior can impact the environment. These skill sets result in an under- or overcompensated ego that, for all creative purposes, is too strong or too weak to focus on pure outcome. This is important because Bandura was able to prove the strong correlation between this with experiments.

Exam Probability: **Medium**

28. *Answer choices:*

(see index for correct answer)

- a. Functional analysis
- b. Reciprocal determinism
- c. Behaviorally anchored rating scales
- d. Licensed behavior analyst

Guidance: level 1

:: Brain ::

The _________ is an organ that serves as the center of the nervous system in all vertebrate and most invertebrate animals. The _________ is located in the head, usually close to the sensory organs for senses such as vision. The _________ is the most complex organ in a vertebrate`s body. In a human, the cerebral cortex contains approximately 14–16 billion neurons, and the estimated number of neurons in the cerebellum is 55–70 billion. Each neuron is connected by synapses to several thousand other neurons. These neurons communicate with one another by means of long protoplasmic fibers called axons, which carry trains of signal pulses called action potentials to distant parts of the _________ or body targeting specific recipient cells.

Exam Probability: **High**

29. *Answer choices:*

(see index for correct answer)

- a. Orbital part of inferior frontal gyrus
- b. Lateral ventricles
- c. Brain
- d. BRAIN Initiative

Guidance: level 1

:: Cognitive science ::

__________ , a theory of cognition, was hypothesized by Allan Paivio of the University of Western Ontario in 1971. In developing this theory, Paivio used the idea that the formation of mental images aids in learning . According to Paivio, there are two ways a person could expand on learned material: verbal associations and visual imagery. __________ postulates that both visual and verbal information is used to represent information . Visual and verbal information are processed differently and along distinct channels in the human mind, creating separate representations for information processed in each channel. The mental codes corresponding to these representations are used to organize incoming information that can be acted upon, stored, and retrieved for subsequent use. Both visual and verbal codes can be used when recalling information . For example, say a person has stored the stimulus concept "dog" as both the word `dog` and as the image of a dog. When asked to recall the stimulus, the person can retrieve either the word or the image individually, or both simultaneously. If the word is recalled, the image of the dog is not lost and can still be retrieved at a later point in time. The ability to code a stimulus two different ways increases the chance of remembering that item compared to if the stimulus was only coded one way.

Exam Probability: **Low**

30. *Answer choices:*

(see index for correct answer)

- a. Associative group analysis
- b. Cognitive map
- c. Congruence bias
- d. Dual-coding theory

Guidance: level 1

:: Problem solving ::

_________ is a fundamental method of problem solving. It is characterised by repeated, varied attempts which are continued until success, or until the agent stops trying.

Exam Probability: **High**

31. *Answer choices:*

(see index for correct answer)

- a. Systems thinking
- b. Encyclopedia of World Problems and Human Potential
- c. Task force
- d. Problem finding

Guidance: level 1

:: Memory ::

In communications and information processing, code is a system of rules to convert information—such as a letter, word, sound, image, or gesture—into another form or representation, sometimes shortened or secret, for communication through a communication channel or storage in a storage medium. An early example is the invention of language, which enabled a person, through speech, to communicate what they saw, heard, felt, or thought to others. But speech limits the range of communication to the distance a voice can carry, and limits the audience to those present when the speech is uttered. The invention of writing, which converted spoken language into visual symbols, extended the range of communication across space and time.

Exam Probability: **High**

32. *Answer choices:*

(see index for correct answer)

- a. Hyperthymesia
- b. Encoding
- c. Ron White
- d. Exosomatic memory

Guidance: level 1

:: Intelligence by type ::

The _________ differentiates human intelligence into specific `modalities`, rather than seeing intelligence as dominated by a single general ability. Howard Gardner proposed this model in his 1983 book Frames of Mind: The _________. According to the theory, an intelligence `modality` must fulfill eight criteria.

Exam Probability: **High**

33. *Answer choices:*

(see index for correct answer)

- a. Social intelligence
- b. Theory of multiple intelligences
- c. Intelligence quotient
- d. Intelligence Test

Guidance: level 1

:: Cognitive linguistics ::

_________ is the practice of forcing another party to act in an involuntary manner by use of threats or force. It involves a set of various types of forceful actions that violate the free will of an individual to induce a desired response, for example: a bully demanding lunch money from a student or the student gets beaten. These actions may include extortion, blackmail, torture, threats to induce favors, or even sexual assault. In law, _________ is codified as a duress crime. Such actions are used as leverage, to force the victim to act in a way contrary to their own interests. _________ may involve the actual infliction of physical pain/injury or psychological harm in order to enhance the credibility of a threat. The threat of further harm may lead to the cooperation or obedience of the person being coerced.

Exam Probability: **Medium**

34. *Answer choices:*

(see index for correct answer)

- a. Conceptual blending
- b. Linguistic frame of reference
- c. Coercion
- d. Linguistic competence

Guidance: level 1

:: Educational psychology ::

A __________ test is a type of test, assessment, or evaluation which yields an estimate of the position of the tested individual in a predefined population, with respect to the trait being measured. The estimate is derived from the analysis of test scores and possibly other relevant data from a sample drawn from the population. That is, this type of test identifies whether the test taker performed better or worse than other test takers, not whether the test taker knows either more or less material than is necessary for a given purpose.

Exam Probability: **High**

35. *Answer choices:*

(see index for correct answer)

- a. Inquiry-based learning
- b. Reading Recovery
- c. Norm-referenced
- d. Structure of Observed Learning Outcome

Guidance: level 1

:: Scientific method ::

In natural and social sciences, and sometimes in other fields, _________ is the systematic empirical investigation of observable phenomena via statistical, mathematical, or computational techniques. The objective of _________ is to develop and employ mathematical models, theories, and hypotheses pertaining to phenomena. The process of measurement is central to _________ because it provides the fundamental connection between empirical observation and mathematical expression of quantitative relationships.

Exam Probability: **High**

36. *Answer choices:*

(see index for correct answer)

- a. Skepticism
- b. Double-blind
- c. Quantitative research
- d. Scientific progress

Guidance: level 1

:: Developmental psychology ::

_________ is a concept related to intelligence. It looks at how a specific individual , at a specific age, performs intellectually, compared to average intellectual performance for that individual`s actual chronological age . The intellectual performance is based on performance in tests and live assessments by a psychologist. The score achieved by the individual is compared to the median average scores at various ages, and the _________ is derived such that the individual`s score equates to the average score at age x.

Exam Probability: **Low**

37. *Answer choices:*

(see index for correct answer)

- a. Motor theory of speech perception
- b. Stage-Crisis View
- c. Developmental psychobiology
- d. Mental age

Guidance: level 1

:: Psychological testing ::

_________ was a French psychologist who invented the first practical IQ test, the Binet–Simon test. In 1904, the French Ministry of Education asked psychologist _________ to devise a method that would determine which students did not learn effectively from regular classroom instruction so they could be given remedial work. Along with his collaborator Théodore Simon, Binet published revisions of his test in 1908 and 1911, the last of which appeared just before his death.

Exam Probability: **Medium**

38. *Answer choices:*

(see index for correct answer)

- a. Alfred Binet

- b. Gudjonsson suggestibility scale
- c. Toronto Alexithymia Scale
- d. Competency evaluation

Guidance: level 1

:: Communication disorders ::

_________ is diagnosed when a child`s language does not develop normally and the difficulties cannot be accounted for by generally slow development, physical abnormality of the speech apparatus, autism spectrum disorder, apraxia, acquired brain damage or hearing loss. Twin studies have shown that it is under genetic influence. Although language impairment can result from a single-gene mutation, this is unusual. More commonly SLI results from the combined influence of multiple genetic variants, each of which is found in the general population, as well as environmental influences.

Exam Probability: **Low**

39. *Answer choices:*

(see index for correct answer)

- a. Nuffield Speech and Language Unit
- b. Specific language impairment
- c. Apraxia of speech
- d. Motor speech disorders

Guidance: level 1

:: Developmental psychology ::

_________ , also known as _________ disorder , is a range of mental disorders of the neurodevelopmental type. It includes autism and Asperger syndrome. Individuals on the spectrum often present with problems with social communication and interaction; and restricted, repetitive patterns of behavior, interests or activities. Symptoms are typically recognized between one and two years of age. Long term issues may include difficulties in performing daily tasks, creating and keeping relationships, and maintaining a job.

Exam Probability: **High**

40. *Answer choices:*

(see index for correct answer)

- a. Autism spectrum
- b. Developmental psychopathology
- c. Orgastic potency
- d. Potty training

Guidance: level 1

:: Reasoning ::

__________ s are steps in reasoning, moving from premises to logical consequences; etymologically, the word infer means to "carry forward". __________ is theoretically traditionally divided into deduction and induction, a distinction that in Europe dates at least to Aristotle . Deduction is __________ deriving logical conclusions from premises known or assumed to be true, with the laws of valid __________ being studied in logic. Induction is __________ from particular premises to a universal conclusion. A third type of __________ is sometimes distinguished, notably by Charles Sanders Peirce, distinguishing abduction from induction, where abduction is __________ to the best explanation.

Exam Probability: **Low**

41. *Answer choices:*

(see index for correct answer)

- a. Logical reasoning
- b. Doxastic logic
- c. Akrasia
- d. Inference

Guidance: level 1

:: Knowledge bases ::

A __________ is a technology used to store complex structured and unstructured information used by a computer system. The initial use of the term was in connection with expert systems which were the first knowledge-based systems.

Exam Probability: **Low**

42. *Answer choices:*

(see index for correct answer)

- a. Classora
- b. Commonsense knowledge base
- c. Knowledge Graph
- d. DBpedia

Guidance: level 1

:: Unconscious ::

The word stems from the old French verb _________ er which means literally to carry something back; and, in the sense of how people relate to each other means that what one person sends out the other sends back. For example, they may realize that they share similar values, beliefs, knowledge, or behaviors around politics, music or sports. This may also mean that the participants engage in reciprocal behaviors such as posture mirroring or in increased coordination in their verbal and nonverbal interactions.

Exam Probability: **High**

43. *Answer choices:*

(see index for correct answer)

- a. Implicit stereotypes

- b. Unconscious communication
- c. Rapport
- d. Psychology from an Empirical Standpoint

Guidance: level 1

:: Neuropsychological assessment ::

_________ is the faculty of the brain by which information is encoded, stored, and retrieved when needed.

Exam Probability: **Low**

44. *Answer choices:*

(see index for correct answer)

- a. Memory
- b. Natural language
- c. forethought
- d. Adaptive memory

Guidance: level 1

:: Knowledge ::

_________ is knowledge that can be readily articulated, codified, stored and accessed. It can be easily transmitted to others. Most forms of _________ can be stored in certain media. _________ is often seen as complementary to tacit knowledge.

Exam Probability: **Low**

45. *Answer choices:*

(see index for correct answer)

- a. Explicit knowledge
- b. Knowledge environment
- c. Too Big to Know
- d. Functional illiteracy

Guidance: level 1

:: Cognitive science ::

_________ is the means to see, hear, or become aware of something or someone through our fundamental senses. The term _________ derives from the Latin word perceptio, and is the organization, identification, and interpretation of sensory information in order to represent and understand the presented information, or the environment.

Exam Probability: **Medium**

46. *Answer choices:*

(see index for correct answer)

- a. Fictive motion
- b. Associative group analysis
- c. Perception
- d. Computational linguistics

Guidance: level 1

:: Machine learning ::

_________ , also known as category learning, concept attainment, and concept formation, is defined by Bruner, Goodnow, & Austin as "the search for and listing of attributes that can be used to distinguish exemplars from non exemplars of various categories". More simply put, concepts are the mental categories to help nts, or ideas, building on the understanding that each object, vent, or idea has a set of co evant features. Thus, _________ is a strategy which requires a learner to compare and contrast groups or categories that contain concept-relevant features with groups or categories that do not contain concept-relevant feature learning task in which a human or machine learner is trained to classify objects by being shown a set of example objects along with their class labels. The learner simplifies what has been observed by condensing it in the form of an example. This simplified version of what has been learned is then applied to future examples. _________ may be simple or complex because learning takes place over many areas. When a concept is difficult, it is less likely that the learner will be able to simplify, and therefore will be less likely to learn. Colloquially, the task is known as learning from examples. Most theories of _________ are based on the storage of exemplars and avoid summarization or overt abstraction of any kind.

Exam Probability: **High**

47. *Answer choices:*

(see index for correct answer)

- a. Predictive state representation
- b. Large margin nearest neighbor
- c. Dimensionality reduction
- d. Metafor Software

Guidance: level 1

:: Intelligence tests ::

The Stanford–Binet Intelligence Scales is an individually administered intelligence test that was revised from the original Binet–Simon Scale by Lewis M. Terman, a psychologist at Stanford University. The Stanford–Binet Intelligence Scale is now in its fifth edition and was released in 2003. It is a cognitive ability and intelligence test that is used to diagnose developmental or intellectual deficiencies in young children. The test measures five weighted factors and consists of both verbal and nonverbal subtests. The five factors being tested are knowledge, quantitative reasoning, visual-spatial processing, working memory, and fluid reasoning.

Exam Probability: **Medium**

48. *Answer choices:*

(see index for correct answer)

- a. IQ classification
- b. Raven%27s Progressive Matrices
- c. Miller Analogies Test
- d. Stanford-Binet

Guidance: level 1

:: Nonverbal communication ::

It includes the use of visual cues such as body language , distance and physical environments/appearance, of voice and of touch . It can also include the use of time and eye contact and the actions of looking while talking and listening, frequency of glances, patterns of fixation, pupil dilation, and blink rate .

Exam Probability: **High**

49. *Answer choices:*

(see index for correct answer)

- a. Nonverbal communication
- b. Silent trade
- c. Joe Navarro
- d. Chronemics

Guidance: level 1

:: Bilingual education ::

_________ involves teaching academic content in two languages, in a native and secondary language with varying amounts of each language used in accordance with the program model. _________ refers to the utilization of two languages as means of instruction for students and considered part of or the entire school curriculum.

Exam Probability: **High**

50. *Answer choices:*

(see index for correct answer)

- a. Bilingual Education Act
- b. National Association for Bilingual Education
- c. Content and language integrated learning
- d. Bilingual education

Guidance: level 1

:: Memory processes ::

__________ is the capacity for holding, but not manipulating, a small amount of information in mind in an active, readily available state for a short period of time. For example, __________ can be used to remember a phone number that has just been recited. The duration of __________ is believed to be in the order of seconds. The most commonly cited capacity is The Magical Number Seven, Plus or Minus Two , despite the fact that Miller himself stated that the figure was intended as "little more than a joke" and that Cowan provided evidence that a more realistic figure is 4±1 units. In contrast, long-term memory can hold the information indefinitely.

Exam Probability: **High**

51. *Answer choices:*

(see index for correct answer)

- a. Prospective memory
- b. Short-term memory
- c. Forgetting curve
- d. Concurrent overlap

Guidance: level 1

:: Educational psychology ::

__________ is a technique of inquiry-based learning and is considered a constructivist based approach to education. It is also referred to as problem-based learning, experiential learning and 21st century learning. It is supported by the work of learning theorists and psychologists Jean Piaget, Jerome Bruner, and Seymour Papert.

Exam Probability: **High**

52. *Answer choices:*

(see index for correct answer)

- a. Criterion-referenced test
- b. Discovery learning
- c. Reading Recovery
- d. Visual learning

Guidance: level 1

:: Research methods ::

_________ is often used to assess thoughts, opinions, and feelings. Surveys can be specific and limited, or they can have more global, widespread goals. Psychologists and sociologists often use surveys to analyze behavior, while it is also used to meet the more pragmatic needs of the media, such as, in evaluating political candidates, public health officials, professional organizations, and advertising and marketing directors. A survey consists of a predetermined set of questions that is given to a sample. With a representative sample, that is, one that is representative of the larger population of interest, one can describe the attitudes of the population from which the sample was drawn. Further, one can compare the attitudes of different populations as well as look for changes in attitudes over time. A good sample selection is key as it allows one to generalize the findings from the sample to the population, which is the whole purpose of _________ .

Exam Probability: **Low**

53. *Answer choices:*

(see index for correct answer)

- a. Nocebo
- b. New Zealand Attitudes and Values Study
- c. Online research community
- d. Methods in Molecular Biology

Guidance: level 1

:: Educational psychology ::

A _________ is an oral presentation intended to present information or teach people about a particular subject, for example by a university or college teacher. _________ s are used to convey critical information, history, background, theories, and equations. A politician`s speech, a minister`s sermon, or even a businessman`s sales presentation may be similar in form to a _________ . Usually the _________ r will stand at the front of the room and recite information relevant to the _________ `s content.

Exam Probability: **Low**

54. *Answer choices:*

(see index for correct answer)

- a. Theme-centered interaction
- b. Culturally relevant teaching
- c. Overjustification effect

- d. Writing motivation

Guidance: level 1

:: Educational psychology ::

A _________ is a group of people who share a craft or a profession. The concept was first proposed by cognitive anthropologist Jean Lave and educational theorist Etienne Wenger in their 1991 book Situated Learning . Wenger then significantly expanded on the concept in his 1998 book Communities of Practice .

Exam Probability: **Low**

55. *Answer choices:*

(see index for correct answer)

- a. Community of practice
- b. E-learning
- c. Educational research
- d. Transfer of learning

Guidance: level 1

:: Death customs ::

A _________ is an inert substance or treatment which is not designed to have a therapeutic value. Common _________ s include inert tablets , inert injections , sham surgery, and other procedures.

Exam Probability: **Low**

56. *Answer choices:*

(see index for correct answer)

- a. Placebo
- b. Archimime
- c. Ushabti
- d. Burial vault

Guidance: level 1

:: Communication disorders ::

A _________ is any disorder that affects an individual`s ability to comprehend, detect, or apply language and speech to engage in discourse effectively with others. The delays and disorders can range from simple sound substitution to the inability to understand or use one`s native language.

Exam Probability: **High**

57. *Answer choices:*

(see index for correct answer)

- a. Multisystem developmental disorder
- b. Cluttering
- c. The Indian Stammering Association
- d. Specific language impairment

Guidance: level 1

:: Collaboration ::

_________ is a cultural value that is characterized by emphasis on cohesiveness among individuals and prioritization of the group over self. Individuals or groups that subscribe to a collectivist worldview tend to find common values and goals as particularly salient and demonstrate greater orientation toward in-group than toward out-group. The term "in-group" is thought to be more diffusely defined for collectivistic individuals to include societal units ranging from the nuclear family to a religious or racial/ethnic group. Meta-analytic findings support that _________ shows a consistent association with discrete values, interpersonal patterns of interaction, cognition, perception and self-construal. While _________ is often defined in contrast to individualism, the notion that _________ -individualism is unidimensional has been challenged by contemporary theorists.

Exam Probability: **Low**

58. *Answer choices:*

(see index for correct answer)

- a. Troupe system

- b. GroupLogic
- c. Collectivism
- d. Sharing economy

Guidance: level 1

:: Scientific method ::

In research design, especially in psychology, social sciences, life sciences, and physics, _________ is a process of defining the measurement of a phenomenon that is not directly measurable, though its existence is inferred by other phenomena. _________ thus defines a fuzzy concept so as to make it clearly distinguishable, measurable, and understandable by empirical observation. In a broader sense, it defines the extension of a concept—describing what is and is not an instance of that concept. For example, in medicine, the phenomenon of health might be operationalized by one or more indicators like body mass index or tobacco smoking. As another example, in visual processing the presence of a certain object in the environment could be inferred by measuring specific features of the light it reflects. In these examples, the phenomena are difficult to directly observe and measure because they are general/abstract or they are latent . _________ helps infer the existence, and some elements of the extension, of the phenomena of interest by means of some observable and measurable effects they have.

Exam Probability: **Low**

59. *Answer choices:*

(see index for correct answer)

- a. Operationalization

- b. Interdisciplinary peer review
- c. Science of team science
- d. Inverse-square law

Guidance: level 1

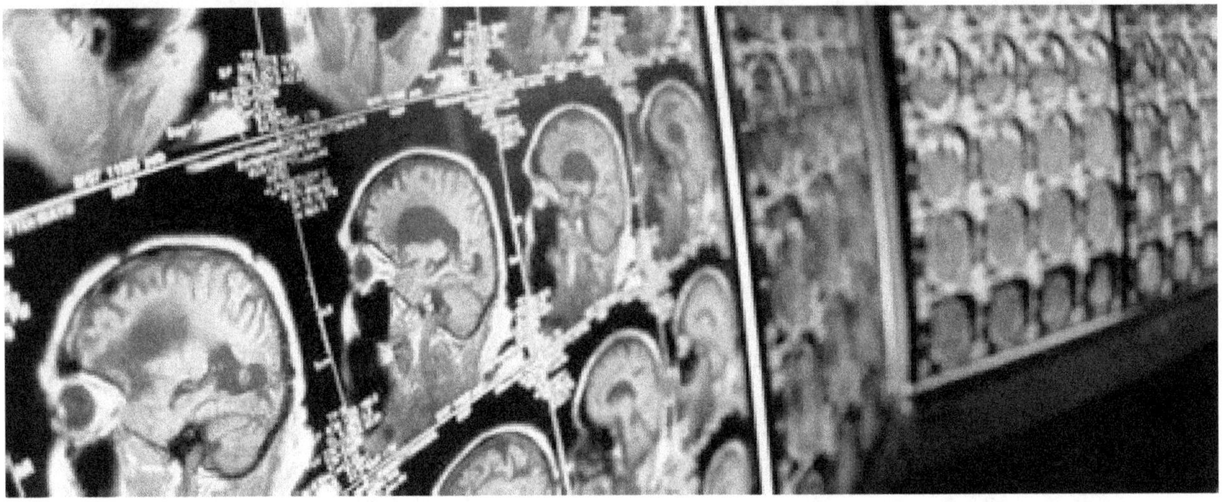

Biopsychology

Behavioral neuroscience, also known as biological psychology, biopsychology, or psychobiology is the application of the principles of biology to the study of physiological, genetic, and developmental mechanisms of behavior in humans and other animals.

The distinguishing characteristic of a behavioral neuroscience experiment is that either the independent variable of the experiment is biological, or some dependent variable is biological. In other words, the nervous system of the organism under study is permanently or temporarily altered, or some aspect of the nervous system is measured (usually to be related to a behavioral variable).

:: Cognitive disorders ::

_________ is a broad category of brain diseases that cause a long-term and often gradual decrease in the ability to think and remember that is great enough to affect a person`s daily functioning. Other common symptoms include emotional problems, difficulties with language, and a decrease in motivation. A person`s consciousness is usually not affected. A _________ diagnosis requires a change from a person`s usual mental functioning and a greater decline than one would expect due to aging. These diseases also have a significant effect on a person`s caregivers.

Exam Probability: **Medium**

1. *Answer choices:*

(see index for correct answer)

- a. Dementia
- b. Frontotemporal lobar degeneration
- c. Cerebellar cognitive affective syndrome
- d. Progressive nonfluent aphasia

Guidance: level 1

:: Neurotransmitters ::

_________ s are synaptic and non synaptic receptors located primarily on the membranes of neuronal and glial cells. Glutamate is abundant in the human body, but particularly in the nervous system and especially prominent in the human brain where it is the body`s most prominent neurotransmitter, the brain`s main excitatory neurotransmitter, and also the precursor for GABA, the brain`s main inhibitory neurotransmitter. _________ s are responsible for the glutamate-mediated postsynaptic excitation of neural cells, and are important for neural communication, memory formation, learning, and regulation.

Exam Probability: **High**

2. *Answer choices:*

(see index for correct answer)

- a. GABAergic
- b. Glutamate receptor
- c. Glutamic acid
- d. Gliotransmitter

Guidance: level 1

:: Exercise physiology ::

_________ is a soft tissue found in most animals. _________ cells contain protein filaments of actin and myosin that slide past one another, producing a contraction that changes both the length and the shape of the cell. _________ s function to produce force and motion. They are primarily responsible for maintaining and changing posture, locomotion, as well as movement of internal organs, such as the contraction of the heart and the movement of food through the digestive system via peristalsis.

Exam Probability: **High**

3. *Answer choices:*

(see index for correct answer)

- a. Muscle hypertrophy
- b. Myograph
- c. Muscle
- d. Exercise-induced nausea

Guidance: level 1

:: Phenomenology ::

_________ is the state or quality of awareness or of being aware of an external object or something within oneself. It has been defined variously in terms of sentience, awareness, qualia, subjectivity, the ability to experience or to feel, wakefulness, having a sense of selfhood or soul, the fact that there is something "that it is like" to "have" or "be" it, and the executive control system of the mind. Despite the difficulty in definition, many philosophers believe that there is a broadly shared underlying intuition about what _________ is. As Max Velmans and Susan Schneider wrote in The Blackwell Companion to _________: "Anything that we are aware of at a given moment forms part of our _________, making conscious experience at once the most familiar and most mysterious aspect of our lives."

Exam Probability: **Medium**

4. *Answer choices:*

(see index for correct answer)

- a. Phenomenology of essences
- b. Schismogenesis
- c. Neurophenomenology
- d. Phenomenology of religion

Guidance: level 1

:: Memory ::

__________ is one of the two main types of long-term human memory. It is acquired and used unconsciously, and can affect thoughts and behaviours. One of its most common forms is procedural memory, which helps people performing certain tasks without conscious awareness of these previous experiences.

Exam Probability: **Medium**

5. *Answer choices:*

(see index for correct answer)

- a. Transactive memory
- b. Positivity effect
- c. Mnemonist
- d. Mnemosyne

Guidance: level 1

:: Computational neuroscience ::

A __________ is a small membranous protrusion from a neuron`s dendrite that typically receives input from a single axon at the synapse. __________ s serve as a storage site for synaptic strength and help transmit electrical signals to the neuron`s cell body. Most spines have a bulbous head , and a thin neck that connects the head of the spine to the shaft of the dendrite. The dendrites of a single neuron can contain hundreds to thousands of spines. In addition to spines providing an anatomical substrate for memory storage and synaptic transmission, they may also serve to increase the number of possible contacts between neurons.

Exam Probability: **Low**

6. *Answer choices:*

(see index for correct answer)

- a. Neurocybernetics
- b. Neuronstudio
- c. Backpropagation through time
- d. Neural decoding

Guidance: level 1

:: Neurological disorders in children ::

_________ is a group of neurological disorders characterized by epileptic seizures. Epileptic seizures are episodes that can vary from brief and nearly undetectable periods to long periods of vigorous shaking. These episodes can result in physical injuries, including occasionally broken bones. In _________ , seizures tend to recur and, as a rule, have no immediate underlying cause. Isolated seizures that are provoked by a specific cause such as poisoning are not deemed to represent _________ . People with _________ may be treated differently in various areas of the world and experience varying degrees of social stigma due to their condition.

Exam Probability: **High**

7. *Answer choices:*

(see index for correct answer)

- a. Epilepsy
- b. Autism
- c. Alexander disease
- d. Panayiotopoulos syndrome

Guidance: level 1

:: Cerebrum ::

The _________ is a sulcus, or fold, in the cerebral cortex in the brains of vertebrates. Also called the central fissure, it was originally called the fissure of Rolando or the Rolandic fissure, after Luigi Rolando. It is sometimes confused with the medial longitudinal fissure.

Exam Probability: **Medium**

8. *Answer choices:*

(see index for correct answer)

- a. Frenulum of superior medullary velum
- b. Inferior temporal gyrus
- c. Cingulate cortex
- d. Lateral globus pallidus

Guidance: level 1

:: Embryology of nervous system ::

In anatomy, the _________ is a flexible rod made out of a material similar to cartilage. If a species has a _________ at any stage of its life cycle, it is, by definition, a chordate. In vertebrates the _________ becomes part of the vertebral column. The _________ lies along the anteroposterior axis, is usually closer to the ventral than the dorsal surface of the animal, and is composed of cells derived from the mesoderm. The _________ has been observed to have many functions including developmental functions. The most commonly cited functions are as a site of muscle attachment, vertebral precursor, and as a midline tissue that provides signals to the surrounding tissue during development.

Exam Probability: **Medium**

9. *Answer choices:*

(see index for correct answer)

- a. Optic vesicle
- b. Colpocephaly
- c. Notochord
- d. Neuroblast

Guidance: level 1

:: Psychedelics, dissociatives and deliriants ::

A __________ is a psychoactive agent which can cause hallucinations, perceptual anomalies, and other substantial subjective changes in thoughts, emotion, and consciousness. The common types of __________ s are psychedelics, dissociatives and deliriants. Although hallucinations are a common symptom of amphetamine psychosis, amphetamines are not considered __________ s as they are not a primary effect of the drugs themselves. While hallucinations can occur when abusing stimulants, the nature of stimulant psychosis is not unlike delirium.

Exam Probability: **Low**

10. *Answer choices:*

(see index for correct answer)

- a. Oneirogen
- b. Hallucinogen
- c. Turn on, tune in, drop out
- d. Cyclorphan

Guidance: level 1

:: Cellular neuroscience ::

In the nervous system, a __________ is a structure that permits a neuron to pass an electrical or chemical signal to another neuron or to the target effector cell.

Exam Probability: **Low**

11. *Answer choices:*

(see index for correct answer)

- a. Repolarization
- b. Synapse
- c. Action potential
- d. Depolarization

Guidance: level 1

:: Peripheral nervous system ::

A __________ is a mixed nerve, which carries motor, sensory, and autonomic signals between the spinal cord and the body. In the human body there are 31 pairs of __________s, one on each side of the vertebral column. These are grouped into the corresponding cervical, thoracic, lumbar, sacral and coccygeal regions of the spine. There are eight pairs of cervical nerves, twelve pairs of thoracic nerves, five pairs of lumbar nerves, five pairs of sacral nerves, and one pair of coccygeal nerves. The __________s are part of the peripheral nervous system.

Exam Probability: **Medium**

12. *Answer choices:*

(see index for correct answer)

- a. General visceral afferent fibers
- b. Spinal nerve

- c. Nerve plexus
- d. Spinocervical pathway

Guidance: level 1

:: Entheogens ::

_________ is a naturally occurring psychedelic alkaloid of the phenethylamine class, known for its hallucinogenic effects comparable to those of LSD and psilocybin.

Exam Probability: **Low**

13. *Answer choices:*

(see index for correct answer)

- a. Psilocybe guilartensis
- b. Psilocybe moseri
- c. Mescaline
- d. Virola

Guidance: level 1

:: Communication disorders ::

__________ s or language impairments are disorders that involve the processing of linguistic information. Problems that may be experienced can involve grammar , semantics , or other aspects of language. These problems may be receptive , expressive , or a combination of both. Examples include specific language impairment and aphasia, among others. __________ s can affect both spoken and written language, and can also affect sign language; typically, all forms of language will be impaired.

Exam Probability: **High**

14. *Answer choices:*

(see index for correct answer)

- a. Language disorder
- b. Cluttering
- c. National Stuttering Association
- d. Motor speech disorders

Guidance: level 1

:: History of neuroscience ::

Aelius __________ us or Claudius __________ us , often Anglicized as __________ and better known as __________ of Pergamon , was a Greek physician, surgeon and philosopher in the Roman Empire. Arguably the most accomplished of all medical researchers of antiquity, __________ influenced the development of various scientific disciplines, including anatomy, physiology, pathology, pharmacology, and neurology, as well as philosophy and logic.

Exam Probability: **Low**

15. *Answer choices:*

(see index for correct answer)

- a. Balloonist theory
- b. Camillo Golgi
- c. Galen
- d. Decade of the Brain

Guidance: level 1

:: Human cells ::

A _________ is a type of lymphocyte which develops in the thymus that plays a central role in the immune response. _________ s can be distinguished from other lymphocytes by the presence of a T-cell receptor on the cell surface. The name _________ originates from the thymus where they develop from precursor cells derived from the bone marrow. The several distinct types of _________ s develop in the thymus, and their differentiation continues after the cells leave the thymus.

Exam Probability: **Low**

16. *Answer choices:*

(see index for correct answer)

- a. Cholangiocyte

- b. T cell
- c. Parietal cell
- d. Osteoclast

Guidance: level 1

:: Cellular neuroscience ::

In biology, _________ is a change within a cell, during which the cell undergoes a shift in electric charge distribution, resulting in less negative charge inside the cell. _________ is essential to the function of many cells, communication between cells, and the overall physiology of an organism.

Exam Probability: **Low**

17. *Answer choices:*

(see index for correct answer)

- a. Synapse
- b. Depolarization
- c. Ephaptic coupling
- d. Autapse

Guidance: level 1

:: Entheogens ::

_________ is a medication used to treat certain types of nerve agent and pesticide poisonings as well as some types of slow heart rate and to decrease saliva production during surgery. It is typically given intravenously or by injection into a muscle. Eye drops are also available which are used to treat uveitis and early amblyopia. The intravenous solution usually begins working within a minute and lasts half an hour to an hour. Large doses may be required to treat some poisonings.

Exam Probability: **Low**

18. *Answer choices:*

(see index for correct answer)

- a. Psilocybe indica
- b. Atropine
- c. Muscimol
- d. Psilocybe caerulipes

Guidance: level 1

:: Aggression ::

_________ is overt or covert, often harmful, social interaction with the intention of inflicting damage or other unpleasantness upon another individual. It may occur either reactively or without provocation. In humans, frustration due to blocked goals can cause _________ . Human _________ can be classified into direct and indirect _________ ; whilst the former is characterized by physical or verbal behavior intended to cause harm to someone, the latter is characterized by behavior intended to harm the social relations of an individual or group.

Exam Probability: **Low**

19. *Answer choices:*

(see index for correct answer)

- a. Bullying
- b. Fighting in ice hockey
- c. On Aggression
- d. Aggression

Guidance: level 1

:: Sleep ::

_________ is a naturally recurring state of mind and body, characterized by altered consciousness, relatively inhibited sensory activity, inhibition of nearly all voluntary muscles, and reduced interactions with surroundings. It is distinguished from wakefulness by a decreased ability to react to stimuli, but more reactive than coma or disorders of consciousness, _________ displaying very different and active brain patterns.

Exam Probability: **Low**

20. *Answer choices:*

(see index for correct answer)

- a. Local sleep
- b. Flowerpot technique
- c. Positive airway pressure
- d. Sleep

Guidance: level 1

:: Aphasias ::

_________ is an acquired neurological disorder causing a loss in the ability to communicate through writing, either due to some form of motor dysfunction or an inability to spell. The loss of writing ability may present with other language or neurological disorders; disorders appearing commonly with _________ are alexia, aphasia, dysarthria, agnosia, and apraxia. The study of individuals with _________ may provide more information about the pathways involved in writing, both language related and motoric. _________ cannot be directly treated, but individuals can learn techniques to help regain and rehabilitate some of their previous writing abilities. These techniques differ depending on the type of _________.

Exam Probability: **High**

21. *Answer choices:*

(see index for correct answer)

- a. Agraphia
- b. Comprehensive Aphasia Test
- c. Global aphasia
- d. Paragrammatism

Guidance: level 1

:: Neuroanatomy ::

The _________ is a brain region that in humans is located in the dorsal portion of the frontal lobe. It is the primary region of the motor system and works in association with other motor areas including premotor cortex, the supplementary motor area, posterior parietal cortex, and several subcortical brain regions, to plan and execute movements. _________ is defined anatomically as the region of cortex that contains large neurons known as Betz cells. Betz cells, along with other cortical neurons, send long axons down the spinal cord to synapse onto the interneuron circuitry of the spinal cord and also directly onto the alpha motor neurons in the spinal cord which connect to the muscles.

Exam Probability: **Medium**

22. *Answer choices:*

(see index for correct answer)

- a. Hypothalamospinal tract
- b. Serotonergic cell groups
- c. Anterior gray column
- d. Primary motor cortex

Guidance: level 1

:: Pheromones ::

A _________ is a secreted or excreted chemical factor that triggers a social response in members of the same species. _________ s are chemicals capable of acting like hormones outside the body of the secreting individual, to impact the behavior of the receiving individuals. There are alarm _________ s, food trail _________ s, sex _________ s, and many others that affect behavior or physiology. _________ s are used from basic unicellular prokaryotes to complex multicellular eukaryotes. Their use among insects has been particularly well documented. In addition, some vertebrates, plants and ciliates communicate by using _________ s.

Exam Probability: **Medium**

23. *Answer choices:*

(see index for correct answer)

- a. Ectocarpene
- b. Pheromone
- c. Major urinary proteins
- d. The Great Pheromone Myth

Guidance: level 1

:: Human–computer interaction ::

_________ is a technique in user experience design in which a person tests a group of subject experts or users to generate a dendrogram or folksonomy. It is a useful approach for designing information architecture, workflows, menu structure, or web site navigation paths.

Exam Probability: **High**

24. *Answer choices:*

(see index for correct answer)

- a. Umoove
- b. Ultra Hal Assistant
- c. Card sorting
- d. Graphics Interface

Guidance: level 1

:: Cerebrum ::

The _________ is a round structure located at the base of the forebrain . The _________ and caudate nucleus together form the dorsal striatum. It is also one of the structures that comprise the basal ganglia. Through various pathways, the _________ is connected to the substantia nigra, the globus pallidus, the claustrum, and the thalamus, in addition to many regions of the cerebral cortex. A primary function of the _________ is to regulate movements at various stages and influence various types of learning. It employs GABA, acetylcholine, and enkephalin to perform its functions. The _________ also plays a role in degenerative neurological disorders, such as Parkinson`s disease.

Exam Probability: **Low**

25. *Answer choices:*

(see index for correct answer)

- a. Vestibular cortex
- b. Frenulum of superior medullary velum
- c. Ventral posterior nucleus
- d. Interpeduncular fossa

Guidance: level 1

:: Cognitive science ::

_________ is the process of acquiring new, or modifying existing, knowledge, behaviors, skills, values, or preferences. The ability to learn is possessed by humans, animals, and some machines; there is also evidence for some kind of _________ in some plants. Some _________ is immediate, induced by a single event , but much skill and knowledge accumulates from repeated experiences. The changes induced by _________ often last a lifetime, and it is hard to distinguish learned material that seems to be "lost" from that which cannot be retrieved.

Exam Probability: **Medium**

26. *Answer choices:*

(see index for correct answer)

- a. Learning
- b. Physical symbol system
- c. Functionalism
- d. Theory of mind

Guidance: level 1

:: Neuroendocrinology ::

In vertebrate anatomy, the __________ , or hypophysis, is an endocrine gland about the size of a pea and weighing 0.5 grams in humans. It is a protrusion off the bottom of the hypothalamus at the base of the brain. The hypophysis rests upon the hypophysial fossa of the sphenoid bone in the center of the middle cranial fossa and is surrounded by a small bony cavity covered by a dural fold . The anterior pituitary is a lobe of the gland that regulates several physiological processes . The intermediate lobe synthesizes and secretes melanocyte-stimulating hormone. The posterior pituitary is a lobe of the gland that is functionally connected to the hypothalamus by the median eminence via a small tube called the pituitary stalk .

Exam Probability: **Low**

27. *Answer choices:*

(see index for correct answer)

- a. Parvocellular neurosecretory cell
- b. Pituitary gland
- c. Magnocellular neurosecretory cell
- d. Posterior pituitary

Guidance: level 1

:: Neurobiology ::

The _________ is the part of an animal that coordinates its actions by transmitting signals to and from different parts of its body. The _________ detects environmental changes that impact the body, then works in tandem with the endocrine system to respond to such events. Nervous tissue first arose in wormlike organisms about 550 to 600 million years ago. In vertebrates it consists of two main parts, the central _________ and the peripheral _________. The CNS consists of the brain and spinal cord. The PNS consists mainly of nerves, which are enclosed bundles of the long fibers or axons, that connect the CNS to every other part of the body. Nerves that transmit signals from the brain are called motor or efferent nerves, while those nerves that transmit information from the body to the CNS are called sensory or afferent. Spinal nerves serve both functions and are called mixed nerves. The PNS is divided into three separate subsystems, the somatic, autonomic, and enteric _________s. Somatic nerves mediate voluntary movement. The autonomic _________ is further subdivided into the sympathetic and the parasympathetic _________s. The sympathetic _________ is activated in cases of emergencies to mobilize energy, while the parasympathetic _________ is activated when organisms are in a relaxed state. The enteric _________ functions to control the gastrointestinal system. Both autonomic and enteric _________s function involuntarily. Nerves that exit from the cranium are called cranial nerves while those exiting from the spinal cord are called spinal nerves.

Exam Probability: **High**

28. *Answer choices:*

(see index for correct answer)

- a. Haemodynamic response

- b. Nervous system
- c. Neuropreservation
- d. Neuroglia

Guidance: level 1

:: Phenethylamines ::

_________ , also known under several other names, is a naturally occurring trace amine derived from the amino acid tyrosine. _________ acts as a catecholamine releasing agent. Notably, it is unable to cross the blood-brain barrier, resulting in only non-psychoactive peripheral sympathomimetic effects following ingestion. A hypertensive crisis can result, however, from ingestion of _________ -rich foods in conjunction with the use of monoamine oxidase inhibitors .

Exam Probability: **Medium**

29. *Answer choices:*

(see index for correct answer)

- a. Tyramine
- b. Meta-Tyramine
- c. Varacin
- d. Terbutaline

Guidance: level 1

:: Qualia ::

In physics, _________ is a vibration that typically propagates as an audible wave of pressure, through a transmission medium such as a gas, liquid or solid.

Exam Probability: **Low**

30. *Answer choices:*

(see index for correct answer)

- a. Flavor
- b. Absent qualia
- c. Color
- d. Odor

Guidance: level 1

:: Brain ::

The _________ is a prefrontal cortex region in the frontal lobes of the brain which is involved in the cognitive process of decision-making. In non-human primates it consists of the association cortex areas Brodmann area 11, 12 and 13; in humans it consists of Brodmann area 10, 11 and 47.

Exam Probability: **Low**

31. *Answer choices:*

(see index for correct answer)

- a. Wilder Brain Collection
- b. Tegmentum
- c. Planum temporale
- d. Orbitofrontal cortex

Guidance: level 1

:: Pyrazolopyrimidines ::

_________, sold as the brand name Viagra among others, is a medication used to treat erectile dysfunction and pulmonary arterial hypertension. It is unclear if it is effective for treating sexual dysfunction in women. It is taken by mouth or injection into a vein. Onset is typically within 20 minutes and lasts for about 2 hours.

Exam Probability: **Medium**

32. *Answer choices:*

(see index for correct answer)

- a. Oxypurinol
- b. BAY 73-6691
- c. DPA-714
- d. DPA-713

Guidance: level 1

:: Central nervous system ::

_________ s , also known collectively as astroglia, are characteristic star-shaped glial cells in the brain and spinal cord. The proportion of _________ s in the brain is not well defined. Depending on the counting technique used, studies have found that the _________ proportion varies by region and ranges from 20% to 40% of all glia. Overall, _________ s outnumber neurons by over fivefold. They perform many functions, including biochemical support of endothelial cells that form the blood–brain barrier, provision of nutrients to the nervous tissue, maintenance of extracellular ion balance, and a role in the repair and scarring process of the brain and spinal cord following traumatic injuries.

Exam Probability: **High**

33. *Answer choices:*

(see index for correct answer)

- a. Posterior funiculus
- b. Reticular activating system
- c. Choroid glomus
- d. Lateral recess

Guidance: level 1

:: Cranial nerves ::

_________ s are the nerves that emerge directly from the brain , in contrast to spinal nerves . 10 of the _________ s originate in the brainstem. _________ s relay information between the brain and parts of the body, primarily to and from regions of the head and neck.

Exam Probability: **Low**

34. *Answer choices:*

(see index for correct answer)

- a. Cranial nerve
- b. Olfactory nerve
- c. Optic nerve
- d. Trigeminal nerve

Guidance: level 1

:: Computing input devices ::

A _________ , plural mice, is a small rodent characteristically having a pointed snout, small rounded ears, a body-length scaly tail and a high breeding rate. The best known _________ species is the common house _________ . It is also a popular pet. In some places, certain kinds of field mice are locally common. They are known to invade homes for food and shelter.

Exam Probability: **High**

35. *Answer choices:*

(see index for correct answer)

- a. SWEEPNIK
- b. Duplex scanning
- c. Mouse
- d. CueCat

Guidance: level 1

:: Human rights abuses ::

__________ , formerly known as electroshock therapy, is a psychiatric treatment in which seizures are electrically induced in patients to provide relief from mental disorders. The ECT procedure was first conducted in 1938 and rapidly replaced less safe and effective forms of biological treatments in use at the time. ECT is often used with informed consent as a safe and effective intervention for major depressive disorder, mania, and catatonia. ECT machines have been placed in the Class III category by the United States Food and Drug Administration since 1976.

Exam Probability: **High**

36. *Answer choices:*

(see index for correct answer)

- a. Protection of Person and Property Act 1881
- b. Body cavity search

- c. Electroconvulsive therapy
- d. David Passaro

Guidance: level 1

:: Vision ::

An _________ is an artifact that depicts visual perception, such as a photograph or other two-dimensional picture, that resembles a subject—usually a physical object—and thus provides a depiction of it. In the context of signal processing, an _________ is a distributed amplitude of color.

Exam Probability: **Medium**

37. *Answer choices:*

(see index for correct answer)

- a. Congenital cataract
- b. Image
- c. Microsaccade
- d. Saccadic masking

Guidance: level 1

:: Embryology of nervous system ::

In the developing chordate , the _________ is the embryonic precursor to the central nervous system, which is made up of the brain and spinal cord. The neural groove gradually deepens as the neural folds become elevated, and ultimately the folds meet and coalesce in the middle line and convert the groove into the closed _________. In humans, _________ closure usually occurs by the fourth week of pregnancy . The ectodermal wall of the tube forms the rudiment of the nervous system. The centre of the tube is the neural canal.

Exam Probability: **High**

38. *Answer choices:*

(see index for correct answer)

- a. Neurogenesis
- b. Neural tube
- c. Rhombomere
- d. Neurula

Guidance: level 1

:: Cerebrum ::

_________s can be found in the primary visual cortex , the secondary visual cortex , and Brodmann area 19 .

Exam Probability: **Medium**

39. *Answer choices:*

(see index for correct answer)

- a. Medial frontal gyrus
- b. Circumventricular organs
- c. Supplementary eye fields
- d. Complex cell

Guidance: level 1

:: Emotion ::

__________ is the study of the neural mechanisms of emotion. This interdisciplinary field combines neuroscience with the psychological study of personality, emotion, and mood. The putative existence of `basic emotions` and their defining attributes represents a long lasting and yet unsettled issue in psychology. However, when reading this article, please note that there are few references to newer studies occurring after 2012 that have changed many of the perspectives in this article. For example, the section relating to emotions and the right hemisphere refer mainly to studies prior to 2006, and these models have been abandoned in favor of the new evidence showing interhemispheric connectivity and the role that the salience network plays in interpreting instinctual emotional responses to the world.

Exam Probability: **High**

40. *Answer choices:*

(see index for correct answer)

- a. Emotional intimacy
- b. Limbic revision
- c. Empathic concern
- d. Emotions in the workplace

Guidance: level 1

:: Psychopharmacology ::

_________ s is an overarching term that covers many drugs including those that increase activity of the central nervous system and the body, drugs that are pleasurable and invigorating, or drugs that have sympathomimetic effects. _________ s are widely used throughout the world as prescription medicines as well as without a prescription as performance-enhancing or recreational drugs. The most frequently prescribed _________ s as of 2013 were lisdexamfetamine, methylphenidate, and amphetamine. It is estimated that the percentage of the population that has abused amphetamine-type _________ s and cocaine combined is between 0.8% and 2.1%.

Exam Probability: **High**

41. *Answer choices:*

(see index for correct answer)

- a. Dopamine receptor D2
- b. Stimulant
- c. Drug resistance
- d. Atypical antipsychotic

Guidance: level 1

:: Agnosia ::

_________ is an impairment in recognition of visually presented objects. It is not due to a deficit in vision , language, memory, or intellect. While cortical blindness results from lesions to primary visual cortex, _________ is often due to damage to more anterior cortex such as the posterior occipital and/or temporal lobe in the brain.[2] There are two types of _________ : apperceptive agnosia and associative agnosia.

Exam Probability: **Medium**

42. *Answer choices:*

(see index for correct answer)

- a. Visual agnosia
- b. Integrative agnosia
- c. Agnosia
- d. Visuospatial dysgnosia

Guidance: level 1

:: Sensory systems ::

The __________ is a portion of sensory space that can elicit neuronal responses when stimulated. The sensory space can be defined in a single dimension , two dimensions or multiple dimensions . The neuronal response can be defined as firing rate or include also subthreshold activity .

Exam Probability: **High**

43. *Answer choices:*

(see index for correct answer)

- a. Secondary sensory endings
- b. Proprioceptor
- c. Hydrodynamic reception
- d. Receptive field

Guidance: level 1

:: Euphoriants ::

__________ , also known as angel dust among other names, is a drug used for its mind-altering effects. PCP may cause hallucinations, distorted perceptions of sounds, and violent behavior. As a recreational drug, it is typically smoked, but may be taken by mouth, snorted, or injected. It may also be mixed with cannabis or tobacco.

Exam Probability: **High**

44. *Answer choices:*

(see index for correct answer)

- a. Hash oil
- b. Dihydromorphine
- c. Amphetamine mixed salts
- d. Phencyclidine

Guidance: level 1

:: Brain ::

The __________ of the brain is that part of the cerebral cortex which processes visual information. It is located in the occipital lobe. Visual nerves run straight from the eye to the primary __________ to the Visual Association cortex.

Exam Probability: **Low**

45. *Answer choices:*

(see index for correct answer)

- a. External granular layer
- b. Visual cortex
- c. Calcar avis
- d. Artery of Percheron

Guidance: level 1

:: Neuroanatomy ::

A _________ is an enclosed, cable-like bundle of _________ fibres called axons, in the peripheral nervous system. A _________ provides a common pathway for the electrochemical _________ impulses called action potentials that are transmitted along each of the axons to peripheral organs or, in the case of sensory _________ s, from the periphery back to the central nervous system. Each axon within the _________ is an extension of an individual neuron, along with other supportive cells such as Schwann cells that coat the axons in myelin.

Exam Probability: **Low**

46. *Answer choices:*

(see index for correct answer)

- a. Anterolateral region of the motor thalamus
- b. Trochlear nucleus
- c. Cerebellopontine angle
- d. Parallel fiber

Guidance: level 1

:: Consciousness ::

A __________ is a disorder of consciousness in which patients with severe brain damage are in a state of partial arousal rather than true awareness. After four weeks in a vegetative state , the patient is classified as in a __________ . This diagnosis is classified as a permanent vegetative state some months after a non-traumatic brain injury or one year after a traumatic injury. Today, doctors and neuroscientists prefer to call the state of consciousness a syndrome, primarily because of ethical questions about whether a patient can be called "vegetative" or not.

Exam Probability: **High**

47. *Answer choices:*

(see index for correct answer)

- a. Self-conscious
- b. Choiceless awareness
- c. Mental substance
- d. Persistent vegetative state

Guidance: level 1

:: Cerebrum ::

The _________ is a large part of the brain containing the cerebral cortex , as well as several subcortical structures, including the hippocampus, basal ganglia, and olfactory bulb. In the human brain, the _________ is the uppermost region of the central nervous system. The prosencephalon is the embryonic structure from which the _________ develops prenatally. In mammals, the dorsal telencephalon, or pallium, develops into the cerebral cortex, and the ventral telencephalon, or subpallium, becomes the basal ganglia. The _________ is also divided into approximately symmetric left and right cerebral hemispheres.

Exam Probability: **High**

48. *Answer choices:*

(see index for correct answer)

- a. Ventromedial prefrontal cortex
- b. Simple cell
- c. Cerebrum
- d. Lateral globus pallidus

Guidance: level 1

:: Opioids ::

__________ s are substances that act on __________ receptors to produce morphine-like effects. Medically they are primarily used for pain relief, including anesthesia. Other medical uses include suppression of diarrhea, replacement therapy for __________ use disorder, reversing __________ overdose, suppressing cough, suppressing __________ induced constipation, as well as for executions in the United States. Extremely potent __________ s such as carfentanil are only approved for veterinary use. __________ s are also frequently used non-medically for their euphoric effects or to prevent withdrawal.

Exam Probability: **Medium**

49. *Answer choices:*

(see index for correct answer)

- a. Heterocodeine
- b. Codeine methylbromide
- c. RWJ-394674
- d. Gluten exorphin

Guidance: level 1

:: Proprioception ::

_________ is the sense of self-movement and body position. It is sometimes described as the "sixth sense". _________ is mediated by mechanically-sensitive proprioceptor neurons distributed throughout an animal`s body. Most vertebrates possess three basic types of proprioceptors: muscle spindles, which are embedded in skeletal muscle fibers, Golgi tendon organs, which lie at the interface of muscles and tendons, and joint receptors, which are low-threshold mechanoreceptors embedded in joint capsules. Many invertebrates, such as insects, also possess three basic proprioceptor types with analogous functional properties: chordotonal neurons, campaniform sensilla, and hair plates.

Exam Probability: **High**

50. *Answer choices:*

(see index for correct answer)

- a. Pinocchio illusion
- b. Spatial disorientation
- c. Proprioception
- d. Agraphesthesia

Guidance: level 1

:: Auditory system ::

The _________ is the innermost part of the vertebrate ear. In vertebrates, the _________ is mainly responsible for sound detection and balance. In mammals, it consists of the bony labyrinth, a hollow cavity in the temporal bone of the skull with a system of passages comprising two main functional parts.

Exam Probability: **High**

51. *Answer choices:*

(see index for correct answer)

- a. Pyramidal eminence
- b. Electrical tuning
- c. Ear canal
- d. Kinocilium

Guidance: level 1

:: Anxiogenics ::

_________ is a selective GABAA antagonist administered via injection or intranasally. Therapeutically, it acts as both an antagonist and antidote to benzodiazepines , through competitive inhibition.

Exam Probability: **Medium**

52. *Answer choices:*

(see index for correct answer)

- a. L-655,708
- b. Flumazenil
- c. Tetrabenazine
- d. Prednisolone

Guidance: level 1

:: Addiction ::

_________ is a brain disorder characterized by compulsive engagement in rewarding stimuli despite adverse consequences. Despite the involvement of a number of psychosocial factors, a biological process – one which is induced by repeated exposure to an addictive stimulus – is the core pathology that drives the development and maintenance of an _________ . The two properties that characterize all addictive stimuli are that they are reinforcing and intrinsically rewarding .

Exam Probability: **Medium**

53. *Answer choices:*

(see index for correct answer)

- a. Three circles
- b. Exercise addiction
- c. Addiction
- d. The Fix

Guidance: level 1

:: Cerebral palsy and other paralytic syndromes ::

_________ is a loss of muscle function for one or more muscles. _________ can be accompanied by a loss of feeling in the affected area if there is sensory damage as well as motor. In the United States, roughly 1 in 50 people have been diagnosed with some form of permanent or transient _________. The word comes from the Greek pas, "disabling of the nerves", itself from pa , "beside, by" and s , "making loose". A _________ accompanied by involuntary tremors is usually called "palsy".

Exam Probability: **Low**

54. *Answer choices:*

(see index for correct answer)

- a. Paralysis
- b. Worster-Drought syndrome
- c. Tetraplegia
- d. Paraplegia

Guidance: level 1

:: Coma ::

A __________ is a deep state of prolonged unconsciousness in which a person cannot be awakened; fails to respond normally to painful stimuli, light, or sound; lacks a normal wake-sleep cycle; and does not initiate voluntary actions. __________ patients exhibit a complete absence of wakefulness and are unable to consciously feel, speak or move. __________ s can be derived by natural causes, or can be medically induced.

Exam Probability: **High**

55. *Answer choices:*

(see index for correct answer)

- a. Fred Plum
- b. Rancho Los Amigos Scale
- c. Coma blister
- d. Induced coma

Guidance: level 1

:: Neuroanatomy ::

Lewy bodies are abnormal aggregates of protein that develop inside nerve cells, contributing to Parkinson`s disease , the __________ dementias , and some other disorders. They are also seen in cases of multiple system atrophy, particularly the parkinsonian variant.

Exam Probability: **Medium**

56. *Answer choices:*

(see index for correct answer)

- a. Lamina pyramidalis interna
- b. Superior olivary complex
- c. Rubro-olivary tract
- d. Lewy body

Guidance: level 1

:: Signal transduction ::

A _________ is any member of a class of signaling molecules produced by glands in multicellular organisms that are transported by the circulatory system to target distant organs to regulate physiology and behavior. _________ s have diverse chemical structures, mainly of three classes: eicosanoids, steroids, and amino acid/protein derivatives . The glands that secrete _________ s comprise the endocrine signaling system. The term _________ is sometimes extended to include chemicals produced by cells that affect the same cell or nearby cells .

Exam Probability: **High**

57. *Answer choices:*

(see index for correct answer)

- a. TRIB3
- b. P70S6 kinase

- c. Hormone
- d. Aurora A kinase

Guidance: level 1

:: Motor control ::

The _________ is the part of the central nervous system that is involved with movement. It consists of the pyramidal and extrapyramidal system.

Exam Probability: **High**

58. *Answer choices:*

(see index for correct answer)

- a. Internal model
- b. Illusions of self-motion
- c. Motor goal
- d. Indirect pathway of movement

Guidance: level 1

:: Headaches ::

__________ is the symptom of pain anywhere in the region of the head or neck. It occurs in migraines , tension-type __________ s, and cluster __________ s. Frequent __________ s can affect relationships and employment. There is also an increased risk of depression in those with severe __________ s.

Exam Probability: **Medium**

59. *Answer choices:*

(see index for correct answer)

- a. Lymphocytic pleocytosis
- b. Headache
- c. External compression headache
- d. Tension headache

Guidance: level 1

Developmental Psychology

Developmental psychology is the scientific study of how and why human beings change over the course of their life. Originally concerned with infants and children, the field has expanded to include adolescence, adult development, aging, and the entire lifespan. Developmental psychologists aim to explain how thinking, feeling, and behaviors change throughout life. This field examines change across three major dimensions: physical development, cognitive development, and socioemotional development. Within these three dimensions are a broad range of topics including motor skills, executive functions, moral understanding, language acquisition, social change, personality, emotional development, self-concept, and identity formation.

:: Moral psychology ::

_________ focuses on the emergence, change, and understanding of morality from infancy through adulthood. Morality develops across a lifetime and is influenced by an individual`s experiences and their behavior when faced with moral issues through different periods` physical and cognitive development. In short, morality concerns an individual`s growing sense of what is right and wrong; it is for this reason that young children have different moral judgement and character than that of a grown adult. Morality in itself is often a synonym for "rightness" or "goodness". It refers to a certain code of conduct that is derived from one`s culture, religion or personal philosophy that guides one`s actions, behaviors and thoughts.

Exam Probability: **Medium**

1. *Answer choices:*

(see index for correct answer)

- a. Moral development
- b. Margaret Urban Walker
- c. Michael Slote
- d. J. David Velleman

Guidance: level 1

:: Friendship ::

_________ is a relationship of mutual affection between people. _________ is a stronger form of interpersonal bond than an association. _________ has been studied in academic fields such as communication, sociology, social psychology, anthropology, and philosophy. Various academic theories of _________ have been proposed, including social exchange theory, equity theory, relational dialectics, and attachment styles.

Exam Probability: **High**

2. *Answer choices:*

(see index for correct answer)

- a. Friendship
- b. Showmance
- c. Romantic friendship
- d. Womance

Guidance: level 1

:: Limbic system ::

The _________ is a major component of the brain of humans and other vertebrates. Humans and other mammals have two hippocampi, one in each side of the brain. The _________ is part of the limbic system, and plays important roles in the consolidation of information from short-term memory to long-term memory, and in spatial memory that enables navigation. The _________ is located under the cerebral cortex in the allocortex, and in primates it is in the medial temporal lobe. It contains two main interlocking parts: the _________ proper and the dentate gyrus.

Exam Probability: **Medium**

3. *Answer choices:*

(see index for correct answer)

- a. Olfactory indicators
- b. Perirhinal
- c. Hippocampus
- d. Olfaction

Guidance: level 1

:: Mood disorders ::

__________ , also called postnatal depression, is a type of mood disorder associated with childbirth, which can affect both sexes. Symptoms may include extreme sadness, low energy, anxiety, crying episodes, irritability, and changes in sleeping or eating patterns. Onset is typically between one week and one month following childbirth. PPD can also negatively affect the newborn child.

Exam Probability: **Low**

4. *Answer choices:*

(see index for correct answer)

- a. Mood disorder
- b. Subcortical ischemic depression

- c. S100A10
- d. Postpartum depression

Guidance: level 1

:: Parenting ::

A _________ is a psychological construct representing standard strategies that parents use in their child rearing. The quality of parenting can be more essential than the quantity of time spent with the child. For instance, a parent can spend an entire afternoon with his or her child, yet the parent may be engaging in a different activity and not demonstrating enough interest towards the child. _________ s are the representation of how parents respond to and make demands on their children. Parenting practices are specific behaviors, while _________ s represent broader patterns of parenting practices. There are various theories and opinions on the best ways to rear children, as well as differing levels of time and effort that parents are willing to invest.

Exam Probability: **High**

5. *Answer choices:*

(see index for correct answer)

- a. Lilian Sperling
- b. Double burden
- c. Ros Draper
- d. Parenting style

Guidance: level 1

:: Infancy ::

An _________ is the more formal or specialised synonym for "baby", the very young offspring of a human. The term may also be used to refer to juveniles of other organisms.

Exam Probability: **Medium**

6. *Answer choices:*

(see index for correct answer)

- a. Bassinet
- b. Galactorrhea
- c. Infant
- d. Reborn doll

Guidance: level 1

:: Educational psychology ::

__________ , also known as reading disorder, is characterized by trouble with reading despite normal intelligence. Different people are affected to varying degrees. Problems may include difficulties in spelling words, reading quickly, writing words, "sounding out" words in the head, pronouncing words when reading aloud and understanding what one reads. Often these difficulties are first noticed at school. When someone who previously could read loses their ability, it is known as alexia. The difficulties are involuntary and people with this disorder have a normal desire to learn.

Exam Probability: **High**

7. *Answer choices:*

(see index for correct answer)

- a. Instructional animation
- b. Experiential education
- c. Dyslexia
- d. Overjustification effect

Guidance: level 1

:: Behaviorism ::

A __________ is a routine of behavior that is repeated regularly and tends to occur subconsciously.

Exam Probability: **High**

8. *Answer choices:*

(see index for correct answer)

- a. Applied behavior analysis
- b. Tootling
- c. Habit
- d. Social disruption

Guidance: level 1

:: Behaviorism ::

__________ is, in contrast to analog observation, a research tool in which a subject is observed in its natural habitat without any manipulation by the observer. During __________, researchers take great care to avoid interfering with the behavior they are observing by using unobtrusive methods. __________ involves two main differences that set it apart from other forms of data gathering. In the context of a __________, the environment is in no way being manipulated by the observer nor was it created by the observer.

Exam Probability: **Medium**

9. *Answer choices:*

(see index for correct answer)

- a. Shaping
- b. Behavior modification facility
- c. Covert conditioning

- d. Psychological behaviorism

Guidance: level 1

:: Neurobiology ::

The _________ is the part of an animal that coordinates its actions by transmitting signals to and from different parts of its body. The _________ detects environmental changes that impact the body, then works in tandem with the endocrine system to respond to such events. Nervous tissue first arose in wormlike organisms about 550 to 600 million years ago. In vertebrates it consists of two main parts, the central _________ and the peripheral _________. The CNS consists of the brain and spinal cord. The PNS consists mainly of nerves, which are enclosed bundles of the long fibers or axons, that connect the CNS to every other part of the body. Nerves that transmit signals from the brain are called motor or efferent nerves, while those nerves that transmit information from the body to the CNS are called sensory or afferent. Spinal nerves serve both functions and are called mixed nerves. The PNS is divided into three separate subsystems, the somatic, autonomic, and enteric _________s. Somatic nerves mediate voluntary movement. The autonomic _________ is further subdivided into the sympathetic and the parasympathetic _________s. The sympathetic _________ is activated in cases of emergencies to mobilize energy, while the parasympathetic _________ is activated when organisms are in a relaxed state. The enteric _________ functions to control the gastrointestinal system. Both autonomic and enteric _________s function involuntarily. Nerves that exit from the cranium are called cranial nerves while those exiting from the spinal cord are called spinal nerves.

Exam Probability: **Medium**

10. *Answer choices:*

(see index for correct answer)

- a. Neuropreservation
- b. Nervous system
- c. Retrograde signaling
- d. Neurovitrification

Guidance: level 1

:: Behavior ::

__________ , used in psychology, education, and communication, holds that portions of an individual's knowledge acquisition can be directly related to observing others within the context of social interactions, experiences, and outside media influences. This theory was advanced by Albert Bandura as an extension of his social learning theory. The theory states that when people observe a model performing a behavior and the consequences of that behavior, they remember the sequence of events and use this information to guide subsequent behaviors. Observing a model can also prompt the viewer to engage in behavior they already learned. In other words, people do not learn new behaviors solely by trying them and either succeeding or failing, but rather, the survival of humanity is dependent upon the replication of the actions of others. Depending on whether people are rewarded or punished for their behavior and the outcome of the behavior, the observer may choose to replicate behavior modeled. Media provides models for a vast array of people in many different environmental settings.

Exam Probability: **Medium**

11. *Answer choices:*

(see index for correct answer)

- a. Meaningful life
- b. Transtheoretical model
- c. Interpersonal complementarity hypothesis
- d. Social cognitive theory

Guidance: level 1

:: Memory ::

_________ is the stage of the Atkinson–Shiffrin memory model where informative knowledge is held indefinitely. It is defined in contrast to short-term and working memory, which persist for only about 18 to 30 seconds. _________ is commonly labelled as explicit memory , as well as episodic memory, semantic memory, autobiographical memory, and implicit memory .

Exam Probability: **Low**

12. *Answer choices:*

(see index for correct answer)

- a. Effects of stress on memory
- b. Priming
- c. Long-term memory
- d. Grand Master of Memory

Guidance: level 1

:: Family ::

__________ , also known as gestation, is the time during which one or more offspring develops inside a woman. A multiple __________ involves more than one offspring, such as with twins. __________ can occur by sexual intercourse or assisted reproductive technology. Childbirth typically occurs around 40 weeks from the start of the last menstrual period . This is just over nine months, where each month averages 31 days. When measured from fertilization it is about 38 weeks. An embryo is the developing offspring during the first eight weeks following fertilization, after which, the term fetus is used until birth. Symptoms of early __________ may include missed periods, tender breasts, nausea and vomiting, hunger, and frequent urination. __________ may be confirmed with a __________ test.

Exam Probability: **High**

13. *Answer choices:*

(see index for correct answer)

- a. Dear husband
- b. Pregnancy
- c. Accident of birth
- d. Carers rights movement

Guidance: level 1

:: Scientific method ::

_________ is a branch of mathematics working with data collection, organization, analysis, interpretation and presentation. In applying _________ to, for example, a scientific, industrial, or social problem, it is conventional to begin with a statistical population or a statistical model process to be studied. Populations can be diverse topics such as "all people living in a country" or "every atom composing a crystal". _________ deals with every aspect of data, including the planning of data collection in terms of the design of surveys and experiments.See glossary of probability and _________ .

Exam Probability: **Medium**

14. *Answer choices:*

(see index for correct answer)

- a. Science of team science
- b. Nano spray dryer
- c. Statistics
- d. Qualitative research

Guidance: level 1

:: Fertility ::

_________ is the natural capability to produce offspring. As a measure, _________ rate is the number of offspring born per mating pair, individual or population. _________ differs from fecundity, which is defined as the potential for reproduction . A lack of _________ is in _________ while a lack of fecundity would be called sterility.

Exam Probability: **Medium**

15. *Answer choices:*

(see index for correct answer)

- a. Virility
- b. Gross reproduction rate
- c. Fertility
- d. Human fertilization

Guidance: level 1

:: Language acquisition ::

_________ refers to the ability to objectify language as a process as well as an artifact. The concept of _________ is helpful in explaining the execution and transfer of linguistic knowledge across languages . Metalinguistics can be classified as the ability to consciously reflect on the nature of language, by using the following skills.

Exam Probability: **High**

16. *Answer choices:*

(see index for correct answer)

- a. Word learning biases
- b. Manual babbling

- c. Distributional semantics
- d. Metalinguistic awareness

Guidance: level 1

:: Gerontology ::

The word " _________ " is sometimes used as a synonym for "life expectancy" in demography. However, the term _________ is sometimes meant to refer only to especially long-lived members of a population, whereas life expectancy is always defined statistically as the average number of years remaining at a given age. For example, a population`s life expectancy at birth is the same as the average age at death for all people born in the same year . _________ is best thought of as a term for general audiences meaning `typical length of life` and specific statistical definitions should be clarified when necessary.

Exam Probability: **High**

17. *Answer choices:*

(see index for correct answer)

- a. Longevity
- b. Oldest people
- c. English Longitudinal Study of Ageing
- d. Oncology

Guidance: level 1

:: Psychometrics ::

Mental chronometry is the study of _________ in perceptual-motor tasks to infer the content, duration, and temporal sequencing of mental operations. Mental chronometry is one of the core methodological paradigms of human experimental and cognitive psychology, but is also commonly analyzed in psychophysiology, cognitive neuroscience, and behavioral neuroscience to help elucidate the biological mechanisms underlying perception, attention, and decision-making across species.

Exam Probability: **Medium**

18. *Answer choices:*

(see index for correct answer)

- a. Polytomous Rasch model
- b. Reaction time
- c. Polychoric correlation
- d. NOMINATE

Guidance: level 1

:: Social psychology ::

_________ , or intent to benefit others, is a social behavior that "benefit[s] other people or society as a whole", "such as helping, sharing, donating, co-operating, and volunteering". Obeying the rules and conforming to socially accepted behaviors are also regarded as _________ s. These actions may be motivated by empathy and by concern about the welfare and rights of others, as well as for egoistic or practical concerns, such as one`s social status or reputation, hope for direct or indirect reciprocity, or adherence to one`s perceived system of fairness. It may also be motivated by altruism, though the existence of pure altruism is somewhat disputed, and some have argued that this falls into philosophical rather than psychological realm of debate. Evidence suggests that pro sociality is central to the well-being of social groups across a range of scales, including schools. _________ in the classroom can have a significant impact on a student`s motivation for learning and contributions to the classroom and larger community. Empathy is a strong motive in eliciting _________ , and has deep evolutionary roots.

Exam Probability: **Low**

19. *Answer choices:*

(see index for correct answer)

- a. Prosocial behavior
- b. Mind-blindness
- c. Externalization
- d. Diffusion of responsibility

Guidance: level 1

:: Cognitive neuroscience ::

_________ is the capacity to understand or feel what another person is experiencing from within their frame of reference, that is, the capacity to place oneself in another`s position. Definitions of _________ encompass a broad range of emotional states. Types of _________ include cognitive _________, emotional _________, and somatic _________.

Exam Probability: **Medium**

20. *Answer choices:*

(see index for correct answer)

- a. Empathy
- b. Listener fatigue
- c. fMRI
- d. Associative Sequence Learning

Guidance: level 1

:: Educational psychology ::

_________ has been defined in many ways, including: the capacity for logic, understanding, self-awareness, learning, emotional knowledge, reasoning, planning, creativity, critical thinking, and problem solving. More generally, it can be described as the ability to perceive or infer information, and to retain it as knowledge to be applied towards adaptive behaviors within an environment or context.

Exam Probability: **High**

21. *Answer choices:*

(see index for correct answer)

- a. Instructional technology
- b. Neurodevelopmental framework for learning
- c. Creativity
- d. Linear-on-the-fly testing

Guidance: level 1

:: Analytical psychology ::

In Neo-Freudian psychology, the _________ , as proposed by Carl Jung in his Theory of Psychoanalysis, is a girl`s psychosexual competition with her mother for possession of her father. In the course of her psychosexual development, the complex is the girl`s phallic stage; a boy`s analogous experience is the Oedipus complex. The _________ occurs in the third—phallic stage —of five psychosexual development stages: the Oral, the Anal, the Phallic, the Latent, and the Genital—in which the source of libido pleasure is in a different erogenous zone of the infant`s body.

Exam Probability: **Medium**

22. *Answer choices:*

(see index for correct answer)

- a. Complex
- b. Self in Jungian psychology

- c. Genetic memory
- d. Electra complex

Guidance: level 1

:: Conformity ::

In sociology, _________ is the process of internalizing the norms and ideologies of society. _________ encompasses both learning and teaching and is thus "the means by which social and cultural continuity are attained".

Exam Probability: **Low**

23. *Answer choices:*

(see index for correct answer)

- a. Mindguard
- b. Sheeple
- c. Deindividuation
- d. Socialization

Guidance: level 1

:: Learning to read ::

A _________ is a set of familiar words within a person`s language. A _________ , usually developed with age, serves as a useful and fundamental tool for communication and acquiring knowledge. Acquiring an extensive _________ is one of the largest challenges in learning a second language.

Exam Probability: **High**

24. *Answer choices:*

(see index for correct answer)

- a. Jolly Phonics
- b. Vocabulary
- c. Sight word
- d. Hooked on Phonics

Guidance: level 1

:: Intelligence by type ::

An intelligence quotient is a total score derived from several standardized tests designed to assess human intelligence. The abbreviation "IQ" was coined by the psychologist William Stern for the German term Intelligenzquotient, his term for a scoring method for _________ s at University of Breslau he advocated in a 1912 book. Historically, IQ is a score obtained by dividing a person`s mental age score, obtained by administering an _________ , by the person`s chronological age, both expressed in terms of years and months. The resulting fraction is multiplied by 100 to obtain the IQ score.

Exam Probability: **Medium**

25. *Answer choices:*

(see index for correct answer)

- a. Systems intelligence
- b. Intelligence test
- c. Theory of multiple intelligences
- d. linguistic intelligence

Guidance: level 1

:: Anxiety disorders ::

__________ s are a group of mental disorders characterized by significant feelings of anxiety and fear. Anxiety is a worry about future events, and fear is a reaction to current events. These feelings may cause physical symptoms, such as a fast heart rate and shakiness. There are several __________ s, including generalized __________ , specific phobia, social __________ , separation __________ , agoraphobia, panic disorder, and selective mutism. The disorder differs by what results in the symptoms. People often have more than one __________ .

Exam Probability: **Low**

26. *Answer choices:*

(see index for correct answer)

- a. Combat Stress Intervention Program
- b. Lick granuloma
- c. Parcopresis
- d. Counting method

Guidance: level 1

:: Developmental psychology ::

_________ is a concept related to intelligence. It looks at how a specific individual , at a specific age, performs intellectually, compared to average intellectual performance for that individual`s actual chronological age . The intellectual performance is based on performance in tests and live assessments by a psychologist. The score achieved by the individual is compared to the median average scores at various ages, and the _________ is derived such that the individual`s score equates to the average score at age x.

Exam Probability: **High**

27. *Answer choices:*

(see index for correct answer)

- a. Orgastic potency
- b. Mental age
- c. Bairn
- d. Positive Disintegration

Guidance: level 1

:: Abuse ::

_________ is an affective feeling towards a person or group member based often on that person`s group membership . The word is often used to refer to preconceived, usually unfavourable, feelings towards people or a person because of their political affiliation, sex, gender, beliefs, values, social class, age, disability, religion, sexuality, race/ethnicity, language, nationality, beauty, occupation, education, criminality, sport team affiliation or other personal characteristics. In this case, it refers to a positive or negative evaluation of another person based on that person`s perceived group membership.

Exam Probability: **High**

28. *Answer choices:*

(see index for correct answer)

- a. Insult comedy
- b. Pharmaceutical lobby
- c. Prejudice
- d. Vicariate of Solidarity Files and Archive Foundation

Guidance: level 1

:: Computational neuroscience ::

A _________ , also known as a _________ e or nerve cell, is an electrically excitable cell that communicates with other cells via specialized connections called synapses. It is the main component of nervous tissue. All animals except sponges and placozoans have _________ s, but other multicellular organisms such as plants do not.

Exam Probability: **Medium**

29. *Answer choices:*

(see index for correct answer)

- a. Neuron
- b. Brian
- c. Activating function
- d. Multi-simulation coordinator

Guidance: level 1

:: Social status ::

_________ is an economic and sociological combined total measure of a person`s work experience and of an individual`s or family`s economic and social position in relation to others, based on household income, earners` education, and occupation are examined, as well as combined income, whereas for an individual`s SES only their own attributes are assessed. However, SES is more commonly used to depict an economic difference in society as a whole.

Exam Probability: **High**

30. *Answer choices:*

(see index for correct answer)

- a. Exploitation
- b. Social exchange
- c. Socioeconomic status

Guidance: level 1

:: Penis ::

A _________ is the primary sexual organ that male animals use to inseminate sexually receptive mates during copulation. Such organs occur in many animals, both vertebrate and invertebrate, but males do not bear a _________ in every animal species, and in those species in which the male does bear a so-called _________, the penes in the various species are not necessarily homologous. For example, the _________ of a mammal is at most analogous to the _________ of a male insect or barnacle.

Exam Probability: **Medium**

31. *Answer choices:*

(see index for correct answer)

- a. Pizzle
- b. Penis
- c. Artery of bulb of penis
- d. Helicine arteries of penis

Guidance: level 1

:: Emotions ::

_________ is an emotion characterized by an unpleasant state of inner turmoil, often accompanied by nervous behaviour such as pacing back and forth, somatic complaints, and rumination. It is the subjectively unpleasant feelings of dread over anticipated events, such as the feeling of imminent death. _________ is not the same as fear, which is a response to a real or perceived immediate threat, whereas _________ involves the expectation of future threat. _________ is a feeling of uneasiness and worry, usually generalized and unfocused as an overreaction to a situation that is only subjectively seen as menacing. It is often accompanied by muscular tension, restlessness, fatigue and problems in concentration. _________ can be appropriate, but when experienced regularly the individual may suffer from an _________ disorder.

Exam Probability: **Low**

32. *Answer choices:*

(see index for correct answer)

- a. Anxiety
- b. Melancholia
- c. Zest
- d. Disgust

Guidance: level 1

:: Behaviorism ::

_________ is a learning process through which the strength of a behavior is modified by reinforcement or punishment. It is also a procedure that is used to bring about such learning.

Exam Probability: **Medium**

33. *Answer choices:*

(see index for correct answer)

- a. Operant conditioning
- b. Psychogenetic system
- c. Single-subject design
- d. Experimental analysis of behavior

Guidance: level 1

:: Memory ::

In communications and information processing, code is a system of rules to convert information—such as a letter, word, sound, image, or gesture—into another form or representation, sometimes shortened or secret, for communication through a communication channel or storage in a storage medium. An early example is the invention of language, which enabled a person, through speech, to communicate what they saw, heard, felt, or thought to others. But speech limits the range of communication to the distance a voice can carry, and limits the audience to those present when the speech is uttered. The invention of writing, which converted spoken language into visual symbols, extended the range of communication across space and time.

Exam Probability: **High**

34. *Answer choices:*

(see index for correct answer)

- a. Encoding
- b. Personal event memory
- c. Hafiz
- d. Transactive memory

Guidance: level 1

:: Cognitive science ::

_________ is "the mental action or process of acquiring knowledge and understanding through thought, experience, and the senses". It encompasses many aspects of intellectual functions and processes such as attention, the formation of knowledge, memory and working memory, judgment and evaluation, reasoning and "computation", problem solving and decision making, comprehension and production of language. Cognitive processes use existing knowledge and generate new knowledge.

Exam Probability: **Medium**

35. *Answer choices:*

(see index for correct answer)

- a. Modularity of mind
- b. Cognition
- c. Legal case management
- d. Embodied cognition

Guidance: level 1

:: Epistemology ::

The term _________ was coined by the psychoanalyst Erik Erikson in 1950 to denote "a concern for establishing and guiding the next generation." He first used the term while defining the Care stage in his theory of the stages of psychosocial development.

Exam Probability: **Low**

36. *Answer choices:*

(see index for correct answer)

- a. Generativity
- b. Knowledge relativity
- c. Paradigm shift
- d. Information source

Guidance: level 1

:: Educational psychology ::

One`s _________ is a collection of beliefs about oneself. Generally, _________ embodies the answer to "Who am I".

Exam Probability: **Medium**

37. *Answer choices:*

(see index for correct answer)

- a. Theme-centered interaction
- b. Reflective practice
- c. Self-concept
- d. Chicago Gifted Community Center

Guidance: level 1

:: Childhood ::

_________ was formally introduced by Sandra Bem in 1981 as a cognitive theory to explain how individuals become gendered in society, and how sex-linked characteristics are maintained and transmitted to other members of a culture.Gender-associated information is predominantly transmuted through society by way of schemata, or networks of information that allow for some information to be more easily assimilated than others. Bem argues that there are individual differences in the degree to which people hold these gender schemata. These differences are manifested via the degree to which individuals are sex-typed.

Exam Probability: **Low**

38. *Answer choices:*

(see index for correct answer)

- a. Genital play
- b. Gender schema theory
- c. Pediatrics
- d. Christian Heinrich Heineken

Guidance: level 1

:: Developmental psychology ::

In Freudian psychology, _________ is a central element of the psychoanalytic sexual drive theory, that human beings, from birth, possess an instinctual libido that develops in five stages. Each stage the oral, the anal, the phallic, the latent, and the genital is characterized by the erogenous zone that is the source of the libidinal drive. Sigmund Freud proposed that if the child experienced sexual frustration in relation to any _________ al stage, they would experience anxiety that would persist into adulthood as a neurosis, a functional mental disorder.

Exam Probability: **Medium**

39. *Answer choices:*

(see index for correct answer)

- a. Life course approach
- b. Psychosexual development
- c. Nonuniversal theory
- d. Ordinal numerical competence

Guidance: level 1

:: Aging-associated diseases ::

_________ , also known as high blood pressure , is a long-term medical condition in which the blood pressure in the arteries is persistently elevated. High blood pressure typically does not cause symptoms. Long-term high blood pressure, however, is a major risk factor for coronary artery disease, stroke, heart failure, atrial fibrillation, peripheral vascular disease, vision loss, chronic kidney disease, and dementia.

Exam Probability: **Medium**

40. *Answer choices:*

(see index for correct answer)

- a. Hypertension
- b. Posterior cortical atrophy
- c. Arthritis
- d. Heart failure

Guidance: level 1

:: Congenital disorders of musculoskeletal system ::

_________ is a birth defect in which there is incomplete closing of the spine and membranes around the spinal cord during early development. There are three main types: _________ occulta, meningocele and myelomeningocele. The most common location is the lower back, but in rare cases it may be the middle back or neck. Occulta has no or only mild signs. Signs of occulta may include a hairy patch, dimple, dark spot or swelling on the back at the site of the gap in the spine. Meningocele typically causes mild problems with a sac of fluid present at the gap in the spine. Myelomeningocele, also known as open _________, is the most severe form. Associated problems include poor ability to walk, problems with bladder or bowel control, accumulation of fluid in the brain , a tethered spinal cord and latex allergy. Learning problems are relatively uncommon.

Exam Probability: **Medium**

41. *Answer choices:*

(see index for correct answer)

- a. Spina bifida
- b. Rapadilino syndrome
- c. Hand deformity
- d. Brachycephaly

Guidance: level 1

:: Anesthesia ::

_________ or anaesthesia is a state of controlled, temporary loss of sensation or awareness that is induced for medical purposes. It may include analgesia , paralysis , amnesia , or unconsciousness. A patient under the effects of anesthetic drugs is referred to as being anesthetized.

Exam Probability: **Low**

42. *Answer choices:*

(see index for correct answer)

- a. Baricity
- b. Anesthesia
- c. FlyNap
- d. Laryngoscopy

Guidance: level 1

:: Congenital disorders ::

_________ is a genetic disorder that affects mostly the lungs, but also the pancreas, liver, kidneys, and intestine. Long-term issues include difficulty breathing and coughing up mucus as a result of frequent lung infections. Other signs and symptoms may include sinus infections, poor growth, fatty stool, clubbing of the fingers and toes, and infertility in most males. Different people may have different degrees of symptoms.

Exam Probability: **Low**

43. *Answer choices:*

(see index for correct answer)

- a. Trichothiodystrophy
- b. Proximal femoral focal deficiency
- c. Ponseti method
- d. Cystic fibrosis

Guidance: level 1

:: Intellectual disability ::

Fetal alcohol spectrum disorders are a group of conditions that can occur in a person whose mother drank alcohol during pregnancy. Problems may include an abnormal appearance, short height, low body weight, small head size, poor coordination, low intelligence, behavior problems, and problems with hearing or seeing. Those affected are more likely to have trouble in school, legal problems, participate in high-risk behaviors, and have trouble with alcohol or other drugs. The most severe form of the condition is known as _________. Other types include partial _________ , alcohol-related neurodevelopmental disorder and alcohol-related birth defects . Some accept only FAS as a diagnosis, seeing the evidence as inconclusive with respect to other types.

Exam Probability: **High**

44. *Answer choices:*

(see index for correct answer)

- a. Phenylketonuria
- b. Fetal alcohol syndrome
- c. Moron
- d. The Men of Atalissa

Guidance: level 1

:: Embryology of nervous system ::

In the developing chordate , the _________ is the embryonic precursor to the central nervous system, which is made up of the brain and spinal cord. The neural groove gradually deepens as the neural folds become elevated, and ultimately the folds meet and coalesce in the middle line and convert the groove into the closed _________ . In humans, _________ closure usually occurs by the fourth week of pregnancy . The ectodermal wall of the tube forms the rudiment of the nervous system. The centre of the tube is the neural canal.

Exam Probability: **High**

45. *Answer choices:*

(see index for correct answer)

- a. Alar plate
- b. Neural tube
- c. Neurogenesis
- d. Optic cup

Guidance: level 1

:: Mental health ::

_________ is the use of psychological methods, particularly when based on regular personal interaction, to help a person change behavior and overcome problems in desired ways. _________ aims to improve an individual`s well-being and mental health, to resolve or mitigate troublesome behaviors, beliefs, compulsions, thoughts, or emotions, and to improve relationships and social skills. Certain psychotherapies are considered evidence-based for treating some diagnosed mental disorders. Others have been criticized as pseudoscience.

Exam Probability: **Medium**

46. *Answer choices:*

(see index for correct answer)

- a. Psychotherapy
- b. Emotional well-being
- c. Behavioral health
- d. Institutional syndrome

Guidance: level 1

:: Ageism ::

_________ is stereotyping and discrimination against individuals or groups on the basis of their age. This may be casual or systematic. The term was coined in 1969 by Robert Neil Butler to describe discrimination against seniors, and patterned on sexism and racism. Butler defined " _________ " as a combination of three connected elements. Among them were prejudicial attitudes towards older people, old age, and the aging process; discriminatory practices against older people; and institutional practices and policies that perpetuate stereotypes about elderly people.

Exam Probability: **High**

47. *Answer choices:*

(see index for correct answer)

- a. Youth On Board
- b. Ageism
- c. Paternalism
- d. Peacefire

Guidance: level 1

:: Learning ::

_________ is a method for teaching reading and writing of the English language by developing learners' phonemic awareness—the ability to hear, identify, and manipulate phonemes—in order to teach the correspondence between these sounds and the spelling patterns that represent them.

Exam Probability: **Low**

48. *Answer choices:*

(see index for correct answer)

- a. Phonics
- b. Youth work
- c. Peer learning
- d. Letterland

Guidance: level 1

:: Developmental psychology ::

_________ is the understanding that objects continue to exist even when they cannot be perceived . This is a fundamental concept studied in the field of developmental psychology, the subfield of psychology that addresses the development of young children`s social and mental capacities. There is not yet scientific consensus on when the understanding of _________ emerges in human development.

Exam Probability: **Low**

49. *Answer choices:*

(see index for correct answer)

- a. U-shaped development
- b. Ontogenetic parade

- c. Object permanence
- d. Mental age

Guidance: level 1

:: History of psychology ::

_________ refers to a learning procedure in which a biologically potent stimulus is paired with a previously neutral stimulus . It also refers to the learning process that results from this pairing, through which the neutral stimulus comes to elicit a response that is usually similar to the one elicited by the potent stimulus.

Exam Probability: **Low**

50. *Answer choices:*

(see index for correct answer)

- a. Classical conditioning
- b. Genetic epistemology
- c. Philosophische Studien
- d. Instincts of the Herd in Peace and War

Guidance: level 1

:: Child abuse ::

_________ or child maltreatment is physical, sexual, and/or psychological maltreatment or neglect of a child or children, especially by a parent or a caregiver. _________ may include any act or failure to act by a parent or a caregiver that results in actual or potential harm to a child, and can occur in a child`s home, or in the organizations, schools or communities the child interacts with.

Exam Probability: **Medium**

51. *Answer choices:*

(see index for correct answer)

- a. Court Appointed Special Advocates
- b. Child abuse
- c. South Ronaldsay child abuse scandal
- d. Ameena case

Guidance: level 1

:: Developmental psychology ::

_________, also known as _________ disorder , is a range of mental disorders of the neurodevelopmental type. It includes autism and Asperger syndrome. Individuals on the spectrum often present with problems with social communication and interaction; and restricted, repetitive patterns of behavior, interests or activities. Symptoms are typically recognized between one and two years of age. Long term issues may include difficulties in performing daily tasks, creating and keeping relationships, and maintaining a job.

Exam Probability: **Low**

52. *Answer choices:*

(see index for correct answer)

- a. Cognitive development
- b. Autism spectrum
- c. Bioecological model
- d. Child

Guidance: level 1

:: Self ::

_________ is the personal sense of one`s own gender. _________ can correlate with assigned sex at birth or can differ from it. All societies have a set of gender categories that can serve as the basis of the formation of a person`s social identity in relation to other members of society.

Exam Probability: **High**

53. *Answer choices:*

(see index for correct answer)

- a. Ecological self
- b. Subjectivity
- c. Deidentification

- d. Self-knowledge

Guidance: level 1

:: Motor control ::

_________ s are the abilities usually acquired during childhood as part of a child`s motor learning. By the time they reach two years of age, almost all children are able to stand up, walk and run, walk up stairs, etc. These skills are built upon, improved and better controlled throughout early childhood, and continue in refinement throughout most of the individual`s years of development into adulthood. These gross movements come from large muscle groups and whole body movement. These skills develop in a head-to-toe order. The children will typically learn head control, trunk stability, and then standing up and walking. It is shown that children exposed to outdoor play time activities will develop better _________ s.

Exam Probability: **Low**

54. *Answer choices:*

(see index for correct answer)

- a. Functional movement
- b. Indirect pathway of movement
- c. Gross motor skill
- d. Direct pathway of movement

Guidance: level 1

:: Cybernetics ::

_________ is the interdisciplinary study of systems. A system is a cohesive conglomeration of interrelated and interdependent parts that is either natural or man-made. Every system is delineated by its spatial and temporal boundaries, surrounded and influenced by its environment, described by its structure and purpose or nature and expressed in its functioning. In terms of its effects, a system can be more than the sum of its parts if it expresses synergy or emergent behavior. Changing one part of the system usually affects other parts and the whole system, with predictable patterns of behavior. For systems that are self-learning and self-adapting, the positive growth and adaptation depend upon how well the system is adjusted with its environment. Some systems function mainly to support other systems by aiding in the maintenance of the other system to prevent failure. The goal of _________ is systematically discovering a system`s dynamics, constraints, conditions and elucidating principles that can be discerned and applied to systems at every level of nesting, and in every field for achieving optimized equifinality.

Exam Probability: **High**

55. *Answer choices:*

(see index for correct answer)

- a. Advanced process control
- b. Systems theory
- c. Computational neuroscience
- d. Centrifugal governor

Guidance: level 1

:: Psychoanalysis ::

__________ is a person`s perception of the aesthetics or sexual attractiveness of their own body. It involves how a person sees themselves, compared to the standards that have been set by society. The Austrian neurologist and psychoanalyst Paul Schilder coined the phrase body-image in his book The Image and Appearance of the Human Body .Human society has at all times placed great value on beauty of the human body, but a person`s perception of their own body may not correspond to society`s standards.

Exam Probability: **Medium**

56. *Answer choices:*

(see index for correct answer)

- a. Basic anxiety
- b. An Outline of Psychoanalysis
- c. Berlin Psychoanalytic Institute
- d. The Question of Lay Analysis

Guidance: level 1

:: Positive psychology ::

__________ , sapience, or sagacity is the ability to think and act using knowledge, experience, understanding, common sense and insight. __________ is associated with attributes such as unbiased judgment, compassion, experiential self-knowledge, self-transcendence and non-attachment, and virtues such as ethics and benevolence.

Exam Probability: **Medium**

57. *Answer choices:*

(see index for correct answer)

- a. Spirituality
- b. Wisdom
- c. Positive organizational behavior
- d. Mental capital

Guidance: level 1

:: Youth ::

__________ is the direct influence on people by peers, or the effect on an individual who gets encouraged to follow their peers by changing their attitudes, values or behaviors to conform to those of the influencing group or individual. This can result in either a positive or negative effect, or both. Social groups affected include both membership groups, in which individuals are "formally" members , and cliques, in which membership is not clearly defined. However, a person does not need to be a member or be seeking membership of a group to be affected by __________ . __________ can decrease one`s confidence. It can affect the lives of the students drastically.

Exam Probability: **Medium**

58. *Answer choices:*

(see index for correct answer)

- a. Middle school
- b. Peer pressure
- c. Teen drama
- d. Anti-oppressive education

Guidance: level 1

:: Perception ::

_________ is the ability to interpret the surrounding environment using light in the visible spectrum reflected by the objects in the environment. This is different from visual acuity, which refers to how clearly a person sees . A person can have problems with visual perceptual processing even if he/she has 20/20 vision.

Exam Probability: **Low**

59. *Answer choices:*

(see index for correct answer)

- a. Natural scene perception
- b. Symbolic behavior

- c. Visual perception
- d. Set

Guidance: level 1

Cognitive Psychology

Cognitive psychology is the study of mental processes such as "attention, language use, memory, perception, problem solving, creativity, and thinking". Much of the work derived from cognitive psychology has been integrated into various other modern disciplines such as Cognitive Science and of psychological study, including educational psychology, social psychology, personality psychology, abnormal psychology, developmental psychology, and economics.

:: Behaviorism ::

_________ is a learning process through which the strength of a behavior is modified by reinforcement or punishment. It is also a procedure that is used to bring about such learning.

Exam Probability: **Low**

1. *Answer choices:*

(see index for correct answer)

- a. Generality
- b. Operant conditioning
- c. Prolonged exposure therapy
- d. Contingency management

Guidance: level 1

:: Problem solving ::

_________ is a cognitive bias that limits a person to use an object only in the way it is traditionally used. The concept of _________ originated in Gestalt psychology, a movement in psychology that emphasizes holistic processing. Karl Duncker defined _________ as being a "mental block against using an object in a new way that is required to solve a problem". This "block" limits the ability of an individual to use components given to them to complete a task, as they cannot move past the original purpose of those components. For example, if someone needs a paperweight, but they only have a hammer, they may not see how the hammer can be used as a paperweight. _________ is this inability to see a hammer's use as anything other than for pounding nails; the person couldn't think to use the hammer in a way other than in its conventional function.

Exam Probability: **Medium**

2. *Answer choices:*

(see index for correct answer)

- a. Cornelian dilemma
- b. Curiosity
- c. Force-field analysis
- d. Creativity techniques

Guidance: level 1

:: Causes of death ::

_________ or brain injury is the destruction or degeneration of brain cells. Brain injuries occur due to a wide range of internal and external factors. In general, _________ refers to significant, undiscriminating trauma-induced damage, while neurotoxicity typically refers to selective, chemically induced neuron damage.

Exam Probability: **Medium**

3. *Answer choices:*

(see index for correct answer)

- a. Ballistic trauma
- b. Solomon curve
- c. Septic shock
- d. Brain damage

Guidance: level 1

:: Behaviorism ::

In behavioral psychology, _________ is a consequence applied that will strengthen an organism`s future behavior whenever that behavior is preceded by a specific antecedent stimulus. This strengthening effect may be measured as a higher frequency of behavior , longer duration , greater magnitude , or shorter latency . There are two types of _________ , known as positive _________ and negative _________ ; positive is where by a reward is offered on expression of the wanted behaviour and negative is taking away an undesirable element in the persons environment whenever the desired behaviour is achieved.

Exam Probability: **Low**

4. *Answer choices:*

(see index for correct answer)

- a. Reinforcement
- b. Purposive behaviorism
- c. Behavior management
- d. Token economy

Guidance: level 1

:: Intelligence by type ::

An intelligence quotient is a total score derived from several standardized tests designed to assess human intelligence. The abbreviation "IQ" was coined by the psychologist William Stern for the German term Intelligenzquotient, his term for a scoring method for _________ s at University of Breslau he advocated in a 1912 book. Historically, IQ is a score obtained by dividing a person's mental age score, obtained by administering an _________ , by the person's chronological age, both expressed in terms of years and months. The resulting fraction is multiplied by 100 to obtain the IQ score.

Exam Probability: **Low**

5. *Answer choices:*

(see index for correct answer)

- a. Emotional intelligence
- b. Intelligence test
- c. Systems intelligence
- d. Theory of multiple intelligences

Guidance: level 1

:: Cognitive science ::

_________ is "the mental action or process of acquiring knowledge and understanding through thought, experience, and the senses". It encompasses many aspects of intellectual functions and processes such as attention, the formation of knowledge, memory and working memory, judgment and evaluation, reasoning and "computation", problem solving and decision making, comprehension and production of language. Cognitive processes use existing knowledge and generate new knowledge.

Exam Probability: **High**

6. *Answer choices:*

(see index for correct answer)

- a. Planning
- b. Stimulus-Response compatibility
- c. Cognition
- d. Cognitive science

Guidance: level 1

:: Neuroanatomy ::

A _________ is an enclosed, cable-like bundle of _________ fibres called axons, in the peripheral nervous system. A _________ provides a common pathway for the electrochemical _________ impulses called action potentials that are transmitted along each of the axons to peripheral organs or, in the case of sensory _________ s, from the periphery back to the central nervous system. Each axon within the _________ is an extension of an individual neuron, along with other supportive cells such as Schwann cells that coat the axons in myelin.

Exam Probability: **Low**

7. *Answer choices:*

(see index for correct answer)

- a. Propriospinal tracts
- b. Pontine raphe nucleus
- c. Nerve
- d. Zona incerta

Guidance: level 1

:: Neural networks ::

__________ is a memory error defined as the production of fabricated, distorted, or misinterpreted memories about oneself or the world, without the conscious intention to deceive. People who confabulate present incorrect memories ranging from "subtle alterations to bizarre fabrications", and are generally very confident about their recollections, despite contradictory evidence.

Exam Probability: **High**

8. *Answer choices:*

(see index for correct answer)

- a. Confabulation
- b. Autoassociative memory
- c. brain plasticity
- d. Long short term memory

Guidance: level 1

:: Neuropsychology ::

_________ is a type of perceptual task requiring attention that typically involves an active scan of the visual environment for a particular object or feature among other objects or features . _________ can take place with or without eye movements. The ability to consciously locate an object or target amongst a complex array of stimuli has been extensively studied over the past 40 years. Practical examples of using _________ can be seen in everyday life, such as when one is picking out a product on a supermarket shelf, when animals are searching for food amongst piles of leaves, when trying to find your friend in a large crowd of people, or simply when playing _________ games such as Where`s Wally Much previous literature on _________ used reaction time in order to measure the time it takes to detect the target amongst its distractors. An example of this could be a green square amongst a set of red circles . However, reaction time measurements do not always distinguish between the role of attention and other factors: a long reaction time might be the result of difficulty directing attention to the target, or slowed decision-making processes or slowed motor responses after attention is already directed to the target and the target has already been detected. Many _________ paradigms have therefore used eye movement as a means to measure the degree of attention given to stimuli.However, vast research to date suggests that eye movements can move independently of attention, and therefore eye movement measures do not completely capture the role of attention.

Exam Probability: **Medium**

9. *Answer choices:*

(see index for correct answer)

- a. Visual search
- b. Salience
- c. Dual-task paradigm
- d. Sleep paralysis

Guidance: level 1

:: Neurological disorders in children ::

_________ is a developmental disorder characterized by difficulties with social interaction and communication, and by restricted and repetitive behavior. Parents usually notice signs during the first three years of their child`s life. These signs often develop gradually, though some children with _________ reach their developmental milestones at a normal pace before worsening.

Exam Probability: **High**

10. *Answer choices:*

(see index for correct answer)

- a. Progressive rubella panencephalitis
- b. Batten disease
- c. Adrenoleukodystrophy
- d. Krabbe disease

Guidance: level 1

:: Memory processes ::

Explicit memory is one of the two main types of long-term human memory. It is the conscious, intentional recollection of factual information, previous experiences, and concepts. Explicit memory can be divided into two categories: episodic memory, which stores specific personal experiences, and semantic memory, which stores factual information.

Exam Probability: **Low**

11. *Answer choices:*

(see index for correct answer)

- a. Declarative memory
- b. Sensory memory
- c. Decay theory
- d. Task appropriate processing

Guidance: level 1

:: Memory ::

In cognitive psychology and neuroscience, _________ is that part of the memory responsible for the recording of information about one`s environment and spatial orientation. For example, a person`s _________ is required in order to navigate around a familiar city, just as a rat`s _________ is needed to learn the location of food at the end of a maze. It is often argued that in both humans and animals, spatial memories are summarized as a cognitive map. _________ has representations within working, short-term memory and long-term memory. Research indicates that there are specific areas of the brain associated with _________. Many methods are used for measuring _________ in children, adults, and animals.

Exam Probability: **Medium**

12. *Answer choices:*

(see index for correct answer)

- a. Interference theory
- b. Muscle memory
- c. Sparse distributed memory
- d. Spatial memory

Guidance: level 1

:: Cognition ::

_________ is a psychological test commonly used to investigate selective attention within the auditory system and is a subtopic of cognitive psychology and neuroscience. Specifically, it is "used as a behavioral test for hemispheric lateralization of speech sound perception." During a standard _________ test, a participant is presented with two different auditory stimuli simultaneously . The different stimuli are directed into different ears over headphones. Participants are asked to pay attention to one or both of the stimuli. Later, they are asked about the content of either the message they were asked to attend to or the message that they were not told to listen to. As a result of focusing to repeat the words, participants noticed little of the message to the other ear, often not even realizing that at some point it changed from English to German. At the same time, participants did notice when the voice in the unattended ear changed from a male`s to a female`s, suggesting that the selectivity of consciousness can work to tune in some information."

Exam Probability: **High**

13. *Answer choices:*

(see index for correct answer)

- a. Orientation
- b. Face perception
- c. Dichotic listening
- d. Listening

Guidance: level 1

:: Memory ::

In communications and information processing, code is a system of rules to convert information—such as a letter, word, sound, image, or gesture—into another form or representation, sometimes shortened or secret, for communication through a communication channel or storage in a storage medium. An early example is the invention of language, which enabled a person, through speech, to communicate what they saw, heard, felt, or thought to others. But speech limits the range of communication to the distance a voice can carry, and limits the audience to those present when the speech is uttered. The invention of writing, which converted spoken language into visual symbols, extended the range of communication across space and time.

Exam Probability: **High**

14. *Answer choices:*

(see index for correct answer)

- a. Transactive memory
- b. Arabian Memory Championship
- c. Encoding
- d. Chester Santos

Guidance: level 1

:: Perception ::

An _________ is a distortion of the senses, which can reveal how the human brain normally organizes and interprets sensory stimulation. Though _________ s distort our perception of reality, they are generally shared by most people.

Exam Probability: **High**

15. *Answer choices:*

(see index for correct answer)

- a. Sensorium
- b. Somebody Else%27s Problem
- c. Illusion
- d. Self-image

Guidance: level 1

:: Molecular neuroscience ::

_________ s are endogenous chemicals that enable neurotransmission. It is a type of chemical messenger which transmits signals across a chemical synapse, such as a neuromuscular junction, from one neuron to another "target" neuron, muscle cell, or gland cell. _________ s are released from synaptic vesicles in synapses into the synaptic cleft, where they are received by _________ receptors on the target cells. Many _________ s are synthesized from simple and plentiful precursors such as amino acids, which are readily available from the diet and only require a small number of biosynthetic steps for conversion. _________ s play a major role in shaping everyday life and functions. Their exact numbers are unknown, but more than 200 chemical messengers have been uniquely identified.

Exam Probability: **Low**

16. *Answer choices:*

(see index for correct answer)

- a. Laboratory rat
- b. Tachykinin receptor
- c. Ubiquitin carboxy-terminal hydrolase L1
- d. Reeler

Guidance: level 1

:: Cognitive neuroscience ::

_________ is the capacity to understand or feel what another person is experiencing from within their frame of reference, that is, the capacity to place oneself in another`s position. Definitions of _________ encompass a broad range of emotional states. Types of _________ include cognitive _________, emotional _________, and somatic _________.

Exam Probability: **Low**

17. *Answer choices:*

(see index for correct answer)

- a. Empathy
- b. Two-streams hypothesis
- c. Decade of the Mind
- d. Listener fatigue

Guidance: level 1

:: Behavior ::

_________ or behaviour is the range of actions and mannerisms made by individuals, organisms, systems, or artificial entities in conjunction with themselves or their environment, which includes the other systems or organisms around as well as the physical environment. It is the computed response of the system or organism to various stimuli or inputs, whether internal or external, conscious or subconscious, overt or covert, and voluntary or involuntary.

Exam Probability: **Low**

18. *Answer choices:*

(see index for correct answer)

- a. Swarm behaviour
- b. Social cognitive theory
- c. Human behavior
- d. Behavior

Guidance: level 1

:: Behavioral concepts ::

__________ is a technical term used in classical conditioning to refer to the observation that a familiar stimulus takes longer to acquire meaning than a new stimulus. The term " __________ " dates back to Lubow and Moore. The LI effect is "latent" in that it is not exhibited in the stimulus pre-exposure phase, but rather in the subsequent test phase. "Inhibition", here, simply connotes that the effect is expressed in terms of relatively poor learning. The LI effect is extremely robust, appearing in all mammalian species that have been tested and across many different learning paradigms, thereby suggesting some adaptive advantages, such as protecting the organism from associating irrelevant stimuli with other, more important, events.

Exam Probability: **Low**

19. *Answer choices:*

(see index for correct answer)

- a. Stimulus
- b. Self-Expansion Model
- c. Latent inhibition
- d. Ethogram

Guidance: level 1

:: Statistical terminology ::

In the design of experiments, treatments are applied to experimental units in the treatment group. In comparative experiments, members of the complementary group, the __________ , receive either no treatment or a standard treatment.

Exam Probability: **Low**

20. *Answer choices:*

(see index for correct answer)

- a. Likelihood
- b. marginal distribution
- c. Floor effect
- d. Independent variable

Guidance: level 1

:: Perception ::

_________ is the ability to interpret the surrounding environment using light in the visible spectrum reflected by the objects in the environment. This is different from visual acuity, which refers to how clearly a person sees . A person can have problems with visual perceptual processing even if he/she has 20/20 vision.

Exam Probability: **High**

21. *Answer choices:*

(see index for correct answer)

- a. Direct experience
- b. Visual perception

- c. Chubb illusion
- d. P300

Guidance: level 1

:: Perception ::

The __________ is a perceptual phenomenon that demonstrates an interaction between hearing and vision in speech perception. The illusion occurs when the auditory component of one sound is paired with the visual component of another sound, leading to the perception of a third sound. The visual information a person gets from seeing a person speak changes the way they hear the sound. If a person is getting poor quality auditory information but good quality visual information, they may be more likely to experience the __________. Integration abilities for audio and visual information may also influence whether a person will experience the effect. People who are better at sensory integration have been shown to be more susceptible to the effect. Many people are affected differently by the __________ based on many factors, including brain damage and other disorders.

Exam Probability: **Low**

22. *Answer choices:*

(see index for correct answer)

- a. Constructive perception
- b. McGurk effect
- c. Categorical perception
- d. Moral perception

Guidance: level 1

:: Communication ::

_________ studies the quantification, storage, and communication of information. It was originally proposed by Claude Shannon in 1948 to find fundamental limits on signal processing and communication operations such as data compression, in a landmark paper entitled "A Mathematical Theory of Communication". Applications of fundamental topics of _________ include lossless data compression , lossy data compression , and channel coding . Its impact has been crucial to the success of the Voyager missions to deep space, the invention of the compact disc, the feasibility of mobile phones, the development of the Internet, the study of linguistics and of human perception, the understanding of black holes, and numerous other fields.

Exam Probability: **Medium**

23. *Answer choices:*

(see index for correct answer)

- a. Speech transmission index
- b. Semantic compaction
- c. Closed-ended question
- d. Misquotation

Guidance: level 1

:: Memory ::

In neuroscience, _________ is a persistent strengthening of synapses based on recent patterns of activity. These are patterns of synaptic activity that produce a long-lasting increase in signal transmission between two neurons. The opposite of LTP is long-term depression, which produces a long-lasting decrease in synaptic strength.

Exam Probability: **Medium**

24. *Answer choices:*

(see index for correct answer)

- a. Long-term potentiation
- b. Metamemory
- c. Exosomatic memory
- d. Hyperthymesia

Guidance: level 1

:: Cognition ::

_________ is a psychological process related to an abstract or physical object, such as a person, situation, or message whereby one is able to think about it and use concepts to deal adequately with that object. _________ is a relation between the knower and an object of _________ . _________ implies abilities and dispositions with respect to an object of knowledge that are sufficient to support intelligent behaviour.

Exam Probability: **Low**

25. *Answer choices:*

(see index for correct answer)

- a. Understanding
- b. International Cognitive Linguistics Association
- c. Imagined interaction
- d. Cognitive holding power

Guidance: level 1

:: Imagination ::

A _________ is a proposed explanation for a phenomenon. For a _________ to be a scientific _________, the scientific method requires that one can test it. Scientists generally base scientific hypotheses on previous observations that cannot satisfactorily be explained with the available scientific theories. Even though the words " _________ " and "theory" are often used synonymously, a scientific _________ is not the same as a scientific theory. A working _________ is a provisionally accepted _________ proposed for further research, in a process beginning with an educated guess or thought.

Exam Probability: **High**

26. *Answer choices:*

(see index for correct answer)

- a. Bovarysme
- b. Mental image

- c. Sexual fantasy
- d. Paracosm

Guidance: level 1

:: History of artificial intelligence ::

The _________ , developed by Alan Turing in 1950, is a test of a machine`s ability to exhibit intelligent behaviour equivalent to, or indistinguishable from, that of a human. Turing proposed that a human evaluator would judge natural language conversations between a human and a machine designed to generate human-like responses. The evaluator would be aware that one of the two partners in conversation is a machine, and all participants would be separated from one another. The conversation would be limited to a text-only channel such as a computer keyboard and screen so the result would not depend on the machine`s ability to render words as speech. If the evaluator cannot reliably tell the machine from the human, the machine is said to have passed the test. The test results do not depend on the machine`s ability to give correct answers to questions, only how closely its answers resemble those a human would give.

Exam Probability: **Medium**

27. *Answer choices:*

(see index for correct answer)

- a. AI winter
- b. Alvey
- c. Turing test
- d. Logic Theorist

Guidance: level 1

:: Second-language acquisition ::

An _________ is an action which is inaccurate or incorrect. In some usages, an _________ is synonymous with a mistake. In statistics, " _________ " refers to the difference between the value which has been computed and the correct value. An _________ could result in failure or in a deviation from the intended performance or behaviour.

Exam Probability: **Low**

28. *Answer choices:*

(see index for correct answer)

- a. Language transfer
- b. Error
- c. Error treatment
- d. Second-language acquisition classroom research

Guidance: level 1

:: Linguistics ::

_________ , according to Literacy Information and Communication System is "the ability of a reader to recognize written words correctly and virtually effortlessly". It is sometimes referred to as "isolated _________ " because it involves a reader`s ability to recognize words individually from a list without needing similar words for contextual help. LINCS continues to say that "rapid and effortless _________ is the main component of fluent reading" and explains that these skills can be improved by "practic[ing] with flashcards, lists, and word grids".

Exam Probability: **Low**

29. *Answer choices:*

(see index for correct answer)

- a. Language documentation
- b. Integrational Theory of Language
- c. Thematic structure
- d. Word recognition

Guidance: level 1

:: Memory processes ::

_________ is the sensory memory register specific to auditory information . The sensory memory for sounds that people have just perceived is the form of _________ . Unlike visual memory, in which our eyes can scan the stimuli over and over, the auditory stimuli cannot be scanned over and over. Overall, echoic memories are stored for slightly longer periods of time than iconic memories . Auditory stimuli are received by the ear one at a time before they can be processed and understood. For instance, hearing the radio is very different from reading a magazine. A person can only hear the radio once at a given time, while the magazine can be read over and over again. It can be said that the _________ is like a "holding tank" concept, because a sound is unprocessed until the following sound is heard, and only then can it be made meaningful. This particular sensory store is capable of storing large amounts of auditory information that is only retained for a short period of time . This echoic sound resonates in the mind and is replayed for this brief amount of time shortly after the presentation of auditory stimuli. _________ encodes only moderately primitive aspects of the stimuli, for example pitch, which specifies localization to the non-association brain regions.

Exam Probability: **Medium**

30. *Answer choices:*

(see index for correct answer)

- a. Memory for the future
- b. Leveling and Sharpening
- c. Match-to-sample task
- d. Echoic memory

Guidance: level 1

:: Aggression ::

_________ is overt or covert, often harmful, social interaction with the intention of inflicting damage or other unpleasantness upon another individual. It may occur either reactively or without provocation. In humans, frustration due to blocked goals can cause _________ . Human _________ can be classified into direct and indirect _________ ; whilst the former is characterized by physical or verbal behavior intended to cause harm to someone, the latter is characterized by behavior intended to harm the social relations of an individual or group.

Exam Probability: **Medium**

31. *Answer choices:*

(see index for correct answer)

- a. Fighting in ice hockey
- b. Character assassination
- c. Monoamine oxidase A
- d. Verbal aggressiveness

Guidance: level 1

:: Apes from language studies ::

_________ is a masculine given name that comes from Hebrew: / , derived from the question mi ka'el, meaning "Who is like God".

Exam Probability: **High**

32. *Answer choices:*

(see index for correct answer)

- a. Kanzi
- b. Michael
- c. Lana
- d. Loulis

Guidance: level 1

:: Mnemonics ::

The __________ is a method of memory enhancement which uses visualizations with the use of spatial memory, familiar information about one`s environment, to quickly and efficiently recall information. The __________ is also known as the memory journey, memory palace, or mind palace technique. This method is a mnemonic device adopted in ancient Roman and Greek rhetorical treatises . Many memory contest champions claim to use this technique to recall faces, digits, and lists of words.

Exam Probability: **High**

33. *Answer choices:*

(see index for correct answer)

- a. Xyzzy
- b. Method of loci
- c. Magic SysRq key

- d. peg system

Guidance: level 1

:: Memory biases ::

The _________ is the tendency for older adults to have increased recollection for events that occurred during their adolescence and early adulthood. It was identified through the study of autobiographical memory and the subsequent plotting of the age of encoding of memories to form the lifespan retrieval curve.

Exam Probability: **Low**

34. *Answer choices:*

(see index for correct answer)

- a. Gender differences in eyewitness memory
- b. Reminiscence bump
- c. Cue-dependent forgetting
- d. Childhood amnesia

Guidance: level 1

:: Death customs ::

A __________ is an inert substance or treatment which is not designed to have a therapeutic value. Common __________ s include inert tablets , inert injections , sham surgery, and other procedures.

Exam Probability: **Medium**

35. *Answer choices:*

(see index for correct answer)

- a. Death anniversary
- b. Roman Catholic funeral
- c. Placebo
- d. Lying in repose

Guidance: level 1

:: Arguments ::

A __________ or premiss is a statement that an argument claims will induce or justify a conclusion. In other words, a __________ is an assumption that something is true.

Exam Probability: **Low**

36. *Answer choices:*

(see index for correct answer)

- a. Premise
- b. Argumentative dialogue
- c. Soiled Dove Plea
- d. Diagonal argument

Guidance: level 1

:: Units of morphological analysis ::

In biology, a _________ is a sequence of nucleotides in DNA or RNA that codes for a molecule that has a function. During _________ expression, the DNA is first copied into RNA. The RNA can be directly functional or be the intermediate template for a protein that performs a function. The transmission of _________s to an organism`s offspring is the basis of the inheritance of phenotypic trait. These _________s make up different DNA sequences called genotypes. Genotypes along with environmental and developmental factors determine what the phenotypes will be. Most biological traits are under the influence of poly_________s as well as _________-environment interactions. Some _________tic traits are instantly visible, such as eye color or number of limbs, and some are not, such as blood type, risk for specific diseases, or the thousands of basic biochemical processes that constitute life.

Exam Probability: **Medium**

37. *Answer choices:*

(see index for correct answer)

- a. Grapheme
- b. Gene

Guidance: level 1

:: Giftedness ::

A _________ is a person who displays exceptional intellectual ability, creative productivity, universality in genres or originality, typically to a degree that is associated with the achievement of new advances in a domain of knowledge. Despite the presence of scholars in many subjects throughout history, many _________ es have shown high achievements in only a single kind of activity.

Exam Probability: **Low**

38. *Answer choices:*

(see index for correct answer)

- a. Marilyn vos Savant
- b. Genius
- c. Personal life of Leonardo da Vinci
- d. William James Sidis

Guidance: level 1

:: Learning ::

_________ is a phenomenon of learning and memory that was first named and described by Ivan Pavlov in his studies of classical conditioning. In that context, it refers to the re-emergence of a previously extinguished conditioned response after a delay. Such a recovery of "lost" behaviors can be observed within a variety of domains, and the recovery of lost human memories is often of particular interest. For a mathematical model for _________ see Further Reading.

Exam Probability: **High**

39. *Answer choices:*

(see index for correct answer)

- a. Discrimination learning
- b. Spontaneous recovery
- c. Initial Teaching Alphabet
- d. Phonetically Intuitive English

Guidance: level 1

:: Memory biases ::

_________, also called infantile amnesia, is the inability of adults to retrieve episodic memories before the age of two to four years, as well as the period before the age of ten of which adults retain fewer memories than might otherwise be expected given the passage of time. The development of a cognitive self is also thought by some to have an effect on encoding and storing early memories.

Exam Probability: **High**

40. *Answer choices:*

(see index for correct answer)

- a. Childhood amnesia
- b. Selective memory loss
- c. Levels-of-processing effect
- d. Google effect

Guidance: level 1

:: Cognitive science ::

_________ is the scientific field that is concerned with the study of the biological processes and aspects that underlie cognition, with a specific focus on the neural connections in the brain which are involved in mental processes. It addresses the questions of how cognitive activities are affected or controlled by neural circuits in the brain. _________ is a branch of both neuroscience and psychology, overlapping with disciplines such as behavioral neuroscience, cognitive psychology, physiological psychology and affective neuroscience. _________ relies upon theories in cognitive science coupled with evidence from neurobiology, and computational modeling.

Exam Probability: **Medium**

41. *Answer choices:*

(see index for correct answer)

- a. Frame semantics
- b. Probability matching
- c. Presence
- d. Mechanical philosophy

Guidance: level 1

:: Behaviorism ::

_________ , also known as graduated exposure therapy, is a type of behavior therapy developed by South African psychiatrist, Joseph Wolpe. It is used in the field of clinical psychology to help many people effectively overcome phobias and other anxiety disorders that are based on classical conditioning, and shares the same elements of both cognitive-behavioral therapy and applied behavior analysis. When used by the behavior analysts, it is based on radical behaviorism and functional analysis, as it incorporates counterconditioning principles, such as meditation and breathing . From the cognitive psychology perspective, however, cognitions and feelings trigger motor actions.

Exam Probability: **High**

42. *Answer choices:*

(see index for correct answer)

- a. Journal of Applied Behavior Analysis
- b. behavior therapy
- c. Systematic desensitization
- d. Functional analytic psychotherapy

Guidance: level 1

:: Information science ::

_________ is the resolution of uncertainty; it is that which answers the question of "what an entity is" and thus defines both its essence and nature of its characteristics. _________ relates to both data and knowledge, as data is meaningful _________ representing values attributed to parameters, and knowledge signifies understanding of a concept. _________ is uncoupled from an observer, which is an entity that can access _________ and thus discern what it specifies; _________ exists beyond an event horizon for example. In the case of knowledge, the _________ itself requires a cognitive observer to be obtained.

Exam Probability: **Low**

43. *Answer choices:*

(see index for correct answer)

- a. Library and information science
- b. Library and Information Science Abstracts
- c. Informedia Digital Library
- d. Information audit

Guidance: level 1

:: Philosophy of psychology ::

_________ is the examination of one`s own conscious thoughts and feelings. In psychology, the process of _________ relies exclusively on observation of one`s mental state, while in a spiritual context it may refer to the examination of one`s soul. _________ is closely related to human self-reflection and is contrasted with external observation.

Exam Probability: **Low**

44. *Answer choices:*

(see index for correct answer)

- a. Cognitivism
- b. Metapsychology
- c. Rationality
- d. Introspection

Guidance: level 1

:: Memory biases ::

The _________ happens when a person`s recall of episodic memories becomes less accurate because of post-event information. For example, in a study published in 1994, subjects were initially shown one of two different series of slides that depicted a college student at the university bookstore, with different objects of the same type changed in some slides. One version of the slides would, for example, show a screwdriver while the other would show a wrench, and the audio narrative accompanying the slides would only refer to the object as a "tool". In the second phase, subjects would read a narrative description of the events in the slides, except this time a specific tool was named, which would be the incorrect tool half the time. Finally, in the third phase, subjects had to list five examples of specific types of objects, such as tools, but were told to only list examples which they had not seen in the slides. Subjects who had read an incorrect narrative were far less likely to list the written object than the control subjects , and were far more likely to incorrectly list the item which they had actually seen .

Exam Probability: **High**

45. *Answer choices:*

(see index for correct answer)

- a. Levels-of-processing effect
- b. Google effect
- c. Misinformation effect
- d. Gender differences in eyewitness memory

Guidance: level 1

:: Communication ::

_________ is the act of conveying meanings from one entity or group to another through the use of mutually understood signs, symbols, and semiotic rules.

Exam Probability: **High**

46. *Answer choices:*

(see index for correct answer)

- a. Asynchronous communication
- b. Universal Accreditation Board
- c. Communication
- d. Orange County Business Council

Guidance: level 1

:: Memory processes ::

During every moment of an organism`s life, sensory information is being taken in by sensory receptors and processed by the nervous system. Sensory information is stored in _________ just long enough to be transferred to short-term memory. Humans have five traditional senses: sight, hearing, taste, smell, touch. _________ allows individuals to retain impressions of sensory information after the original stimulus has ceased. A common demonstration of SM is a child`s ability to write letters and make circles by twirling a sparkler at night. When the sparkler is spun fast enough, it appears to leave a trail which forms a continuous image. This "light trail" is the image that is represented in the visual sensory store known as iconic memory. The other two types of SM that have been most extensively studied are echoic memory, and haptic memory; however, it is reasonable to assume that each physiological sense has a corresponding memory store. Children for example have been shown to remember specific "sweet" tastes during incidental learning trials but the nature of this gustatory store is still unclear.

Exam Probability: **Low**

47. *Answer choices:*

(see index for correct answer)

- a. Leveling and Sharpening
- b. Declarative memory
- c. Sensory memory
- d. Verbal memory

Guidance: level 1

:: Human behavior ::

_________ is a cognitive system with a limited capacity that is responsible for temporarily holding information available for processing. _________ is important for reasoning and the guidance of decision-making and behavior. _________ is often used synonymously with short-term memory, but some theorists consider the two forms of memory distinct, assuming that _________ allows for the manipulation of stored information, whereas short-term memory only refers to the short-term storage of information. _________ is a theoretical concept central to cognitive psychology, neuropsychology, and neuroscience.

Exam Probability: **High**

48. *Answer choices:*

(see index for correct answer)

- a. Loner
- b. Working Memory
- c. Ultracrepidarianism
- d. Critical positivity ratio

Guidance: level 1

:: Mental health ::

_________ is defined as the level of psychological well-being or an absence of mental illness. It is the state of someone who is "functioning at a satisfactory level of emotional and behavioural adjustment". From the perspectives of positive psychology or of holism, _________ may include an individual`s ability to enjoy life, and to create a balance between life activities and efforts to achieve psychological resilience.According to the World Health Organization , _________ includes "subjective well-being, perceived self-efficacy, autonomy, competence, inter-generational dependence, and self-actualization of one`s intellectual and emotional potential, among others." The WHO further states that the well-being of an individual is encompassed in the realization of their abilities, coping with normal stresses of life, productive work and contribution to their community.Cultural differences, subjective assessments, and competing professional theories all affect how one defines " _________ ".

Exam Probability: **Medium**

49. *Answer choices:*

(see index for correct answer)

- a. Self-help groups for mental health
- b. Mental health
- c. Care programme approach
- d. Global mental health

Guidance: level 1

:: Evaluation ::

__________ is asystematic determination of a subject`s merit, worth and significance, using criteria governed by a set of standards. It can assist an organization, program, design, project or any other intervention or initiative to assess any aim, realisable concept/proposal, or any alternative, to help in decision-making; or to ascertain the degree of achievement or value in regard to the aim and objectives and results of any such action that has been completed. The primary purpose of __________ , in addition to gaining insight into prior or existing initiatives, is to enable reflection and assist in the identification of future change.

Exam Probability: **Medium**

50. *Answer choices:*

(see index for correct answer)

- a. Evaluation
- b. Impact evaluation
- c. Registration, Evaluation, Authorisation and Restriction of Chemicals
- d. Goddard College

Guidance: level 1

:: Neuropsychological tests ::

Functionally, __________ is to measure the number of discrete units over which the individual can successively distribute his attention and still organize them into a working unit. To generalize, it refers to the ability of an individual to reproduce immediately, after one presentation, a series of discrete stimuli in their original order.

Exam Probability: **Medium**

51. *Answer choices:*

(see index for correct answer)

- a. Memory span
- b. Wisconsin Card Sorting Test
- c. 1-2-AX working memory task
- d. Wechsler Adult Intelligence Scale

Guidance: level 1

:: Cerebrum ::

The _________ is involved in processing sensory input into derived meanings for the appropriate retention of visual memory, language comprehension, and emotion association.

Exam Probability: **Medium**

52. *Answer choices:*

(see index for correct answer)

- a. Temporal lobe
- b. Frenulum of superior medullary velum
- c. Pulvinar nuclei
- d. Superior temporal gyrus

Guidance: level 1

:: Knowledge ::

Dictionaries traditionally define _________ as the ability to read and write. In the modern world, this is one way of interpreting _________ . One more broad interpretation sees _________ as knowledge and competence in a specific area. The concept of _________ has evolved in meaning. The modern term`s meaning has been expanded to include the ability to use language, numbers, images, computers, and other basic means to understand, communicate, gain useful knowledge, solve mathematical problems and use the dominant symbol systems of a culture. The concept of _________ is expanding across OECD countries to include skills to access knowledge through technology and ability to assess complex contexts. A person who travels and resides in a foreign country but is unable to read or write in the language of the host country would be regarded by the locals as illiterate.

Exam Probability: **Low**

53. *Answer choices:*

(see index for correct answer)

- a. Interdisciplinarity
- b. Knowledge ark
- c. Ignorance
- d. Knowledge mobilization

Guidance: level 1

:: Fiction ::

A _________ is a figure of speech that, for rhetorical effect, directly refers to one thing by mentioning another. It may provide clarity or identify hidden similarities between two ideas. Antithesis, hyperbole, metonymy and simile are all types of _________ . One of the most commonly cited examples of a _________ in English literature is the "All the world`s a stage" monologue from As You Like It.

Exam Probability: **Low**

54. *Answer choices:*

(see index for correct answer)

- a. Metaphor
- b. Fantasy world
- c. A-Plot
- d. Epilogue

Guidance: level 1

:: Human–computer interaction ::

_________ is a theory of attention developed in 1980 by Anne Treisman and Garry Gelade that suggests that when perceiving a stimulus, features are "registered early, automatically, and in parallel, while objects are identified separately" and at a later stage in processing. The theory has been one of the most influential psychological models of human visual attention.

Exam Probability: **Medium**

55. *Answer choices:*

(see index for correct answer)

- a. Feature integration theory
- b. User virtualization
- c. Scratch input
- d. Collaborative information seeking

Guidance: level 1

:: Personality ::

_________ is a psychological attribute that indicates how people explain to themselves why they experience a particular event, either positive or negative.

Exam Probability: **Low**

56. *Answer choices:*

(see index for correct answer)

- a. Personality development
- b. Positive affectivity
- c. Subpersonality
- d. Bicultural identity

Guidance: level 1

:: Philosophy of life ::

_________ or moral philosophy is a branch of philosophy that involves systematizing, defending, and recommending concepts of right and wrong conduct. The field of _________ , along with aesthetics, concerns matters of value, and thus comprises the branch of philosophy called axiology.

Exam Probability: **High**

57. *Answer choices:*

(see index for correct answer)

- a. Ethics
- b. Alternative lifestyle
- c. Atheist existentialism
- d. Nihilism

Guidance: level 1

:: Discrimination ::

In human social behavior, __________ is treatment or consideration of, or making a distinction towards, a person based on the group, class, or category to which the person is perceived to belong. These include age, colour, criminal record, height, disability, ethnicity, family status, gender identity, generation, genetic characteristics, marital status, nationality, race, religion, sex, and sexual orientation. __________ consists of treatment of an individual or group, based on their actual or perceived membership in a certain group or social category, "in a way that is worse than the way people are usually treated". It involves the group`s initial reaction or interaction going on to influence the individual`s actual behavior towards the group leader or the group, restricting members of one group from opportunities or privileges that are available to another group, leading to the exclusion of the individual or entities based on illogical or irrational decision making.

Exam Probability: **Low**

58. *Answer choices:*

(see index for correct answer)

- a. Dalit
- b. Discrimination
- c. Anti-Igbo sentiment
- d. Ableism

Guidance: level 1

:: Inductive fallacies ::

The __________ is a mental shortcut that relies on immediate examples that come to a given person`s mind when evaluating a specific topic, concept, method or decision. The __________ operates on the notion that if something can be recalled, it must be important, or at least more important than alternative solutions which are not as readily recalled. Subsequently, under the __________, people tend to heavily weigh their judgments toward more recent information, making new opinions biased toward that latest news.

Exam Probability: **Low**

59. *Answer choices:*

(see index for correct answer)

- a. Availability heuristic
- b. Hasty generalization
- c. Cherry picking
- d. Overwhelming exception

Guidance: level 1

Abnormal Psychology

Abnormal psychology is the branch of psychology that studies unusual patterns of behavior, emotion and thought, which may or may not be understood as precipitating a mental disorder. Although many behaviors could be considered as abnormal, this branch of psychology generally deals with behavior in a clinical context. There is a long history of attempts to understand and control behavior deemed to be aberrant or deviant (statistically, functionally, morally or in some other sense), and there is often cultural variation in the approach taken. The field of abnormal psychology identifies multiple causes for different conditions, employing diverse theories from the general field of psychology and elsewhere, and much still hinges on what exactly is meant by "abnormal".

:: Human behavior ::

A _________, also known as a sex role, is a social role encompassing a range of behaviors and attitudes that are generally considered acceptable, appropriate, or desirable for people based on their actual or perceived sex. _________ s are usually centered on conceptions of femininity and masculinity, although there are exceptions and variations. The specifics regarding these gendered expectations may vary substantially among cultures, while other characteristics may be common throughout a range of cultures. There is ongoing debate as to what extent _________ s and their variations are biologically determined, and to what extent they are socially constructed.

Exam Probability: **Medium**

1. *Answer choices:*

(see index for correct answer)

- a. Maternal sensitivity
- b. Spoiled child
- c. Evolutionary psychology
- d. Gender role

Guidance: level 1

:: Anxiety disorders ::

__________ is a Japanese culture-specific syndrome. The term __________ translates into the disorder of fear of interpersonal relations . Those who have __________ are likely to be extremely embarrassed about themselves or fearful of displeasing others when it comes to the functions of their bodies or their appearances. These bodily functions and appearances include their faces, odor, actions, or even looks. They do not want to embarrass other people with their presence. This culture-bound syndrome is a social phobia based on fear and anxiety.

Exam Probability: **High**

2. *Answer choices:*

(see index for correct answer)

- a. Lick granuloma
- b. Stage fright
- c. Taijin kyofusho
- d. Compulsive behavior

Guidance: level 1

:: Social work ::

_________ is an evidence-based therapeutic intervention for patients and their loved ones that provides information and support to better understand and cope with illness. _________ is most often associated with serious mental illness, including dementia, schizophrenia, clinical depression, anxiety disorders, psychotic illnesses, eating disorders, personality disorders and autism, although the term has also been used for programs that address physical illnesses, such as cancer.

Exam Probability: **High**

3. *Answer choices:*

(see index for correct answer)

- a. LifeRing Secular Recovery
- b. Social learning tools
- c. Psychoeducation
- d. 6-15-99 Club

Guidance: level 1

:: Clinical psychology ::

_________ is the perception and actuality that one is cared for, has assistance available from other people, and most popularly, that one is part of a supportive social network. These supportive resources can be emotional , informational , or companionship ; tangible or intangible .

Exam Probability: **Low**

4. *Answer choices:*

(see index for correct answer)

- a. Cognitive behavioral therapy
- b. Services for mental disorders
- c. Mindfulness
- d. Social support

Guidance: level 1

:: Mental health ::

__________ is the use of psychological methods, particularly when based on regular personal interaction, to help a person change behavior and overcome problems in desired ways. __________ aims to improve an individual`s well-being and mental health, to resolve or mitigate troublesome behaviors, beliefs, compulsions, thoughts, or emotions, and to improve relationships and social skills. Certain psychotherapies are considered evidence-based for treating some diagnosed mental disorders. Others have been criticized as pseudoscience.

Exam Probability: **Medium**

5. *Answer choices:*

(see index for correct answer)

- a. Self-help groups for mental health
- b. Stig-9

- c. Testamentary capacity
- d. Dark therapy

Guidance: level 1

:: Positive psychology ::

_________ , sapience, or sagacity is the ability to think and act using knowledge, experience, understanding, common sense and insight. _________ is associated with attributes such as unbiased judgment, compassion, experiential self-knowledge, self-transcendence and non-attachment, and virtues such as ethics and benevolence.

Exam Probability: **Low**

6. *Answer choices:*

(see index for correct answer)

- a. Humanity
- b. Wisdom
- c. UK Kindness Movement
- d. Positive organizational behavior

Guidance: level 1

:: Euphoriants ::

_________, sold under the trade name Ritalin, among others, is a stimulant medication used to treat attention deficit hyperactivity disorder and narcolepsy. It is a first line medication for ADHD. It is taken by mouth or applied to the skin. Different formulations have different durations of effect.

Exam Probability: **High**

7. *Answer choices:*

(see index for correct answer)

- a. Cathine
- b. Mitragynine pseudoindoxyl
- c. Methylphenidate
- d. Oxycodone

Guidance: level 1

:: Tricyclic antidepressants ::

_________, sold under the brand name Tofranil among others, is a tricyclic antidepressant which is used mainly in the treatment of depression. It can also reduce symptoms of agitation and anxiety. The drug is also used to treat bedwetting. It is taken by mouth. A long-acting form for injection into muscle is also available.

Exam Probability: **Low**

8. *Answer choices:*

(see index for correct answer)

- a. Opipramol
- b. Butriptyline
- c. Doxepin
- d. Imipramine

Guidance: level 1

:: Pharmacology ::

In medicine, a side effect is an effect, whether therapeutic or adverse, that is secondary to the one intended; although the term is predominantly employed to describe adverse effects, it can also apply to beneficial, but unintended, consequences of the use of a drug. Developing drugs is a complicated process, because no two people are exactly the same, so even drugs that have virtually no _________ , might be difficult for some people. Also, it is difficult to make a drug that targets one part of the body but that doesn't affect other parts, the fact that increases the risk of _________ in the untargeted parts.

Exam Probability: **High**

9. *Answer choices:*

(see index for correct answer)

- a. cross-tolerance
- b. Side effects

Guidance: level 1

:: Personality disorders ::

_________ s are a class of mental disorders characterized by enduring maladaptive patterns of behavior, cognition, and inner experience, exhibited across many contexts and deviating from those accepted by the individual`s culture. These patterns develop early, are inflexible, and are associated with significant distress or disability. The definitions may vary somewhat, according to source. Official criteria for diagnosing _________ s are listed in the Diagnostic and Statistical Manual of Mental Disorders and the fifth chapter of the International Classification of Diseases .

Exam Probability: **High**

10. *Answer choices:*

(see index for correct answer)

- a. Sadistic personality disorder
- b. Personality disorder
- c. Schizoid personality disorder
- d. Schizotypal personality disorder

Guidance: level 1

:: Philosophy of sexuality ::

_________ is a motivational state and an interest in "sexual objects or activities, or as a wish, or drive to seek out sexual objects or to engage in sexual activities". Synonyms for _________ are libido, sexual attraction and lust. _________ is an aspect of a person`s sexuality, which varies significantly from one person to another, and also varies depending on circumstances at a particular time. Not every person experiences _________; those who do not experience it may be labelled asexual.

Exam Probability: **High**

11. *Answer choices:*

(see index for correct answer)

- a. The History of Sexuality
- b. Homosexuality: A Philosophical Inquiry
- c. Sexual desire
- d. Lust

Guidance: level 1

:: Alcohol abuse ::

_________ is a mental disorder that can develop after a person is exposed to a traumatic event, such as sexual assault, warfare, traffic collisions, or other threats on a person`s life. Symptoms may include disturbing thoughts, feelings, or dreams related to the events, mental or physical distress to trauma-related cues, attempts to avoid trauma-related cues, alterations in how a person thinks and feels, and an increase in the fight-or-flight response. These symptoms last for more than a month after the event. Young children are less likely to show distress, but instead may express their memories through play. A person with PTSD is at a higher risk for suicide and intentional self-harm.

Exam Probability: **Low**

12. *Answer choices:*

(see index for correct answer)

- a. Sinclair Method
- b. National Institute on Alcohol Abuse and Alcoholism
- c. Iomazenil
- d. Children of Light

Guidance: level 1

:: Psychosis ::

_________ is a period of psychosis whose duration is short, is not caused by another condition, and which may or may not be recurrent.

Exam Probability: **Low**

13. *Answer choices:*

(see index for correct answer)

- a. Occupational psychosis
- b. Mystical psychosis
- c. Delusion
- d. Substance-induced psychosis

Guidance: level 1

:: Applied psychology ::

_________ is a psychological specialty that encompasses research and applied work in several broad domains: counseling process and outcome; supervision and training; career development and counseling; and prevention and health. Some unifying themes among counseling psychologists include a focus on assets and strengths, person–environment interactions, educational and career development, brief interactions, and a focus on intact personalities.

Exam Probability: **High**

14. *Answer choices:*

(see index for correct answer)

- a. Applied psychology
- b. Social marketing

- c. Genopolitics
- d. Community psychology

Guidance: level 1

:: Emotion ::

_________ is, e.g., the purification and purgation of emotions—particularly pity and fear—through art or any extreme change in emotion that results in renewal and restoration. It is a metaphor originally used by Aristotle in the Poetics, comparing the effects of tragedy on the mind of a spectator to the effect of a cathartic on the body. New work shows that metaphor is not allowed in definitions for Aristotle and thus, for a number of other reasons, too, Aristotle could not have written himself the word katharsis in that location, which helps explain why no one in 1000 years has been able to translate it to the satisfaction of the specialists in Aristotle.

Exam Probability: **High**

15. *Answer choices:*

(see index for correct answer)

- a. Self-conscious emotions
- b. Jealousy in religion
- c. Catharsis
- d. Emotional Intelligence 2.0

Guidance: level 1

:: Dopamine agonists ::

_________ is a potent central nervous system stimulant that is mainly used as a recreational drug and less commonly as a second-line treatment for attention deficit hyperactivity disorder and obesity. _________ was discovered in 1893 and exists as two enantiomers: levo-_________ and dextro-_________ . _________ properly refers to a specific chemical, the racemic free base, which is an equal mixture of levo _________ and dextro _________ in their pure amine forms. It is rarely prescribed over concerns involving human neurotoxicity and potential for recreational use as an aphrodisiac and euphoriant, among other concerns, as well as the availability of safer substitute drugs with comparable treatment efficacy. Dextro _________ is a much stronger CNS stimulant than levo _________ .

Exam Probability: **Medium**

16. *Answer choices:*

(see index for correct answer)

- a. Metergoline
- b. Methamphetamine
- c. Dopexamine
- d. Ro10-5824

Guidance: level 1

:: Self ::

__________ is a term that has been used in various psychology theories, often in different ways. The term was originally introduced by the organismic theorist Kurt Goldstein for the motive to realize one`s full potential. In Goldstein`s view, it is the organism`s master motive, the only real motive: "the tendency to actualize itself as fully as possible is the basic drive ... the drive of __________ ." Carl Rogers similarly wrote of "the curative force in psychotherapy man`s tendency to actualize himself, to become his potentialities ... to express and activate all the capacities of the organism." The concept was brought most fully to prominence in Abraham Maslow`s hierarchy of needs theory as the final level of psychological development that can be achieved when all basic and mental needs are essentially fulfilled and the "actualization" of the full personal potential takes place, although he adapted this viewpoint later on in life to be more flexible.

Exam Probability: **Low**

17. *Answer choices:*

(see index for correct answer)

- a. Nafs
- b. Individualism
- c. Self-compassion
- d. Self-denial

Guidance: level 1

:: Smoking ::

_________ is a practice in which a substance is burned and the resulting smoke breathed in to be tasted and absorbed into the bloodstream. Most commonly the substance is the dried leaves of the tobacco plant which have been rolled into a small square of rice paper to create a small, round cylinder called a "cigarette". _________ is primarily practiced as a route of administration for recreational drug use because the combustion of the dried plant leaves vaporizes and delivers active substances into the lungs where they are rapidly absorbed into the bloodstream and reach bodily tissue. In the case of cigarette _________ these substances are contained in a mixture of aerosol particles and gasses and include the pharmacologically active alkaloid nicotine; the vaporization creates heated aerosol and gas into a form that allows inhalation and deep penetration into the lungs where absorption into the bloodstream of the active substances occurs. In some cultures, _________ is also carried out as a part of various rituals, where participants use it to help induce trance-like states that, they believe, can lead them to spiritual enlightenment.

Exam Probability: **High**

18. *Answer choices:*

(see index for correct answer)

- a. Public Finance Balance of Smoking in the Czech Republic
- b. Cigarette receptacles
- c. Electronic cigarette
- d. Smoking

Guidance: level 1

:: Motivation ::

_________ is an individual`s subjective evaluation of their own worth. _________ encompasses beliefs about oneself as well as emotional states, such as triumph, despair, pride, and shame. Smith and Mackie defined it by saying "The self-concept is what we think about the self; _________ , is the positive or negative evaluations of the self, as in how we feel about it."

Exam Probability: **High**

19. *Answer choices:*

(see index for correct answer)

- a. Cognitive evaluation theory
- b. Goal orientation
- c. Morale
- d. Self-esteem

Guidance: level 1

:: Behaviorism ::

A flood is an overflow of water that submerges land that is usually dry. In the sense of "flowing water", the word may also be applied to the inflow of the tide. Floods are an area of study of the discipline hydrology and are of significant concern in agriculture, civil engineering and public health.

Exam Probability: **Medium**

20. *Answer choices:*

(see index for correct answer)

- a. Community reinforcement and family training
- b. Analog observation
- c. Flooding
- d. Clinical behavior analysis

Guidance: level 1

:: Developmental psychology ::

_________ entails the biological, psychological and emotional changes that occur in human beings between birth and the conclusion of adolescence, as the individual progresses from dependency to increasing autonomy. It is a continuous process with a predictable sequence, yet having a unique course for every child. It does not progress at the same rate and each stage is affected by the preceding developmental experiences. Because these developmental changes may be strongly influenced by genetic factors and events during prenatal life, genetics and prenatal development are usually included as part of the study of _________ . Related terms include developmental psychology, referring to development throughout the lifespan, and pediatrics, the branch of medicine relating to the care of children. Developmental change may occur as a result of genetically-controlled processes known as maturation, or as a result of environmental factors and learning, but most commonly involves an interaction between the two. It may also occur as a result of human nature and our ability to learn from our environment.

Exam Probability: **Medium**

21. *Answer choices:*

(see index for correct answer)

- a. Speech perception
- b. Domain-specific learning
- c. Child development
- d. Personal fable

Guidance: level 1

:: Communication of falsehoods ::

_________ is the fabricating of symptoms of mental or physical disorders for a variety of reasons such as financial compensation ; avoiding school, work or military service; obtaining drugs; or as a mitigating factor for sentencing in criminal cases. It is not a medical diagnosis. _________ is typically conceptualized as being distinct from other forms of excessive illness behavior such as somatization disorder and factitious disorder, e.g., in DSM-5, although not all mental health professionals agree with this formulation.

Exam Probability: **Low**

22. *Answer choices:*

(see index for correct answer)

- a. Making false statements
- b. Malingering
- c. Jactitation

- d. False light

Guidance: level 1

:: Behaviorism ::

_________ refers to behavior-change procedures that were employed during the 1970s and early 1980s. Based on methodological behaviorism, overt behavior was modified with presumed consequences, including artificial positive and negative reinforcement contingencies to increase desirable behavior, or administering positive and negative punishment and/or extinction to reduce problematic behavior. For the treatment of phobias, habituation and punishment were the basic principles used in flooding, a subcategory of desensitization.

Exam Probability: **Low**

23. *Answer choices:*

(see index for correct answer)

- a. Programmed instruction
- b. Teaching-family model
- c. Behaviorally anchored rating scales
- d. Professional practice of behavior analysis

Guidance: level 1

:: Child sexual abuse ::

_________ is human sexual activity between family members or close relatives. This typically includes sexual activity between people in consanguinity , and sometimes those related by affinity , adoption, clan, or lineage.

Exam Probability: **Medium**

24. *Answer choices:*

(see index for correct answer)

- a. KoreKorea
- b. To Catch a Predator
- c. Project Safe Childhood
- d. Franklin child prostitution ring allegations

Guidance: level 1

:: Stress ::

A _________ is a chemical or biological agent, environmental condition, external stimulus or an event that causes stress to an organism. Psychologically speaking, a _________ can be events or environments that an individual would consider demanding, challenging, and or threaten the individual`s safety.

Exam Probability: **Low**

25. *Answer choices:*

(see index for correct answer)

- a. Stress ball
- b. Traumatic stress
- c. Military sexual trauma
- d. Occupational burnout

Guidance: level 1

:: Research methods ::

A _________ is a research design that involves repeated observations of the same variables over short or long periods of time . It is often a type of observational study, although they can also be structured as longitudinal randomized experiments.

Exam Probability: **Low**

26. *Answer choices:*

(see index for correct answer)

- a. Online research methods
- b. Qualtrics
- c. Muringa vila
- d. Longitudinal study

Guidance: level 1

:: Antidepressants ::

_________ , sold under the brand names Wellbutrin and Zyban among others, is a medication primarily used to treat major depressive disorder and to support stopping smoking. It is an effective antidepressant on its own, but is also used as an add-on medication in cases of incomplete response to first-line SSRI antidepressants. _________ is taken in tablet form and is available only by prescription in most countries.

Exam Probability: **High**

27. *Answer choices:*

(see index for correct answer)

- a. Paraxazone
- b. Pirlindole
- c. Bupropion
- d. Mucuna pruriens

Guidance: level 1

:: Psychoanalytic terminology ::

A defence mechanism is an unconscious psychological mechanism that reduces anxiety arising from unacceptable or potentially harmful stimuli.

Exam Probability: **Low**

28. *Answer choices:*

(see index for correct answer)

- a. Reparation
- b. Oceanic feeling
- c. Narcissistic personality
- d. Defense mechanism

Guidance: level 1

:: Psychiatry ::

A _________ is a physician who specializes in psychiatry, the branch of medicine devoted to the diagnosis, prevention, study, and treatment of mental disorders. _________ s are medical doctors, unlike psychologists, and must evaluate patients to determine whether their symptoms are the result of a physical illness, a combination of physical and mental ailments, or strictly psychiatric. A _________ usually works as the clinical leader of the multi-disciplinary team, which may comprise psychologists, social workers, occupational therapists and nursing staff. _________ s have broad training in a bio-psycho-social approach to assessment and management of mental illness.

Exam Probability: **High**

29. *Answer choices:*

(see index for correct answer)

- a. Self-directedness
- b. Stilted speech
- c. Psychiatrist
- d. A Stranger in The Family: Culture, Families, and Therapy

Guidance: level 1

:: Scientific method ::

_________ is the active acquisition of information from a primary source. In living beings, _________ employs the senses. In science, _________ can also involve the recording of data via the use of scientific instruments. The term may also refer to any data collected during the scientific activity. _________s can be qualitative, that is, only the absence or presence of a property is noted, or quantitative if a numerical value is attached to the observed phenomenon by counting or measuring.

Exam Probability: **High**

30. *Answer choices:*

(see index for correct answer)

- a. Open-label trial
- b. Consilience
- c. Self-experimentation

- d. Observation

Guidance: level 1

:: Psychiatric diagnosis ::

Intellectual disability , also known as general learning disability and _________ , is a generalized neurodevelopmental disorder characterized by significantly impaired intellectual and adaptive functioning. It is defined by an IQ under 70 in addition to deficits in two or more adaptive behaviors that affect everyday, general living.

Exam Probability: **Low**

31. *Answer choices:*

(see index for correct answer)

- a. Onychophagia
- b. Mental retardation
- c. Psychiatric Epidemiology
- d. generalized anxiety

Guidance: level 1

:: Psychiatry ::

The _________ , published by the American Psychiatric Association , offers a common language and standard criteria for the classification of mental disorders. It is used, or relied upon, by clinicians, researchers, psychiatric drug regulation agencies, health insurance companies, pharmaceutical companies, the legal system, and policy makers together with alternatives such as the ICD-10 Classification of Mental and Behavioural Disorders, produced by the WHO.

Exam Probability: **High**

32. *Answer choices:*

(see index for correct answer)

- a. Diagnostic and Statistical Manual of Mental Disorders
- b. Shell shock
- c. Autokabalesis
- d. Psychopathology

Guidance: level 1

:: Euphoriants ::

_________ , also known as diamorphine among other names, is an opioid most commonly used as a recreational drug for its euphoric effects. It is used medically in several countries to relieve pain or in opioid replacement therapy. It is typically injected, usually into a vein, but it can also be smoked, snorted, or inhaled. The onset of effects is usually rapid and lasts for a few hours.

Exam Probability: **Low**

33. *Answer choices:*

(see index for correct answer)

- a. Heroin
- b. Fentanyl
- c. Phenmetrazine
- d. Adderall

Guidance: level 1

:: Psychotherapy ::

_________ is a brief, attachment-focused psychotherapy that centers on resolving interpersonal problems and symptomatic recovery. It is an empirically supported treatment that follows a highly structured and time-limited approach and is intended to be completed within 12–16 weeks. IPT is based on the principle that relationships and life events impact mood and that the reverse is also true. It was developed by Gerald Klerman and Myrna Weissman for major depression in the 1970s and has since been adapted for other mental disorders. IPT is an empirically validated intervention for depressive disorders, and is more effective when used in combination with psychiatric medications. Along with cognitive behavioral therapy , IPT is recommended in treatment guidelines as a psychosocial treatment of choice, and IPT and CBT are the only psychosocial interventions in which psychiatry residents in the United States are mandated to be trained for professional practice.

Exam Probability: **High**

34. *Answer choices:*

(see index for correct answer)

- a. Atavistic regression
- b. Dream dictionary
- c. Psychotherapy and social action model
- d. Melodic intonation therapy

Guidance: level 1

:: Autism ::

_________ is defined as the unsolicited repetition of vocalizations made by another person . In its profound form it is automatic and effortless. It is one of the echophenomena, closely related to echopraxia, the automatic repetition of movements made by another person; both are "subsets of imitative behavior" whereby sounds or actions are imitated "without explicit awareness". _________ may be an immediate reaction to a stimulus or may be delayed.

Exam Probability: **High**

35. *Answer choices:*

(see index for correct answer)

- a. International Meeting for Autism Research
- b. Naoki Higashida
- c. Weak central coherence theory
- d. Autism therapies

Guidance: level 1

:: Behavioral neuroscience ::

In medicine, _________ or recidivism is a recurrence of a past condition. For example, multiple sclerosis and malaria often exhibit peaks of activity and sometimes very long periods of dormancy, followed by _________ or recrudescence.

Exam Probability: **Low**

36. *Answer choices:*

(see index for correct answer)

- a. Behavioral and Brain Functions
- b. Water maze
- c. SHIRPA
- d. Paula Tallal

Guidance: level 1

:: Childhood psychiatric disorders ::

An _________ —sometimes called exogenous, reactive, or situational depression—occurs when an individual is unable to adjust to or cope with a particular stress or a major life event. Since people with this disorder normally have symptoms that depressed people do, such as general loss of interest, feelings of hopelessness, and crying, this disorder is sometimes known as situational depression. Unlike major depression, the disorder is caused by an outside stressor and generally resolves once the individual is able to adapt to the situation. One hypothesis about AD is that it may represent a sub-threshold clinical syndrome.

Exam Probability: **Medium**

37. *Answer choices:*

(see index for correct answer)

- a. Regressive autism
- b. Pediatric acute-onset neuropsychiatric syndrome
- c. Adjustment disorder
- d. Autism Diagnostic Observation Schedule

Guidance: level 1

:: Behavior ::

_________ refers to behavior that enables a person to get along in his or her environment with greatest success and least conflict with others. This is a term used in the areas of psychology and special education. _________ relates to every day skills or tasks that the average person is able to complete, similar to the term life skills.

Exam Probability: **High**

38. *Answer choices:*

(see index for correct answer)

- a. National Training Laboratories
- b. Adaptive behavior
- c. Behavioral ethics
- d. The Imp of the Perverse

Guidance: level 1

:: Neurotransmitters ::

_________ is the reabsorption of a neurotransmitter by a neurotransmitter transporter located along the plasma membrane of an axon terminal or glial cell after it has performed its function of transmitting a neural impulse.

Exam Probability: **Low**

39. *Answer choices:*

(see index for correct answer)

- a. Gasotransmitter
- b. Phasic transmitter
- c. Aspartic acid
- d. Glutamate receptor

Guidance: level 1

:: Freudian psychology ::

In Freudian psychoanalysis, the term _________ or hemitaxia denotes the first psychosexual development stage wherein the mouth of the infant is his or her primary erogenous zone. Spanning the life period from birth to the age of 18 months, the _________ is the first of the five Freudian psychosexual development stages: the oral, the anal, the phallic, the latent, and the genital. Moreover, because it is the infant`s first human relationship—biological and psychological —its duration depends upon the child-rearing mores of the mother`s society. Sociologically speaking, the duration of infantile nursing is determined normatively; in some societies it is common for a child to be nursed by its mother for several years but in others this period is much shorter.

Exam Probability: **Low**

40. *Answer choices:*

(see index for correct answer)

- a. Transference neurosis
- b. Anal expulsiveness
- c. Content
- d. International Psychoanalytical Association

Guidance: level 1

:: Euphoriants ::

_________ , also known as angel dust among other names, is a drug used for its mind-altering effects. PCP may cause hallucinations, distorted perceptions of sounds, and violent behavior. As a recreational drug, it is typically smoked, but may be taken by mouth, snorted, or injected. It may also be mixed with cannabis or tobacco.

Exam Probability: **Medium**

41. *Answer choices:*

(see index for correct answer)

- a. Opium
- b. Dextrorphan
- c. Hydromorphone
- d. Oxymorphone

Guidance: level 1

:: Psychoanalysis ::

_________ is a class of functional mental disorders involving chronic distress but neither delusions nor hallucinations. The term is no longer used by the professional psychiatric community in the United States, having been eliminated from the Diagnostic and Statistical Manual of Mental Disorders in 1980 with the publication of DSM III. It is still used in the ICD-10 Chapter V F40–48.

Exam Probability: **Low**

42. *Answer choices:*

(see index for correct answer)

- a. Healthy narcissism
- b. Affect theory
- c. Barbara Johnson
- d. Neurosis

Guidance: level 1

:: Psychometrics ::

A _________ is a set of categories designed to elicit information about a quantitative or a qualitative attribute. In the social sciences, particularly psychology, common examples are the Likert response scale and 1-10 _________ s in which a person selects the number which is considered to reflect the perceived quality of a product.

Exam Probability: **Low**

43. *Answer choices:*

(see index for correct answer)

- a. Rating scale
- b. Riddle scale

- c. Highlands Ability Battery
- d. Fuzzy concept

Guidance: level 1

:: Aphrodisiacs ::

_________ is the primary male sex hormone and an anabolic steroid. In male humans, _________ plays a key role in the development of male reproductive tissues such as testes and prostate, as well as promoting secondary sexual characteristics such as increased muscle and bone mass, and the growth of body hair. In addition, _________ is involved in health and well-being, and the prevention of osteoporosis. Insufficient levels of _________ in men may lead to abnormalities including frailty and bone loss.

Exam Probability: **Medium**

44. *Answer choices:*

(see index for correct answer)

- a. THIQ
- b. Aphrodisiac
- c. PF-00446687
- d. Cow cod soup

Guidance: level 1

:: Opioids ::

The term _________ originally referred medically to any psychoactive compound with sleep-inducing properties. In the United States, it has since become associated with opiates and opioids, commonly morphine and heroin, as well as derivatives of many of the compounds found within raw opium latex. The primary three are morphine, codeine, and thebaine .

Exam Probability: **Low**

45. *Answer choices:*

(see index for correct answer)

- a. Pholcodine
- b. Thiambutenes
- c. Butinazocine
- d. Narcotic

Guidance: level 1

:: Behavior ::

_________ is a concept introduced during the 1970s by Mark Snyder, that shows how much people monitor their self-presentations, expressive behavior, and nonverbal affective displays. Human beings generally differ in substantial ways in their abilities and desires to engage in expressive controls . It is defined as a personality trait that refers to an ability to regulate behavior to accommodate social situations. People concerned with their expressive self-presentation tend to closely monitor their audience in order to ensure appropriate or desired public appearances. Self-monitors try to understand how individuals and groups will perceive their actions. Some personality types commonly act spontaneously and others are more apt to purposely control and consciously adjust their behavior . Recent studies suggest that a distinction should be made between acquisitive and protective _________ due to their different interactions with metatraits. This differentiates the motive behind _________ behaviours: for the purpose of acquiring appraisal from others or protecting oneself from social disapproval .

Exam Probability: **High**

46. *Answer choices:*

(see index for correct answer)

- a. High-velocity human factors
- b. Cat intelligence
- c. Self-monitoring
- d. Model of hierarchical complexity

Guidance: level 1

:: Childhood psychiatric disorders ::

_________ is voluntary or involuntary passage of feces outside of toilet trained contexts in children who are four years or older and after an organic cause has been excluded. Children with _________ often leak stool into their undergarments.

Exam Probability: **Medium**

47. *Answer choices:*

(see index for correct answer)

- a. PANDAS
- b. Encopresis
- c. Regressive autism
- d. Diagnosis of Asperger syndrome

Guidance: level 1

:: Behaviorism ::

A _________ is a routine of behavior that is repeated regularly and tends to occur subconsciously.

Exam Probability: **Low**

48. *Answer choices:*

(see index for correct answer)

- a. Contingency management
- b. Beyond Freedom and Dignity
- c. Equipotentiality
- d. Howard Rachlin

Guidance: level 1

:: Educational psychology ::

One`s _________ is a collection of beliefs about oneself. Generally, _________ embodies the answer to "Who am I".

Exam Probability: **Low**

49. *Answer choices:*

(see index for correct answer)

- a. Poisonous pedagogy
- b. Creativity
- c. Self-concept
- d. Goal theory

Guidance: level 1

:: Psychological schools ::

_________ pertains to the theory and practice of Alfred Adler , whose school of psychotherapy is called individual psychology .

Exam Probability: **High**

50. *Answer choices:*

(see index for correct answer)

- a. Ecological psychology
- b. Filipino psychology
- c. Isomorphism
- d. Adlerian

Guidance: level 1

:: Cognitive disorders ::

_________ , also known as acute confusional state, is an organically caused decline from a previous baseline level of mental function that develops over a short period of time, typically hours to days. _________ is a syndrome encompassing disturbances in attention, consciousness, and cognition. It may also involve other neurological deficits, such as psychomotor disturbances , impaired sleep-wake cycle, emotional disturbances, and perceptual disturbances , although these features are not required for diagnosis.

Exam Probability: **High**

51. *Answer choices:*

(see index for correct answer)

- a. Frontotemporal dementia and parkinsonism linked to chromosome 17
- b. Vascular dementia
- c. Delirium
- d. Progressive nonfluent aphasia

Guidance: level 1

:: Psychotherapy ::

__________ , a concept developed by the humanistic psychologist Carl Rogers, is the basic acceptance and support of a person regardless of what the person says or does, especially in the context of client-centered therapy. Its founder, Carl Rogers, writes.

Exam Probability: **High**

52. *Answer choices:*

(see index for correct answer)

- a. Hakomi
- b. Logotherapy
- c. Unconditional positive regard
- d. Autogenic training

Guidance: level 1

:: Behaviorism ::

_________ is a third generation behavior therapy for treating depression. It is one of many functional analytic psychotherapies which are based on a Skinnerian psychological model of behavior change, generally referred to as applied behavior analysis. This area is also a part of what is called clinical behavior analysis and makes up one of the most effective practices in the professional practice of behavior analysis.

Exam Probability: **Low**

53. *Answer choices:*

(see index for correct answer)

- a. Covert conditioning
- b. Prolonged exposure therapy
- c. Behavioral activation
- d. Token economy

Guidance: level 1

:: Behaviorism ::

_________ is most-widely used in the field of substance abuse, often implemented as part of clinical behavior analysis. CM refers to the application of the three-term contingency , which uses stimulus control and positive reinforcement to change behavior. Patients` behaviors are rewarded ; generally, adherence to or failure to adhere to program rules and regulations or their treatment plan. CM derives from the science of applied behavior analysis , and by most evaluations, its procedures produces one of the largest effect sizes out of all mental health and educational interventions.

Exam Probability: **High**

54. *Answer choices:*

(see index for correct answer)

- a. Howard Rachlin
- b. Covert conditioning
- c. Curriculum-based measurement
- d. Contingency management

Guidance: level 1

:: Memory ::

The _________ , also known as the paleomammalian cortex, is a set of brain structures located on both sides of the thalamus, immediately beneath the medial temporal lobe of the cerebrum primarily in the midbrain.

Exam Probability: **Medium**

55. *Answer choices:*

(see index for correct answer)

- a. Limbic system
- b. Long-term memory
- c. Long-term potentiation
- d. Spaced repetition

Guidance: level 1

:: Dopamine agonists ::

_________ , also known as acid, is a hallucinogenic drug. Effects typically include altered thoughts, feelings, and awareness of one`s surroundings. Many users see or hear things that do not exist. Dilated pupils, increased blood pressure, and increased body temperature are typical. Effects typically begin within half an hour and can last for up to 12 hours. It is used mainly as a recreational drug and for spiritual reasons.

Exam Probability: **Medium**

56. *Answer choices:*

(see index for correct answer)

- a. Lysergic acid diethylamide
- b. Methamphetamine
- c. Diphenyl-2-pyridylmethane
- d. Azapride

Guidance: level 1

:: Behavioural sciences ::

_________ is an integration of science, theory, and clinical knowledge for the purpose of understanding, preventing, and relieving psychologically-based distress or dysfunction and to promote subjective well-being and personal development. Central to its practice are psychological assessment, clinical formulation, and psychotherapy, although clinical psychologists also engage in research, teaching, consultation, forensic testimony, and program development and administration. In many countries, _________ is a regulated mental health profession.

Exam Probability: **Medium**

57. *Answer choices:*

(see index for correct answer)

- a. Clinical psychology
- b. Direct Behavior Rating
- c. Criminology
- d. Occupational health psychology

Guidance: level 1

:: Psychology ::

A _________ is the formulation of general concepts from specific instances by abstracting common properties. _________ s posit the existence of a domain or set of elements, as well as one or more common characteristics shared by those elements . As such, they are the essential basis of all valid deductive inferences. The process of verification is necessary to determine whether a _________ holds true for any given situation.

Exam Probability: **Low**

58. *Answer choices:*

(see index for correct answer)

- a. Gestaltzerfall
- b. Stimulus control
- c. Hybristophilia
- d. Norman Adler

Guidance: level 1

:: Abnormal psychology ::

_________ s are conditions that involve disruptions or breakdowns of memory, awareness, identity, or perception. People with _________ s use dissociation as a defense mechanism, pathologically and involuntarily. Some _________ s are triggered by psychological trauma, but _________ s such as depersonalization/derealization disorder may be preceded only by stress, psychoactive substances, or no identifiable trigger at all.

Exam Probability: **Medium**

59. *Answer choices:*

(see index for correct answer)

- a. Rumination
- b. Dissociative disorder
- c. Self-neglect
- d. Hamilton Anxiety Rating Scale

Guidance: level 1

Social Psychology

Social psychology is the scientific study of how people's thoughts, feelings, and behaviors are influenced by the actual, imagined, or implied presence of others. In this definition, scientific refers to the empirical investigation using the scientific method. The terms thoughts, feelings, and behavior refer to psychological variables that can be measured in humans. The statement that others' presence may be imagined or implied suggests that humans are malleable to social influences even when alone, such as when watching television or following internalized cultural norms. Social psychologists typically explain human behavior as a result of the interaction of mental states and social situations.

:: Human behavior ::

_________ is the quality of being self-assured and confident without being aggressive. In the field of psychology and psychotherapy, it is a learnable skill and mode of communication. Dorland`s Medical Dictionary defines _________ as.

Exam Probability: **High**

1. *Answer choices:*

(see index for correct answer)

- a. Taunting
- b. Impulse
- c. Reasoned action approach
- d. Accismus

Guidance: level 1

:: Freudian psychology ::

The _________ in psychoanalysis is the term used by Sigmund Freud to describe the final stage of human psychosexual development. The individual develops a strong sexual interest in people outside of the family.

Exam Probability: **Medium**

2. *Answer choices:*

(see index for correct answer)

- a. British Psychoanalytical Society
- b. Signorelli parapraxis
- c. Mortido
- d. Genital stage

Guidance: level 1

:: Family ::

In the context of human society, a _________ is a group of people related either by consanguinity , affinity , or co-residence or some combination of these. Members of the immediate _________ may include spouses, parents, brothers, sisters, sons, and daughters. Members of the extended _________ may include grandparents, aunts, uncles, cousins, nephews, nieces, and siblings-in-law. Sometimes these are also considered members of the immediate _________ , depending on an individual's specific relationship with them.

Exam Probability: **Low**

3. *Answer choices:*

(see index for correct answer)

- a. Family Home Evening
- b. Family Equality Council
- c. Parent-in-law
- d. International Year of the Family

Guidance: level 1

:: Psychological theories ::

The ________ is a theory of love developed by Robert Sternberg, a member of the Psychology Department at Yale University. During his time as a professor, Sternberg emphasized his research in the fields of intelligence, creativity, wisdom, leadership, thinking styles, ethical reasoning, love, and hate. In the context of interpersonal relationships, "the three components of love, according to the triangular theory, are an intimacy component, a passion component, and a decision/commitment component."

Exam Probability: **Low**

4. *Answer choices:*

(see index for correct answer)

- a. Triangular theory of love
- b. Privacy regulation theory
- c. Contextual cueing
- d. Script theory

Guidance: level 1

:: Behavioural syndromes associated with physiological disturbances and physical factors ::

__________ , also known as impotence, is a type of sexual dysfunction characterized by the inability to develop or maintain an erection of the penis during sexual activity. __________ can have psychological consequences as it can be tied to relationship difficulties and self-image.

Exam Probability: **High**

5. *Answer choices:*

(see index for correct answer)

- a. Hyperorgasmia
- b. Premature ejaculation
- c. Sexual anhedonia
- d. Hypoactive sexual desire disorder

Guidance: level 1

:: Abnormal psychology ::

A __________ is a type of anxiety disorder, defined by a persistent and excessive fear of an object or situation. The __________ typically results in a rapid onset of fear and is present for more than six months. The affected person goes to great lengths to avoid the situation or object, to a degree greater than the actual danger posed. If the feared object or situation cannot be avoided, the affected person experiences significant distress. With blood or injury __________ , fainting may occur. Agora __________ is often associated with panic attacks. Usually a person has __________ s to a number of objects or situations.

Exam Probability: **High**

6. *Answer choices:*

(see index for correct answer)

- a. Phobia
- b. Dissociative disorder
- c. Somatoform disorder
- d. Amotivational syndrome

Guidance: level 1

:: Aesthetic beauty ::

_________ is the ascription of a property or characteristic to an animal, idea, object, person or place that provides a perceptual experience of pleasure or satisfaction. _________ is studied as part of aesthetics, culture, social psychology, philosophy and sociology. An "ideal _________ " is an entity which is admired, or possesses features widely attributed to _________ in a particular culture, for perfection. Ugliness is the opposite of _________ .

Exam Probability: **High**

7. *Answer choices:*

(see index for correct answer)

- a. Aesthetic canon
- b. Beautification

- c. Mathematical beauty
- d. Beauty

Guidance: level 1

:: LGBT-related legislation ::

_________ is the marriage of two persons of the same sex or gender, entered into in a civil or religious ceremony.

Exam Probability: **Medium**

8. *Answer choices:*

(see index for correct answer)

- a. Same-sex marriage
- b. Section 213 of the Norwegian Penal Code
- c. Section 377A of the Penal Code
- d. Section 171 of the Criminal Code of Cyprus

Guidance: level 1

:: Thought ::

_________ is the analysis of facts to form a judgment. The subject is complex, and several different definitions exist, which generally include the rational, skeptical, unbiased analysis, or evaluation of factual evidence. _________ is self-directed, self-disciplined, self-monitored, and self-corrective thinking. It presupposes assent to rigorous standards of excellence and mindful command of their use. It entails effective communication and problem-solving abilities as well as a commitment to overcome native egocentrism and sociocentrism.

Exam Probability: **Low**

9. *Answer choices:*

(see index for correct answer)

- a. Truth condition
- b. DSRP
- c. Polymath
- d. Dianoia

Guidance: level 1

:: Sexual fetishism ::

_________ is the act of exposing in a public or semi-public context those parts of one`s body that are not normally exposed for example, the breasts, genitals or buttocks. The practice may arise from a desire or compulsion to expose themselves in such a manner to groups of friends or acquaintances, or to strangers for their amusement or sexual satisfaction or to shock the bystander. Exposing oneself only to an intimate partner is normally not regarded as _________ . In law, the act of _________ may be called indecent exposure, "exposing one`s person", or other expressions.

Exam Probability: **High**

10. *Answer choices:*

(see index for correct answer)

- a. Wetlook
- b. Asian fetish
- c. Glasses fetishism
- d. Exhibitionism

Guidance: level 1

:: Sexuality ::

_________ is difficulty experienced by an individual or a couple during any stage of a normal sexual activity, including physical pleasure, desire, preference, arousal or orgasm. According to the DSM-5, _________ requires a person to feel extreme distress and interpersonal strain for a minimum of six months . _________ s can have a profound impact on an individual`s perceived quality of sexual life. The term sexual disorder may not only refer to physical _________ , but to paraphilias as well; this is sometimes termed disorder of sexual preference.

Exam Probability: **High**

11. *Answer choices:*

(see index for correct answer)

- a. Paraphilia
- b. Media and American adolescent sexuality
- c. Sexual orientation hypothesis
- d. Sexual dysfunction

Guidance: level 1

:: Behavior ::

__________ is a theory of learning process and social behavior which proposes that new behaviors can be acquired by observing and imitating others. It states that learning is a cognitive process that takes place in a social context and can occur purely through observation or direct instruction, even in the absence of motor reproduction or direct reinforcement. In addition to the observation of behavior, learning also occurs through the observation of rewards and punishments, a process known as vicarious reinforcement. When a particular behavior is rewarded regularly, it will most likely persist; conversely, if a particular behavior is constantly punished, it will most likely desist. The theory expands on traditional behavioral theories, in which behavior is governed solely by reinforcements, by placing emphasis on the important roles of various internal processes in the learning individual.

Exam Probability: **Medium**

12. *Answer choices:*

(see index for correct answer)

- a. Melioration theory
- b. Theory of reasoned action
- c. Adaptive behavior
- d. Quorum sensing

Guidance: level 1

:: Collaboration ::

_________ is the process of groups of organisms working or acting together for common, mutual, or some underlying benefit, as opposed to working in competition for selfish benefit. Many animal and plant species cooperate both with other members of their own species and with members of other species .

Exam Probability: **High**

13. *Answer choices:*

(see index for correct answer)

- a. Operational transformation
- b. IvanAnywhere
- c. Collaboration graph
- d. Buddy system

Guidance: level 1

:: Social psychology ::

__________ is a sociopsychological phenomenon whereby a person is less likely to take responsibility for action or inaction when others are present. Considered a form of attribution, the individual assumes that others either are responsible for taking action or have already done so. Assumption of responsibility tends to decrease when the potential helping group is larger, resulting in little aiding behavior demonstrated by the bystander. Causes range from psychological effects of anonymity to differences in sex. Implication of behaviours related to __________ can be threatening as there have been increases in moral disengagement and helping behaviour. The infamous murder case of Kitty Genovese and increased murders in WWII can be attributed to __________.

Exam Probability: **Low**

14. *Answer choices:*

(see index for correct answer)

- a. Mnemic neglect
- b. Motivated tactician
- c. Reflected appraisal
- d. Diffusion of responsibility

Guidance: level 1

:: Motivation ::

In personality psychology, _________ is the degree to which people believe that they have control over the outcome of events in their lives, as opposed to external forces beyond their control. Understanding of the concept was developed by Julian B. Rotter in 1954, and has since become an aspect of personality studies. A person`s "locus" is conceptualized as internal or external .

Exam Probability: **Low**

15. *Answer choices:*

(see index for correct answer)

- a. Self-efficacy
- b. Exertion
- c. Locus of control
- d. Psychological resilience

Guidance: level 1

:: Domestic violence ::

__________ is violence or other abuse by one person against another in a domestic setting, such as in marriage or cohabitation. It may be termed intimate partner violence when committed by a spouse or partner in an intimate relationship against the other spouse or partner, and can take place in heterosexual or same-sex relationships, or between former spouses or partners. __________ can also involve violence against children, parents, or the elderly. It takes a number of forms, including physical, verbal, emotional, economic, religious, reproductive, and sexual abuse, which can range from subtle, coercive forms to marital rape and to violent physical abuse such as choking, beating, female genital mutilation, and acid throwing that results in disfigurement or death. Domestic murders include stoning, bride burning, honor killings, and dowry deaths.

Exam Probability: **Medium**

16. *Answer choices:*

(see index for correct answer)

- a. Marital rape
- b. Francine Hughes
- c. Domestic violence
- d. One Minute to Nine

Guidance: level 1

:: Child abuse ::

_________ or child maltreatment is physical, sexual, and/or psychological maltreatment or neglect of a child or children, especially by a parent or a caregiver. _________ may include any act or failure to act by a parent or a caregiver that results in actual or potential harm to a child, and can occur in a child`s home, or in the organizations, schools or communities the child interacts with.

Exam Probability: **High**

17. *Answer choices:*

(see index for correct answer)

- a. Child Exploitation Tracking System
- b. Auguste Ambroise Tardieu
- c. Lloyd deMause
- d. Child abuse

Guidance: level 1

:: Second-language acquisition ::

An _________ is an action which is inaccurate or incorrect. In some usages, an _________ is synonymous with a mistake. In statistics, " _________ " refers to the difference between the value which has been computed and the correct value. An _________ could result in failure or in a deviation from the intended performance or behaviour.

Exam Probability: **Medium**

18. *Answer choices:*

(see index for correct answer)

- a. Second-language phonology
- b. Comprehensible output
- c. Input enhancement
- d. Theories of second-language acquisition

Guidance: level 1

:: Sexual and gender prejudices ::

__________ encompasses a range of negative attitudes and feelings toward homosexuality or people who are identified or perceived as being lesbian, gay, bisexual or transgender . It has been defined as contempt, prejudice, aversion, hatred or antipathy, may be based on irrational fear, and is often related to religious beliefs.

Exam Probability: **High**

19. *Answer choices:*

(see index for correct answer)

- a. Homophobia
- b. Straight pride
- c. Effemimania
- d. Nakusha

Guidance: level 1

:: Communication ::

In the history of radio communications, the term "detector" was first used for a device that detected the simple presence or absence of a radio signal, since all communications were in Morse code. The term is still in use today to describe a component that extracts a particular signal from all of the electromagnetic waves present. _________ is usually based on the frequency of the carrier signal, as in the familiar frequencies of radio broadcasting, but it may also involve filtering a faint signal from noise, as in radio astronomy, or reconstructing a hidden signal, as in steganography.

Exam Probability: **Medium**

20. *Answer choices:*

(see index for correct answer)

- a. Organizational dissent
- b. Interface
- c. Sliding window protocol
- d. Superluminal communication

Guidance: level 1

:: Artificial insemination ::

__________ is the deliberate introduction of sperm into a female`s cervix or uterine cavity for the purpose of achieving a pregnancy through in vivo fertilization by means other than sexual intercourse. It is a fertility treatment for humans, and is common practice in animal breeding, including dairy cattle and pigs.

Exam Probability: **Medium**

21. *Answer choices:*

(see index for correct answer)

- a. Breeding mount
- b. Semen collection
- c. Electroejaculation

Guidance: level 1

:: Behavioural sciences ::

__________ is an integration of science, theory, and clinical knowledge for the purpose of understanding, preventing, and relieving psychologically-based distress or dysfunction and to promote subjective well-being and personal development. Central to its practice are psychological assessment, clinical formulation, and psychotherapy, although clinical psychologists also engage in research, teaching, consultation, forensic testimony, and program development and administration. In many countries, __________ is a regulated mental health profession.

Exam Probability: **High**

22. *Answer choices:*

(see index for correct answer)

- a. Personnel selection
- b. Clinical psychology
- c. Correlates of crime
- d. Behavioural genetics

Guidance: level 1

:: Cognitive science ::

_________ is "the mental action or process of acquiring knowledge and understanding through thought, experience, and the senses". It encompasses many aspects of intellectual functions and processes such as attention, the formation of knowledge, memory and working memory, judgment and evaluation, reasoning and "computation", problem solving and decision making, comprehension and production of language. Cognitive processes use existing knowledge and generate new knowledge.

Exam Probability: **Medium**

23. *Answer choices:*

(see index for correct answer)

- a. Choice theory

- b. Cognition
- c. Cognitive approaches to grammar
- d. Embodied cognition

Guidance: level 1

:: Philosophy of love ::

_________ is a stage of romantic relationships in humans whereby two people meet socially with the aim of each assessing the other's suitability as a prospective partner in an intimate relationship or marriage. It is a form of courtship, consisting of social activities done by the couple, either alone or with others. The protocols and practices of _________, and the terms used to describe it, vary considerably from country to country and over time. While the term has several meanings, the most frequent usage refers to two people exploring whether they are romantically or sexually compatible by participating in dates with the other. With the use of modern technology, people can date via telephone or computer or meet in person.

Exam Probability: **Medium**

24. *Answer choices:*

(see index for correct answer)

- a. Dating
- b. The Four Loves
- c. Works of Love
- d. Agape

Guidance: level 1

:: Human development ::

A _________ is a caregiver of the offspring in their own species. In humans, a _________ is the caretaker of a child . A biological _________ is a person whose gamete resulted in a child, a male through the sperm, and a female through the ovum. Biological _________ s are first-degree relatives and have 50% genetic meet. A female can also become a _________ through surrogacy. Some _________ s may be adoptive _________ s, who nurture and raise an offspring, but are not biologically related to the child. Orphans without adoptive _________ s can be raised by their grand _________ s or other family members.

Exam Probability: **Medium**

25. *Answer choices:*

(see index for correct answer)

- a. Parent
- b. Developmental dysfluency
- c. Zone of proximal development
- d. Barry Bogin

Guidance: level 1

:: Sexual acts ::

__________ is the sexual stimulation of one`s own genitals for sexual arousal or other sexual pleasure, usually to the point of orgasm. The stimulation may involve hands, fingers, everyday objects, sex toys such as vibrators, or combinations of these. Manual stimulation of a partner, such as fingering, a handjob or mutual __________, is a common sexual act and can be a substitute for penetration. Studies have found that __________ is frequent in humans of both sexes and all ages, although there is variation. Various medical and psychological benefits have been attributed to a healthy attitude toward sexual activity in general and to __________ in particular. No causal relationship is known between __________ and any form of mental or physical disorder.

Exam Probability: **Low**

26. *Answer choices:*

(see index for correct answer)

- a. Penis fencing
- b. Serosorting
- c. Urophagia
- d. Scrotal inflation

Guidance: level 1

:: Twelve-step programs ::

__________ is a self-enforced restraint from indulging in bodily activities that are widely experienced as giving pleasure. Most frequently, the term refers to sexual __________, or __________ from alcohol, drugs, or food.

Exam Probability: **Low**

27. *Answer choices:*

(see index for correct answer)

- a. Horizon Services
- b. Survivors of Incest Anonymous
- c. Celebrate Recovery
- d. Pagans in Recovery

Guidance: level 1

:: Racism ::

_________ is the belief in the superiority of one race over another, which often results in discrimination and prejudice towards people based on their race or ethnicity. The use of the term " _________ " does not easily fall under a single definition.

Exam Probability: **High**

28. *Answer choices:*

(see index for correct answer)

- a. Operation AntiSec
- b. Ha Ling Peak
- c. Racism

- d. Racial politics

Guidance: level 1

:: Consciousness ::

__________ is the capacity for introspection and the ability to recognize oneself as an individual separate from the environment and other individuals. It is not to be confused with consciousness in the sense of qualia. While consciousness is being aware of one`s environment and body and lifestyle, __________ is the recognition of that awareness. __________ is how an individual consciously knows and understands their own character, feelings, motives, and desires. There are two broad categories of __________ : internal __________ and external __________ .

Exam Probability: **Low**

29. *Answer choices:*

(see index for correct answer)

- a. Choiceless awareness
- b. Class consciousness
- c. Self-conscious
- d. Self-awareness

Guidance: level 1

:: Human behavior ::

__________ is behavior among two or more organisms within the same species, and encompasses any behavior in which one member affects the other. This is due to an interaction among those members. __________ can be seen as similar to an exchange of goods, with the expectation that when you give, you will receive the same. This behavior can be effected by both the qualities of the individual and the environmental factors. Therefore, __________ arises as a result of an interaction between the two—the organism and its environment. This means that, in regards to humans, __________ can be determined by both the individual characteristics of the person, and the situation they are in.

Exam Probability: **High**

30. *Answer choices:*

(see index for correct answer)

- a. Phi complex
- b. Angry mob
- c. Social behavior
- d. Reasoned action approach

Guidance: level 1

:: Freudian psychology ::

In Freudian psychoanalysis, the _________ is the third stage of psychosexual development, spanning the ages of three to six years, wherein the infant`s libido centers upon his or her genitalia as the erogenous zone. When children become aware of their bodies, the bodies of other children, and the bodies of their parents, they gratify physical curiosity by undressing and exploring each other and their genitals, the center of the _________, in course of which they learn the physical differences between "male" and "female", and the gender differences between "boy" and "girl", experiences which alter the psychologic dynamics of the parent and child relationship. The _________ is the third of five Freudian psychosexual development stages: the oral, the anal, the phallic, the latent, and the genital.

Exam Probability: **Medium**

31. *Answer choices:*

(see index for correct answer)

- a. Decathexis
- b. Uncanny
- c. British Psychoanalytical Society
- d. Phallic stage

Guidance: level 1

:: Youth ::

_________ is the direct influence on people by peers, or the effect on an individual who gets encouraged to follow their peers by changing their attitudes, values or behaviors to conform to those of the influencing group or individual. This can result in either a positive or negative effect, or both. Social groups affected include both membership groups, in which individuals are "formally" members , and cliques, in which membership is not clearly defined. However, a person does not need to be a member or be seeking membership of a group to be affected by _________ . _________ can decrease one`s confidence. It can affect the lives of the students drastically.

Exam Probability: **Low**

32. *Answer choices:*

(see index for correct answer)

- a. Positive youth development
- b. Peer pressure
- c. Popular culture
- d. Youth philanthropy

Guidance: level 1

:: Emotion ::

_________ is a mental state associated with the nervous system brought on by chemical changes variously associated with thoughts, feelings, behavioural responses, and a degree of pleasure or displeasure. There is currently no scientific consensus on a definition. _________ is often intertwined with mood, temperament, personality, disposition, and motivation.

Exam Probability: **High**

33. *Answer choices:*

(see index for correct answer)

- a. Conditioned emotional response
- b. Affective neuroscience
- c. Emotional selection
- d. Emotion

Guidance: level 1

:: Social psychology ::

_________, or intent to benefit others, is a social behavior that "benefit[s] other people or society as a whole", "such as helping, sharing, donating, co-operating, and volunteering". Obeying the rules and conforming to socially accepted behaviors are also regarded as _________ s. These actions may be motivated by empathy and by concern about the welfare and rights of others, as well as for egoistic or practical concerns, such as one`s social status or reputation, hope for direct or indirect reciprocity, or adherence to one`s perceived system of fairness. It may also be motivated by altruism, though the existence of pure altruism is somewhat disputed, and some have argued that this falls into philosophical rather than psychological realm of debate. Evidence suggests that pro sociality is central to the well-being of social groups across a range of scales, including schools. _________ in the classroom can have a significant impact on a student`s motivation for learning and contributions to the classroom and larger community. Empathy is a strong motive in eliciting _________, and has deep evolutionary roots.

Exam Probability: **Low**

34. *Answer choices:*

(see index for correct answer)

- a. Prosocial behavior
- b. Availability, salience and vividness
- c. Proteans
- d. Closing time effect

Guidance: level 1

:: Behaviorism ::

_________ is defined as improvement in individual performance when working with other people rather than alone. Compared to their performance when alone, when in the presence of others, they tend to perform better on simple or well-rehearsed tasks and worse on complex or new ones. In addition to working together with other people, _________ also occurs in mere presence of other people. Previous research have found that individual performance are improved by coaction, performing a task in presence of others who are performing a similar task, and as well as having a mere audience while performing a certain task. An example of coaction triggering _________ can be seen in instances where cyclists` performances are improved when cycling along with other cyclists as compared to cycling alone. An instance where having an audience triggers _________ can be observed in situation where weightlifter lifts heavier weight in presence of audience.

Exam Probability: **Medium**

35. *Answer choices:*

(see index for correct answer)

- a. Habit
- b. Tact
- c. Social facilitation
- d. Reward system

Guidance: level 1

:: Racism ::

A _________ is a metaphor used to represent an invisible barrier that keeps a given demographic from rising beyond a certain level in a hierarchy.

Exam Probability: **Low**

36. *Answer choices:*

(see index for correct answer)

- a. Programme to Combat Racism
- b. Glass ceiling
- c. Bongo Bongo Land
- d. Racial politics

Guidance: level 1

:: Phenomenology ::

_________ is any of several aspects of perception and consciousness in such fields as psychology, philosophy and epistemology.

Exam Probability: **High**

37. *Answer choices:*

(see index for correct answer)

- a. Bracketing
- b. Urdoxa
- c. Counter-experience
- d. Visual space

Guidance: level 1

:: Conformity ::

In sociology, _________ is the process of internalizing the norms and ideologies of society. _________ encompasses both learning and teaching and is thus "the means by which social and cultural continuity are attained".

Exam Probability: **Medium**

38. *Answer choices:*

(see index for correct answer)

- a. Socialization
- b. The Lonely Crowd
- c. Deindividuation
- d. Information cascade

Guidance: level 1

:: Affirmative action ::

_________ , also known as reservation in India and Nepal, positive discrimination / action in the United Kingdom, and employment equity in Canada and South Africa, is the policy of promoting the education and employment of members of groups that are known to have previously suffered from discrimination. Historically and internationally, support for _________ has sought to achieve goals such as bridging inequalities in employment and pay, increasing access to education, promoting diversity, and redressing apparent past wrongs, harms, or hindrances.

Exam Probability: **Low**

39. *Answer choices:*

(see index for correct answer)

- a. Minority rights
- b. Affirmative action

- c. Special rights
- d. Affirmative Action Around the World

Guidance: level 1

:: Neurotransmitters ::

_________ or 5-hydroxytryptamine is a monoamine neurotransmitter. It has a popular image as a contributor to feelings of well-being and happiness, though its actual biological function is complex and multifaceted, modulating cognition, reward, learning, memory, and numerous physiological processes.

Exam Probability: **High**

40. *Answer choices:*

(see index for correct answer)

- a. Serotonin
- b. Phasic transmitter
- c. Aspartic acid
- d. Stearoylethanolamide

Guidance: level 1

:: Self ::

_________ is a process of communication by which one person reveals information about themself to another. The information can be descriptive or evaluative, and can include thoughts, feelings, aspirations, goals, failures, successes, fears, and dreams, as well as one`s likes, dislikes, and favorites.

Exam Probability: **High**

41. *Answer choices:*

(see index for correct answer)

- a. Self-disclosure
- b. Self-righteousness
- c. Selfishness
- d. Self-actualization

Guidance: level 1

:: Love ::

_________ is the attraction between people which leads to the development of platonic or romantic relationships. It is distinct from perceptions such as physical attractiveness, and involves views of what is and what is not considered beautiful or attractive.

Exam Probability: **Medium**

42. *Answer choices:*

(see index for correct answer)

- a. Love dart
- b. Crystallization
- c. -phil-
- d. Platonic love

Guidance: level 1

:: Psychology experiments ::

The implicit-association test is a measure within social psychology designed to detect the strength of a person's automatic association between mental representations of objects in memory. The IAT was introduced in the scientific literature in 1998 by Anthony Greenwald, Debbie McGhee, and Jordan Schwartz. The IAT is now widely used in social psychology research and, to some extent, in clinical, cognitive, and developmental psychology research. The IAT is the subject of much controversy regarding precisely what it measures, and the lack of reproducibility of many of its results.

Exam Probability: **High**

43. *Answer choices:*

(see index for correct answer)

- a. Concord Prison Experiment
- b. International Affective Picture System
- c. Air-defense experiments

- d. Project Pigeon

Guidance: level 1

:: Psychology terminology ::

__________ is a situational predicament in which people are or feel themselves to be at risk of conforming to stereotypes about their social group. __________ is purportedly a contributing factor to long-standing racial and gender gaps in academic performance. It may occur whenever an individual`s performance might confirm a negative stereotype because __________ is thought to arise from a particular situation, rather than from an individual`s personality traits or characteristics. Since most people have at least one social identity which is negatively stereotyped, most people are vulnerable to __________ if they encounter a situation in which the stereotype is relevant. Situational factors that increase __________ can include the difficulty of the task, the belief that the task measures their abilities, and the relevance of the stereotype to the task. Individuals show higher degrees of __________ on tasks they wish to perform well on and when they identify strongly with the stereotyped group. These effects are also increased when they expect discrimination due to their identification with a negatively stereotyped group. Repeated experiences of __________ can lead to a vicious circle of diminished confidence, poor performance, and loss of interest in the relevant area of achievement.

Exam Probability: **High**

44. *Answer choices:*

(see index for correct answer)

- a. Stereotype threat

- b. Mental toughness
- c. sociocultural perspective
- d. Relapse prevention

Guidance: level 1

:: Self ::

_________ is how one thinks of oneself in terms of to whom one is romantically or sexually attracted. _________ may also refer to sexual orientation identity, which is when people identify or dis-identify with a sexual orientation or choose not to identify with a sexual orientation. _________ and sexual behavior are closely related to sexual orientation, but they are distinguished, with identity referring to an individual`s conception of themselves, behavior referring to actual sexual acts performed by the individual, and sexual orientation referring to romantic or sexual attractions toward persons of the opposite sex or gender, the same sex or gender, to both sexes or more than one gender, or to no one.

Exam Probability: **Medium**

45. *Answer choices:*

(see index for correct answer)

- a. Amour-propre
- b. Self-knowledge
- c. Sexual identity
- d. The Self-Discrepancy Theory

Guidance: level 1

:: Cognitive science ::

_________ is the process of acquiring new, or modifying existing, knowledge, behaviors, skills, values, or preferences. The ability to learn is possessed by humans, animals, and some machines; there is also evidence for some kind of _________ in some plants. Some _________ is immediate, induced by a single event , but much skill and knowledge accumulates from repeated experiences. The changes induced by _________ often last a lifetime, and it is hard to distinguish learned material that seems to be "lost" from that which cannot be retrieved.

Exam Probability: **Medium**

46. *Answer choices:*

(see index for correct answer)

- a. Cognitive specialization
- b. Informatics
- c. Numerical cognition
- d. Learning

Guidance: level 1

:: Human female reproductive system ::

The _________ s, also known as oviducts, uterine tubes, or salpinges are uterine appendages, lined from inside with ciliated simple columnar epithelium, leading from the ovaries of female mammals into the uterus, via the uterotubal junction. They enable the passage of egg cells from the ovaries to the uterus. In non-mammalian vertebrates, the equivalent structures are just called oviducts.

Exam Probability: **Low**

47. *Answer choices:*

(see index for correct answer)

- a. Vulva
- b. Fallopian tube
- c. Human female reproductive system
- d. Ovary

Guidance: level 1

:: Cognitive biases ::

In psychology, _________ is the phenomenon of perceiving a relationship between variables even when no such relationship exists. A false association may be formed because rare or novel occurrences are more salient and therefore tend to capture one`s attention. This phenomenon is one way stereotypes form and endure. found that stereotypes can lead people to expect certain groups and traits to fit together, and then to overestimate the frequency with which these correlations actually occur.

Exam Probability: **High**

48. *Answer choices:*

(see index for correct answer)

- a. Curse of knowledge
- b. Illusory correlation
- c. Negativity effect
- d. Fading affect bias

Guidance: level 1

:: Sexual abuse ::

_________ , also referred to as molestation, is usually undesired sexual behavior by one person upon another. It is often perpetrated using force or by taking advantage of another. When force is immediate, of short duration, or infrequent, it is called sexual assault. The offender is referred to as a _________r or molester. The term also covers any behavior by an adult or older adolescent towards a child to stimulate any of the involved sexually. The use of a child, or other individuals younger than the age of consent, for sexual stimulation is referred to as child _________ or statutory rape.

Exam Probability: **Medium**

49. *Answer choices:*

(see index for correct answer)

- a. Agraphobia
- b. Rochdale sex trafficking gang
- c. Sexual abuse
- d. Telford sex gang

Guidance: level 1

:: Social psychology ::

The _________ , or bystander apathy, is a social psychological phenomenon in which individuals are less likely to offer help to a victim when other people are present. The greater the number of bystanders, the less likely it is that one of them will help. Several factors contribute to the _________ , including ambiguity, group cohesiveness, and diffusion of responsibility that reinforces mutual denial of a situation's severity.

Exam Probability: **Medium**

50. *Answer choices:*

(see index for correct answer)

- a. Death row phenomenon
- b. Bystander effect
- c. Identity Formation, Agency, and Culture
- d. Externalization

Guidance: level 1

:: Sexual fidelity ::

_________ is a violation of a couple`s assumed or stated contract regarding emotional and/or sexual exclusivity. Other scholars define _________ as a violation according to the subjective feeling that one`s partner has violated a set of rules or relationship norms; this violation results in feelings of jealousy, sexual jealousy, and rivalry.

Exam Probability: **Low**

51. *Answer choices:*

(see index for correct answer)

- a. Infidelity
- b. serial monogamy
- c. Ashley Madison
- d. Cuckquean

Guidance: level 1

:: Nonverbal communication ::

It includes the use of visual cues such as body language , distance and physical environments/appearance, of voice and of touch . It can also include the use of time and eye contact and the actions of looking while talking and listening, frequency of glances, patterns of fixation, pupil dilation, and blink rate .

Exam Probability: **High**

52. *Answer choices:*

(see index for correct answer)

- a. Paralanguage
- b. Nonverbal communication
- c. Occupy movement hand signals
- d. Chronemics

Guidance: level 1

:: Interpersonal relationships ::

An _________ is a strong, deep, or close association or acquaintance between two or more people that may range in duration from brief to enduring.The context can vary from family or kinship relations, friendship, marriage, relations with associates, work, clubs, neighborhoods, and places of worship. They may be regulated by law, custom, or mutual agreement, and are the basis of social groups and society as a whole.

Exam Probability: **Low**

53. *Answer choices:*

(see index for correct answer)

- a. Romantic comedy film
- b. Workplace relationships

- c. Interpersonal relationship
- d. Confidant

Guidance: level 1

:: Emotions ::

_________ is a state of having simultaneous conflicting reactions, beliefs, or feelings towards some object. Stated another way, _________ is the experience of having an attitude towards someone or something that contains both positively and negatively valenced components. The term also refers to situations where "mixed feelings" of a more general sort are experienced, or where a person experiences uncertainty or indecisiveness.

Exam Probability: **Low**

54. *Answer choices:*

(see index for correct answer)

- a. Happiness
- b. Ambivalence
- c. Worry
- d. Rage

Guidance: level 1

:: Fertility ::

_________ is the natural capability to produce offspring. As a measure, _________ rate is the number of offspring born per mating pair, individual or population. _________ differs from fecundity, which is defined as the potential for reproduction . A lack of _________ is in _________ while a lack of fecundity would be called sterility.

Exam Probability: **High**

55. *Answer choices:*

(see index for correct answer)

- a. Fertility
- b. Monocarpic
- c. Human fertilization
- d. American Fertility Association

Guidance: level 1

:: Genderqueer ::

_________ is the combination of masculine and feminine characteristics into an ambiguous form. _________ may be expressed with regard to biological sex, gender identity, gender expression, or sexual identity. The different meanings of _________ point to the complex interrelationship between aspects of sex, gender, and sexuality.

Exam Probability: **Low**

56. *Answer choices:*

(see index for correct answer)

- a. Genderless
- b. Androgyny
- c. Fantasia Fair
- d. Femme conference

Guidance: level 1

:: Statistical terminology ::

In mathematical modeling, statistical modeling and experimental sciences, the values of _________ s depend on the values of in _________ s. The _________ s represent the output or outcome whose variation is being studied. The in _________ s, also known in a statistical context as regressors, represent inputs or causes, that is, potential reasons for variation. In an experiment, any variable that the experimenter manipulates can be called an in _________ . Models and experiments test the effects that the in _________ s have on the _________ s. Sometimes, even if their influence is not of direct interest, in _________ s may be included for other reasons, such as to account for their potential confounding effect.

Exam Probability: **High**

57. *Answer choices:*

(see index for correct answer)

- a. Dependent variable

- b. Control group
- c. Floor effect
- d. Likelihood

Guidance: level 1

:: Collaboration ::

_________ is a cultural value that is characterized by emphasis on cohesiveness among individuals and prioritization of the group over self. Individuals or groups that subscribe to a collectivist worldview tend to find common values and goals as particularly salient and demonstrate greater orientation toward in-group than toward out-group. The term "in-group" is thought to be more diffusely defined for collectivistic individuals to include societal units ranging from the nuclear family to a religious or racial/ethnic group. Meta-analytic findings support that _________ shows a consistent association with discrete values, interpersonal patterns of interaction, cognition, perception and self-construal. While _________ is often defined in contrast to individualism, the notion that _________ -individualism is unidimensional has been challenged by contemporary theorists.

Exam Probability: **Medium**

58. *Answer choices:*

(see index for correct answer)

- a. Implicit collaboration
- b. Mobile collaboration
- c. Loffice

- d. Operational transformation

Guidance: level 1

:: Scientific method ::

In the social sciences and life sciences, a _________ is a research method involving an up-close, in-depth, and detailed examination of a subject of study , as well as its related contextual conditions.

Exam Probability: **Low**

59. *Answer choices:*

(see index for correct answer)

- a. Operationalization
- b. The Logic of Modern Physics
- c. Serendipity
- d. Case study

Guidance: level 1

Applied Psychology

Applied psychology is the use of psychological methods and findings of scientific psychology to solve practical problems of human and animal behavior and experience. Mental health, organizational psychology, business management, education, health, product design, ergonomics, and law are just a few of the areas that have been influenced by the application of psychological principles and findings. Some of the areas of applied psychology include clinical psychology, counseling psychology, evolutionary psychology, industrial and organizational psychology, legal psychology, neuropsychology, occupational health psychology, human factors, forensic psychology, engineering psychology, school psychology, sports psychology, traffic psychology, community psychology, medical psychology.

__________ is a psychological specialty that encompasses research and applied work in several broad domains: counseling process and outcome; supervision and training; career development and counseling; and prevention and health. Some unifying themes among counseling psychologists include a focus on assets and strengths, person–environment interactions, educational and career development, brief interactions, and a focus on intact personalities.

Exam Probability: **Medium**

1. *Answer choices:*

(see index for correct answer)

- a. Traffic psychology
- b. Counseling psychology
- c. Psycho-oncology
- d. Sport psychology

Guidance: level 1

:: Educational psychology ::

The __________, also known as method of Elenchus, elenctic method, or Socratic debate, is a form of cooperative argumentative dialogue between individuals, based on asking and answering questions to stimulate critical thinking and to draw out ideas and underlying presuppositions. It is a dialectical method, involving a discussion in which the defense of one point of view is questioned; one participant may lead another to contradict themselves in some way, thus weakening the defender`s point. This method is named after the Classical Greek philosopher Socrates and is introduced by him in Plato`s Theaetetus as midwifery because it is employed to bring out definitions implicit in the interlocutors` beliefs, or to help them further their understanding.

Exam Probability: **High**

2. *Answer choices:*

(see index for correct answer)

- a. Socratic method
- b. Human performance technology
- c. Team-based learning
- d. Student engagement

Guidance: level 1

:: Scientific method ::

_________ is the active acquisition of information from a primary source. In living beings, _________ employs the senses. In science, _________ can also involve the recording of data via the use of scientific instruments. The term may also refer to any data collected during the scientific activity. _________ s can be qualitative, that is, only the absence or presence of a property is noted, or quantitative if a numerical value is attached to the observed phenomenon by counting or measuring.

Exam Probability: **High**

3. *Answer choices:*

(see index for correct answer)

- a. Total Balance
- b. Observation
- c. Evidence-based practice
- d. Mertonian norms

Guidance: level 1

:: Epistemology ::

_________ literally means "proposition of the law" and is used in philosophy , psychology, and law with differing meanings. In psychology, _________ measures are contrasted to ipsative or idiothetic measures, where _________ measures are measures that are observed on a relatively large sample and have a more general outlook while the idiographic approach is relating to a more singular case as is done in case studies.

Exam Probability: **Medium**

4. *Answer choices:*

(see index for correct answer)

- a. Systemography
- b. Paradigm shift
- c. Nomothetic
- d. Argument from illusion

Guidance: level 1

:: Scientific method ::

In the social sciences and life sciences, a _________ is a research method involving an up-close, in-depth, and detailed examination of a subject of study , as well as its related contextual conditions.

Exam Probability: **High**

5. *Answer choices:*

(see index for correct answer)

- a. Woozle effect
- b. Scientific formalism
- c. Cybermethodology
- d. Case study

Guidance: level 1

:: Psychometrics ::

_________ is a body of related psychometric theory that predicts outcomes of psychological testing such as the difficulty of items or the ability of test-takers. It is a theory of testing based on the idea that a person's observed or obtained score on a test is the sum of a true score and an error score. Generally speaking, the aim of _________ is to understand and improve the reliability of psychological tests.

Exam Probability: **Medium**

6. *Answer choices:*

(see index for correct answer)

- a. Citizen survey
- b. Online assessment
- c. Classical test theory
- d. Fuzzy concept

Guidance: level 1

:: Philosophers of mind ::

__________ was an English anthropologist, social scientist, linguist, visual anthropologist, semiotician, and cyberneticist whose work intersected that of many other fields. In the 1940s, he helped extend systems theory and cybernetics to the social and behavioral sciences. He spent the last decade of his life developing a "meta-science" of epistemology to bring together the various early forms of systems theory developing in different fields of science. His writings include Steps to an Ecology of Mind and Mind and Nature . Angels Fear was co-authored by his daughter Mary Catherine Bateson.

Exam Probability: **Low**

7. *Answer choices:*

(see index for correct answer)

- a. Hans-Werner Bothe
- b. Gregory Bateson
- c. Robert Lawrence Kuhn
- d. Paul Boghossian

Guidance: level 1

:: Philosophy of science ::

An __________ definition is the articulation of __________ ization used in defining the terms of a process needed to determine the nature of an item or phenomenon and its properties such as duration, quantity, extension in space, chemical composition, etc. Since the degree of __________ ization can vary itself, it can result in a more or less __________ definition. The procedures included in definitions should be repeatable by anyone or at least by peers.

Exam Probability: **Medium**

8. *Answer choices:*

(see index for correct answer)

- a. Sense experience
- b. Universology
- c. Bayesian probability
- d. Historiography of science

Guidance: level 1

:: Psychoanalysis ::

_________ is a class of functional mental disorders involving chronic distress but neither delusions nor hallucinations. The term is no longer used by the professional psychiatric community in the United States, having been eliminated from the Diagnostic and Statistical Manual of Mental Disorders in 1980 with the publication of DSM III. It is still used in the ICD-10 Chapter V F40–48.

Exam Probability: **High**

9. *Answer choices:*

(see index for correct answer)

- a. Unthought known
- b. Daimonic

- c. Ljubljana school of psychoanalysis
- d. Feminist psychology

Guidance: level 1

:: Psychological testing ::

The ________ is a psychological test that measures suggestibility. It was created in 1983 by Icelandic psychologist Gísli Hannes Guðjónsson and involves reading the subject a short story and testing their recall. It has been used in court cases in several jurisdictions but has been the subject of various criticisms.

Exam Probability: **Medium**

10. *Answer choices:*

(see index for correct answer)

- a. Cambridge Neuropsychological Test Automated Battery
- b. Trier social stress test
- c. Vineland Adaptive Behavior Scale
- d. Gudjonsson suggestibility scale

Guidance: level 1

:: Neuropsychological tests ::

The ________ is one of the most widely used neuropsychological tests in North America. As an instrument, it represents a relatively new approach to clinical psychology and the cognitive science of memory. It measures of episodic verbal learning and memory, and demonstrates sensitivity to a range of clinical conditions. The test does this by attempting to link memory deficits with impaired performance on specific tasks. It assesses encoding, recall and recognition in a single modality of item presentation . The CVLT is considered to be a more sensitive measure of episodic memory than other verbal learning tests. It was designed to not only measure how much a subject learned, but also reveal strategies employed and the types of errors made. The CVLT indexes free and cued recall, serial position effects , semantic clustering, intrusions, interference and recognition. Delis et al. released the ________ for Children . The ________ -II is an updated version of the original CVLT, which has been standardized and provides normative data.

Exam Probability: **Medium**

11. *Answer choices:*

(see index for correct answer)

- a. Serial sevens
- b. California Verbal Learning Test
- c. Compensatory tracking task
- d. Pain stimulus

Guidance: level 1

:: Neuropsychological tests ::

The __________ is a neuropsychological test of visual attention and task switching. It consists of two parts in which the subject is instructed to connect a set of 25 dots as quickly as possible while still maintaining accuracy. The test can provide information about visual search speed, scanning, speed of processing, mental flexibility, as well as executive functioning. It is sensitive to detecting cognitive impairment associated with dementia, for example, Alzheimer`s disease.

Exam Probability: **Low**

12. *Answer choices:*

(see index for correct answer)

- a. Clinical Dementia Rating
- b. Epworth Sleepiness Scale
- c. Purdue Pegboard Test
- d. Serial sevens

Guidance: level 1

:: Organizational behavior ::

Greenberg introduced the concept of __________ with regard to how an employee judges the behaviour of the organization and the employee`s resulting attitude and behaviour. .

Exam Probability: **High**

13. *Answer choices:*

(see index for correct answer)

- a. organizational climate
- b. Behavioral systems analysis
- c. Managerial grid model
- d. Organizational justice

Guidance: level 1

:: Discrimination ::

The term _________ has a range of meanings within the contexts of sociology, of political philosophy, and of colloquial use. In sociology and in everyday usage, it is a synonym for "ethnic pluralism", with the two terms often used interchangeably, for example, a cultural pluralism in which various ethnic groups collaborate and enter into a dialogue with one another without having to sacrifice their particular identities. It can describe a mixed ethnic community area where multiple cultural traditions exist or a single country within which they do . Groups associated with an aboriginal or autochthonous ethnic group and foreigner ethnic groups are often the focus.

Exam Probability: **Low**

14. *Answer choices:*

(see index for correct answer)

- a. Multiculturalism
- b. A Class Divided

- c. Legacy preferences
- d. The Price of Admission

Guidance: level 1

:: Psychological tools ::

A _________ is a pictorial display of a person`s family relationships and medical history. It goes beyond a traditional family tree by allowing the user to visualize hereditary patterns and psychological factors that punctuate relationships. It can be used to identify repetitive patterns of behavior and to recognize hereditary tendencies.

Exam Probability: **High**

15. *Answer choices:*

(see index for correct answer)

- a. Eco-map
- b. Case study in psychology
- c. Culturagram
- d. Monitoring competence

Guidance: level 1

:: Human behavior ::

__________ is the changing of one`s behaviour to assume a role, either unconsciously to fill a social role, or consciously to act out an adopted role. While the Oxford English Dictionary offers a definition of __________ as "the changing of one`s behaviour to fulfill a social role", in the field of psychology, the term is used more loosely in four senses.

Exam Probability: **Medium**

16. *Answer choices:*

(see index for correct answer)

- a. Role-playing
- b. Ritualization
- c. Accismus
- d. Impulse

Guidance: level 1

:: Organizational psychology ::

_________ is a theory of leadership where a leader works with teams to identify needed change, creating a vision to guide the change through inspiration, and executing the change in tandem with committed members of a group; it is an integral part of the Full Range Leadership Model. _________ serves to enhance the motivation, morale, and job performance of followers through a variety of mechanisms; these include connecting the follower`s sense of identity and self to a project and to the collective identity of the organization; being a role model for followers in order to inspire them and to raise their interest in the project; challenging followers to take greater ownership for their work, and understanding the strengths and weaknesses of followers, allowing the leader to align followers with tasks that enhance their performance.

Exam Probability: **Low**

17. *Answer choices:*

(see index for correct answer)

- a. Snakes in Suits
- b. Onboarding
- c. Organizational psychology
- d. The Intangibles of Leadership

Guidance: level 1

:: Human resource management ::

Frederick Herzberg, an American psychologist, originally developed the concept of ` __________ ` in 1968, in an article that he published on pioneering studies at A T&T. The concept stemmed from Herzberg`s motivator-hygiene theory, which is based on the premise that job attitude is a construct of two independent factors, namely job satisfaction and job dissatisfaction. Job satisfaction encompasses intrinsic factors that arise from the work itself, including achievement and advancement; whilst job dissatisfaction stems from factors external to the actual work, including company policy and the quality of supervision.

Exam Probability: **High**

18. *Answer choices:*

(see index for correct answer)

- a. Electronic human resources
- b. Co-determination
- c. Idea portal
- d. Job enrichment

Guidance: level 1

:: Educational psychology ::

_________ is a field that applies principles of educational psychology, developmental psychology, clinical psychology, community psychology, and applied behavior analysis to meet children`s and adolescents` behavioral health and learning needs in a collaborative manner with educators and parents. School psychologists are educated in psychology, child and adolescent development, child and adolescent psychopathology, education, family and parenting practices, learning theories, and personality theories. They are knowledgeable about effective instruction and effective schools. They are trained to carry out psychological testing and psychoeducational assessment, counseling, and consultation, and in the ethical, legal and administrative codes of their profession.

Exam Probability: **Low**

19. *Answer choices:*

(see index for correct answer)

- a. Multipotentiality
- b. Shuhari
- c. Educational research
- d. School psychology

Guidance: level 1

:: Personality tests ::

The _________ is a personality test measuring normal personality developed by J. P. Guilford and Wayne S. Zimmerman in 1948. It is currently marketed by Pearson Assessments.

Exam Probability: **Low**

20. *Answer choices:*

(see index for correct answer)

- a. Eysenck Personality Questionnaire
- b. Test Construction Strategies
- c. Barratt Impulsiveness Scale
- d. Guilford-Zimmerman Temperament Survey

Guidance: level 1

:: Psychology terminology ::

_________ is a type of validity that is used to determine whether a new psychometric assessment will increase the predictive ability beyond that provided by an existing method of assessment. In other words, _________ seeks to answer if the new test adds much information that might be obtained with simpler, already existing methods.

Exam Probability: **Medium**

21. *Answer choices:*

(see index for correct answer)

- a. Emotional safety
- b. Golem effect

- c. Tip of the tongue
- d. Mowgli syndrome

Guidance: level 1

:: Survey methodology ::

An _________ , often simply referred to as a poll or a survey, is a human research survey of public opinion from a particular sample. _________ s are usually designed to represent the opinions of a population by conducting a series of questions and then extrapolating generalities in ratio or within confidence intervals.

Exam Probability: **Low**

22. *Answer choices:*

(see index for correct answer)

- a. Opinion poll
- b. Self-report
- c. Sampling
- d. Group concept mapping

Guidance: level 1

:: Anxiety disorders ::

__________ is an adaptive, short-term psychological helping-process that focuses solely on an immediate and identifiable problem. It can include pre-incident preparedness to acute crisis management to post-crisis follow-up. Its purpose is to enable people to return to their daily routine more quickly and with less likelihood of experiencing post-traumatic stress disorder . Evidence-based reviews, however, have concluded that CISM is ineffective for primary trauma victims, and should only be used for secondary victims, such as responding emergency services personnel. CISM was never intended to treat primary victims of trauma.

Exam Probability: **Low**

23. *Answer choices:*

(see index for correct answer)

- a. Critical incident stress management
- b. Social anxiety disorder
- c. Dermatophagia
- d. Limited symptom attack

Guidance: level 1

:: Educational psychology ::

An _________ is a component of a competence to do a certain kind of work at a certain level. Outstanding _________ can be considered "talent". An _________ may be physical or mental. _________ is inborn potential to do certain kinds of work whether developed or undeveloped. Ability is developed knowledge, understanding, learned or acquired abilities or attitude. The innate nature of _________ is in contrast to skills and achievement, which represent knowledge or ability that is gained through learning.

Exam Probability: **Medium**

24. *Answer choices:*

(see index for correct answer)

- a. Inquiry in Motion
- b. Educational measurement
- c. Aptitude
- d. Picture superiority effect

Guidance: level 1

:: Educational psychology ::

One`s _________ is a collection of beliefs about oneself. Generally, _________ embodies the answer to "Who am I".

Exam Probability: **Low**

25. *Answer choices:*

(see index for correct answer)

- a. Self-concept
- b. Inquiry education
- c. Generation effect
- d. Transfer of learning

Guidance: level 1

:: Second-language acquisition ::

An _________ is an action which is inaccurate or incorrect. In some usages, an _________ is synonymous with a mistake. In statistics, " _________ " refers to the difference between the value which has been computed and the correct value. An _________ could result in failure or in a deviation from the intended performance or behaviour.

Exam Probability: **Medium**

26. *Answer choices:*

(see index for correct answer)

- a. Second-language acquisition classroom research
- b. Willingness to communicate
- c. Error
- d. CANAL-F

Guidance: level 1

:: Recruitment ::

_________ in criminal law is a period of supervision over an offender, ordered by the court instead of serving time in prison.

Exam Probability: **High**

27. *Answer choices:*

(see index for correct answer)

- a. Recession-proof job
- b. S.I.R. Method of Recruiting
- c. Salary
- d. Probation

Guidance: level 1

:: Segregation ::

_________ or marginalization , or social marginalisation, is the social disadvantage and relegation to the fringe of society. It is a term used widely in Europe and was first used in France. It is used across disciplines including education, sociology, psychology, politics and economics.

Exam Probability: **Medium**

28. *Answer choices:*

(see index for correct answer)

- a. Residential segregation
- b. Separatism
- c. Social exclusion
- d. Separate but equal

Guidance: level 1

:: Psychometrics ::

_________ is a survey-based statistical technique used in market research that helps determine how people value different attributes that make up an individual product or service.

Exam Probability: **Medium**

29. *Answer choices:*

(see index for correct answer)

- a. Item bank
- b. Polychoric correlation
- c. Missing completely at random
- d. IPPQ

Guidance: level 1

:: Human resource management ::

A _________ is a process through which feedback from an employee`s subordinates, colleagues, and supervisor, as well as a self-evaluation by the employee themselves is gathered. Such feedback can also include, when relevant, feedback from external sources who interact with the employee, such as customers and suppliers or other interested stakeholders. _________ is so named because it solicits feedback regarding an employee`s behavior from a variety of points of view . It therefore may be contrasted with "downward feedback" , or "upward feedback" delivered to supervisory or management employees by subordinates only.

Exam Probability: **Medium**

30. *Answer choices:*

(see index for correct answer)

- a. Fresh tracks
- b. 360-degree feedback
- c. Training and development
- d. Contextual performance

Guidance: level 1

:: Human resource management ::

_________ is the strategic approach to the effective management of people in an organization so that they help the business to gain a competitive advantage. It is designed to maximize employee performance in service of an employer`s strategic objectives. HR is primarily concerned with the management of people within organizations, focusing on policies and on systems. HR departments are responsible for overseeing employee-benefits design, employee recruitment, training and development, performance appraisal, and Reward management . HR also concerns itself with organizational change and industrial relations, that is, the balancing of organizational practices with requirements arising from collective bargaining and from governmental laws.

Exam Probability: **Low**

31. *Answer choices:*

(see index for correct answer)

- a. Workforce management
- b. Human resource management
- c. Talent management system
- d. Skills management

Guidance: level 1

:: Intelligence tests ::

The __________ is a group-administered test developed by Robert Yerkes and six others in order to evaluate the many U.S. military recruits during World War I. It was first introduced in 1917 due to a demand for a systematic method of evaluating the intellectual and emotional functioning of soldiers. The test measured "verbal ability, numerical ability, ability to follow directions, and knowledge of information". Scores on the __________ were used to determine a soldier`s capability of serving, his job classification, and his potential for a leadership position. Soldiers who were illiterate or foreign speaking would take the Army Beta, the nonverbal equivalent of the exam.

Exam Probability: **High**

32. *Answer choices:*

(see index for correct answer)

- a. Army alpha
- b. Porteus Maze Test
- c. Mental Rotations Test
- d. Raven%27s Progressive Matrices

Guidance: level 1

:: Human resource management ::

An __________ is a formal scheme used to promote or encourage specific actions or behavior by a specific group of people during a defined period of time. __________ s are particularly used in business management to motivate employees and in sales to attract and retain customers. Scientific literature also refers to this concept as pay for performance.

Exam Probability: **Medium**

33. *Answer choices:*

(see index for correct answer)

- a. Idea portal
- b. ROWE
- c. Trust fall
- d. Herrmann Brain Dominance Instrument

Guidance: level 1

:: Human resource management ::

A _________ usually refers to a group of individuals who work together from different geographic locations and rely on communication technology such as email, FAX, and video or voice conferencing services in order to collaborate. The term can also refer to groups or teams that work together asynchronously or across organizational levels. Powell, Piccoli and Ives define _________ s as "groups of geographically, organizationally and/or time dispersed workers brought together by information and telecommunication technologies to accomplish one or more organizational tasks." According to Ale Ebrahim et. al. , _________ s can also be defined as "small temporary groups of geographically, organizationally and/or time dispersed knowledge workers who coordinate their work predominantly with electronic information and communication technologies in order to accomplish one or more organization tasks."

Exam Probability: **Low**

34. *Answer choices:*

(see index for correct answer)

- a. Job sharing
- b. On-ramping
- c. Open plan
- d. Virtual team

Guidance: level 1

:: Mood disorders ::

The _________ is a 10-item questionnaire that was developed to identify women who have postpartum depression. Items of the scale correspond to various clinical depression symptoms, such as guilt feeling, sleep disturbance, low energy, anhedonia, and suicidal ideation. Overall assessment is done by total score, which is determined by adding together the scores for each of the 10 items. Higher scores indicate more depressive symptoms. The EPDS may be used within 8 weeks postpartum and it also can be applied for depression screening during pregnancy.

Exam Probability: **Medium**

35. *Answer choices:*

(see index for correct answer)

- a. Post-vacation blues
- b. Edinburgh Postnatal Depression Scale

- c. S100A10
- d. Bipolar disorder

Guidance: level 1

:: Alcohol abuse ::

_________ is a mental disorder that can develop after a person is exposed to a traumatic event, such as sexual assault, warfare, traffic collisions, or other threats on a person`s life. Symptoms may include disturbing thoughts, feelings, or dreams related to the events, mental or physical distress to trauma-related cues, attempts to avoid trauma-related cues, alterations in how a person thinks and feels, and an increase in the fight-or-flight response. These symptoms last for more than a month after the event. Young children are less likely to show distress, but instead may express their memories through play. A person with PTSD is at a higher risk for suicide and intentional self-harm.

Exam Probability: **Medium**

36. *Answer choices:*

(see index for correct answer)

- a. Children of Light
- b. Sobriety
- c. Disease theory of alcoholism
- d. Alcoholic lung disease

Guidance: level 1

:: Psychological testing ::

__________ is a personality trait defined by the search for experiences and feelings, that are "varied, novel, complex and intense", and by the readiness to "take physical, social, legal, and financial risks for the sake of such experiences." Risk is not an essential part of the trait, as many activities associated with it are not risky. However, risk may be ignored, tolerated, or minimized and may even be considered to add to the excitement of the activity. The concept was developed by Marvin Zuckerman of the University of Delaware. In order to assess this trait he created a personality test called the __________ Scale. This test assesses individual differences in terms of sensory stimulation preferences. So there are people who prefer a strong stimulation and display a behavior that manifests a greater desire for sensations and there are those who prefer a low sensory stimulation. The scale is a questionnaire designed to measure how much stimulation a person requires and the extent to which they enjoy the excitement. Zuckerman hypothesized that people who are high sensation seekers require a lot of stimulation to reach their Optimal Level of Arousal. When the stimulation or sensory input is not met, the person finds the experience unpleasant.

Exam Probability: **High**

37. *Answer choices:*

(see index for correct answer)

- a. Washington University Sentence Completion Test
- b. Cambridge Neuropsychological Test Automated Battery
- c. Inhibitory control test
- d. Sensation seeking

Guidance: level 1

:: Applied psychology ::

An _________ is a psychologist whose differentiating functions may include diagnostic and psycho-educational assessment, psychological counseling in educational communities , community-type psycho-educational intervention, and mediation, coordination, and referral to other professionals, at all levels of the educational system. Many countries use this term to signify those who provide services to students, their teachers, and families while other countries use this term to signify academic expertise in teaching Educational Psychology.

Exam Probability: **Medium**

38. *Answer choices:*

(see index for correct answer)

- a. Counseling psychology
- b. Sport psychology
- c. Traffic psychology
- d. Biodata

Guidance: level 1

:: Applied psychology ::

_________ studies the individuals` contexts within communities and the wider society, and the relationships of the individual to communities and society. Community psychologists seek to understand the quality of life of individuals within groups, organizations and institutions, communities, and society. Their aim is to enhance quality of life through collaborative research and action.

Exam Probability: **Low**

39. *Answer choices:*

(see index for correct answer)

- a. Genopolitics
- b. Zero-sum mentality
- c. Medical-psychological assessment
- d. Community psychology

Guidance: level 1

:: Psychotherapy ::

_________ is a set of related therapies arising from what proponents see as a disparity between the origin of most psychological theories and the majority of people seeking counseling being female. It focuses on societal, cultural, and political causes and solutions to issues faced in the counseling process. It openly encourages the client to participate in the world in a more social and political way.

Exam Probability: **High**

40. *Answer choices:*

(see index for correct answer)

- a. Feminist therapy
- b. Therapy interfering behavior
- c. Solution focused brief therapy
- d. Guided affective imagery

Guidance: level 1

:: Educational psychology research methods ::

A __________ is a psychometric scale commonly involved in research that employs questionnaires. It is the most widely used approach to scaling responses in survey research, such that the term is often used interchangeably with rating scale, although there are other types of rating scales.

Exam Probability: **Low**

41. *Answer choices:*

(see index for correct answer)

- a. Reliability
- b. Likert scale
- c. Effect size

- d. Visual analogue scale

Guidance: level 1

:: Organizational behavior ::

In industrial and organizational psychology, _________ is a person`s voluntary commitment within an organization or company that is not part of his or her contractual tasks.

Exam Probability: **Medium**

42. *Answer choices:*

(see index for correct answer)

- a. Administrative Behavior
- b. Managerial grid model
- c. Organizational justice
- d. Organizational citizenship behavior

Guidance: level 1

:: Heuristics ::

__________ science is the application of science to criminal and civil laws, mainly—on the criminal side—during criminal investigation, as governed by the legal standards of admissible evidence and criminal procedure.

Exam Probability: **Medium**

43. *Answer choices:*

(see index for correct answer)

- a. Affect heuristic
- b. Forensic
- c. Meta-optimization
- d. Human biocomputer

Guidance: level 1

:: History of psychology ::

__________ refers to a learning procedure in which a biologically potent stimulus is paired with a previously neutral stimulus . It also refers to the learning process that results from this pairing, through which the neutral stimulus comes to elicit a response that is usually similar to the one elicited by the potent stimulus.

Exam Probability: **Low**

44. *Answer choices:*

(see index for correct answer)

- a. Radical behaviorism
- b. Law of effect
- c. Extraordinary Popular Delusions and the Madness of Crowds
- d. Classical conditioning

Guidance: level 1

:: Cognitive therapy ::

_________ was an American psychologist who in 1955 developed Rational Emotive Behavior Therapy . He held MA and PhD degrees in clinical psychology from Columbia University and the American Board of Professional Psychology . He also founded and was the President of the New York City-based _________ Institute for decades. He is generally considered to be one of the originators of the cognitive revolutionary paradigm shift in psychotherapy and one of the founders of cognitive-behavioral therapies.

Exam Probability: **Medium**

45. *Answer choices:*

(see index for correct answer)

- a. Cognitive interventions
- b. Cognitive therapies for dementia
- c. Marsha M. Linehan
- d. Albert Ellis

Guidance: level 1

:: Perception ::

In research, the _________ of a study means that the methods, materials and setting of the study must approximate the real-world that is being examined. Unlike internal and external validity, _________ is not necessary to the overall validity of a study.

Exam Probability: **Medium**

46. *Answer choices:*

(see index for correct answer)

- a. Set
- b. Ecological validity
- c. Kinesis
- d. Chubb illusion

Guidance: level 1

:: Validity (statistics) ::

_________ is the validity of applying the conclusions of a scientific study outside the context of that study. In other words, it is the extent to which the results of a study can be generalized to and across other situations, people, stimuli, and times. In contrast, internal validity is the validity of conclusions drawn within the context of a particular study. Because general conclusions are almost always a goal in research, _________ is an important property of any study. Mathematical analysis of _________ concerns a determination of whether generalization across heterogeneous populations is feasible, and devising statistical and computational methods that produce valid generalizations.

Exam Probability: **Low**

47. *Answer choices:*

(see index for correct answer)

- a. External validity
- b. Convergent validity
- c. Test validity
- d. Nomological validity

Guidance: level 1

:: Social psychology ::

_________ is a term originated by the US military. The US Department of Defense gives this definition.

Exam Probability: **High**

48. *Answer choices:*

(see index for correct answer)

- a. Norm of reciprocity
- b. Rabin fairness
- c. Psychographic
- d. Greater Good Science Center

Guidance: level 1

:: Applied psychology ::

_________ is a form of advertising, it has been a large industry for some time now. Originally with newspapers and billboards, but now we have advanced to huge LCD screens and online advertisement on social medias and websites. The most common use of _________ in today`s society is through social media.. It has the primary goal of achieving "social good". Traditional commercial marketing aims are primarily financial, though they can have positive social affects as well. In the context of public health, _________ would promote general health, raise awareness and induce changes in behaviour. To see _________ as only the use of standard commercial marketing practices to achieve non-commercial goals is an oversimplified view.

Exam Probability: **Low**

49. *Answer choices:*

(see index for correct answer)

- a. Psycho-oncology
- b. Medical-psychological assessment
- c. Social marketing
- d. Counseling psychology

Guidance: level 1

:: Educational psychology ::

The _________ is the finding that long-term memory is often increased when some of the learning period is devoted to retrieving the to-be-remembered information. The effect is also sometimes referred to as retrieval practice, practice testing, or test-enhanced learning. The _________ on memory should be distinguished from more general practice effects, defined in the APA Dictionary of Psychology as "any change or improvement that results from practice or repetition of task items or activities." The term _________ is also sometimes used in a more general sense; The Oxford Dictionary of Psychology defines a _________ as "any effect of taking tests on the respondents, a typical example being test sophistication." Whereas psychologists who develop tests for personality and intelligence want to avoid practice effects, cognitive psychologists working with educators have begun to understand how to take advantage of tests—not as an assessment tool, but as a teaching/learning tool.

Exam Probability: **Low**

50. *Answer choices:*

(see index for correct answer)

- a. Rasch model

- b. Validity
- c. Testing effect
- d. Formal education

Guidance: level 1

:: Human–computer interaction ::

A _________ is a small, but demographically diverse group of people and whose reactions are studied especially in market research or political analysis in guided or open discussions about a new product or something else to determine the reactions that can be expected from a larger population. It is a form of qualitative research consisting of interviews in which a group of people are asked about their perceptions, opinions, beliefs, and attitudes towards a product, service, concept, advertisement, idea, or packaging. Questions are asked in an interactive group setting where participants are free to talk with other group members. During this process, the researcher either takes notes or records the vital points he or she is getting from the group. Researchers should select members of the _________ carefully for effective and authoritative responses.

Exam Probability: **Medium**

51. *Answer choices:*

(see index for correct answer)

- a. Google
- b. Wikirating
- c. Needs analysis

- d. Focus group

Guidance: level 1

:: Educational psychology ::

A __________ is a type of test, assessment, or evaluation which yields an estimate of the position of the tested individual in a predefined population, with respect to the trait being measured. The estimate is derived from the analysis of test scores and possibly other relevant data from a sample drawn from the population. That is, this type of test identifies whether the test taker performed better or worse than other test takers, not whether the test taker knows either more or less material than is necessary for a given purpose.

Exam Probability: **High**

52. *Answer choices:*

(see index for correct answer)

- a. Norm-referenced test
- b. Integrative learning
- c. Risk inclination formula
- d. Information design

Guidance: level 1

:: Cognitive science ::

_________ is the process of acquiring new, or modifying existing, knowledge, behaviors, skills, values, or preferences. The ability to learn is possessed by humans, animals, and some machines; there is also evidence for some kind of _________ in some plants. Some _________ is immediate, induced by a single event , but much skill and knowledge accumulates from repeated experiences. The changes induced by _________ often last a lifetime, and it is hard to distinguish learned material that seems to be "lost" from that which cannot be retrieved.

Exam Probability: **Medium**

53. *Answer choices:*

(see index for correct answer)

- a. Mental rotation
- b. Computational neurogenetic modeling
- c. Psychic apparatus
- d. Dual-coding theory

Guidance: level 1

:: Scientific method ::

_________ is an interdisciplinary approach to clinical practice that has been gaining ground following its formal introduction in 1992. It started in medicine as evidence-based medicine and spread to allied health professions, educational fields, and others. EBP is traditionally defined in terms of a "three legged stool" integrating three basic principles: the best available research evidence bearing on whether and why a treatment works, clinical expertise to rapidly identify each patient`s unique health state and diagnosis, their individual risks and benefits of potential interventions, and client preferences and values.

Exam Probability: **Low**

54. *Answer choices:*

(see index for correct answer)

- a. Skepticism
- b. Retrodiction
- c. Pasteur's quadrant
- d. Evidence-based practice

Guidance: level 1

:: Validity (statistics) ::

__________ is a type of evidence that can be gathered to defend the use of a test for predicting other outcomes. It is a parameter used in sociology, psychology, and other psychometric or behavioral sciences. __________ is demonstrated when a test correlates well with a measure that has previously been validated. The two measures may be for the same construct, but more often used for different, but presumably related, constructs.

Exam Probability: **High**

55. *Answer choices:*

(see index for correct answer)

- a. Criterion validity
- b. Convergent validity
- c. Concurrent validity
- d. Face validity

Guidance: level 1

:: Neuropsychological tests ::

The __________ , introduced in 1983 by Edith Kaplan, Harold Goodglass and Sandra Weintraub, is a widely used neuropsychological assessment tool to measure confrontational word retrieval in individuals with aphasia or other language disturbance caused by stroke, Alzheimer`s disease, or other dementing disorder. A common and debilitating feature is anomic aphasia, an impairment in the ability to name objects. The BNT contains 60 line drawings graded in difficulty. Patients with anomia often have greater difficulties with the naming of not only difficult and low frequency objects but also easy and high frequency objects. Naming difficulties may be rank ordered along a continuum. Items are rank ordered in terms of their ability to be named, which is correlated with their frequency. This type of picture-naming test is also useful in the examination of children with learning disabilities and the evaluation of brain-injured adults.

Exam Probability: **High**

56. *Answer choices:*

(see index for correct answer)

- a. Pain stimulus
- b. Four boxes test
- c. California Verbal Learning Test
- d. Boston Naming Test

Guidance: level 1

:: Survey methodology ::

A ________ study is a type of survey, questionnaire, or poll in which respondents read the question and select a response by themselves without researcher interference. A ________ is any method which involves asking a participant about their feelings, attitudes, beliefs and so on. Examples of ________s are questionnaires and interviews; ________s are often used as a way of gaining participants' responses in observational studies and experiments.

Exam Probability: **High**

57. *Answer choices:*

(see index for correct answer)

- a. World Association for Public Opinion Research
- b. Self-report
- c. Sampling
- d. Political forecasting

Guidance: level 1

:: Branches of psychology ::

_________ is a subfield of Industrial and Organizational Psychology. _________ is the area of industrial/organizational psychology that primarily deals with the recruitment, selection and evaluation of personnel, and other job aspects such as morale, job satisfaction, and relationships between managers and workers in the workplace. It is the field of study that concentrates on the selection and evaluation of employees; this area of psychology deals with job analysis and defines and measures job performance, performance appraisal, employment testing, employment interviews, personnel selection and employee training, and human factors and ergonomics.

Exam Probability: **Medium**

58. *Answer choices:*

(see index for correct answer)

- a. Personnel psychology
- b. Psychology of science
- c. Theoretical psychology
- d. Medical psychology

Guidance: level 1

:: Organizational behavior ::

__________ is a persistent pattern of mistreatment from others in the workplace that causes either physical or emotional harm. It can include such tactics as verbal, nonverbal, psychological, physical abuse and humiliation. This type of workplace aggression is particularly difficult because, unlike the typical school bully, workplace bullies often operate within the established rules and policies of their organization and their society. In the majority of cases, bullying in the workplace is reported as having been by someone who has authority over their victim. However, bullies can also be peers, and occasionally subordinates. Research has also investigated the impact of the larger organizational context on bullying as well as the group-level processes that impact on the incidence and maintenance of bullying behaviour. Bullying can be covert or overt. It may be missed by superiors; it may be known by many throughout the organization. Negative effects are not limited to the targeted individuals, and may lead to a decline in employee morale and a change in organizational culture. It can also take place as overbearing supervision, constant criticism, and blocking promotions.

Exam Probability: **Low**

59. *Answer choices:*

(see index for correct answer)

- a. Managerial grid model
- b. Span of control
- c. Micro-initiative
- d. Workplace bullying

Guidance: level 1

People

Psychologists can be seen as practicing within two general categories of psychology: applied psychology which includes "practitioners" or "professionals", and research-orientated psychology which includes "scientists", or "scholars". The training models endorsed by the American Psychological Association (APA) require that applied psychologists be trained as both researchers and practitioners,[3] and that they possess advanced degrees.

Psychologists typically have one of two degrees (PsyD or PhD). The PhD prepares a psychologist to conduct scientific research for a career in academia; whereas, the PsyD prepares for clinical practice (e.g. testing, psychotherapy). Both PsyD and PhD programs can prepare students to be licensed psychologists, and training in these types of programs prepares graduates to take state licensing exams.

Within the two main categories are many further types of psychologists as reflected by the 56 professional classifications recognized by the APA, including clinical, counseling, and educational psychologists. Such professionals work with persons in a variety of therapeutic contexts. People often think of the discipline as involving only such clinical or counseling psychologists. While counseling and psychotherapy are common activities for psychologists, these applied fields are just two branches in the larger domain of psychology. There are other classifications such as industrial, organizational and community psychologists, whose professionals mainly apply psychological research, theories, and techniques to "real-world" problems of business, industry, social benefit organizations, government, and academia.

:: Blood diamonds ::

The National Union for the Total Independence of Angola is the second-largest political party in Angola. Founded in 1966, _________ fought alongside the Popular Movement for the Liberation of Angola in the Angolan War for Independence and then against the MPLA in the ensuing civil war . The war was one of the most prominent Cold War proxy wars, with _________ receiving military aid from the United States and South Africa while the MPLA received support from the Soviet Union and its allies.

Exam Probability: **Low**

1. *Answer choices:*

(see index for correct answer)

- a. Annansi Clothing Co.
- b. United Nations Security Council Resolution 1237
- c. United Nations Security Council Resolution 1459
- d. UNITA

Guidance: level 1

:: War in Darfur ::

The _________ is a Sudanese rebel group based in the region of Darfur. The group was formed when it broke away from the Justice and Equality Movement in 2004. The NMRD came into existence because its founding members felt that JEM focused too much on the political rather than the social and economic needs of the Fur people. JEM merged with the Alliance of Revolutionary Forces of West Sudan on January 20, 2006.

Exam Probability: **High**

2. *Answer choices:*

(see index for correct answer)

- a. United Nations Security Council Resolution 1769
- b. National Redemption Front

- c. National Movement for Reform and Development
- d. Google Darfur

Guidance: level 1

:: Racism ::

_________ is any system in which principles of property law are applied to people, allowing individuals to own, buy and sell other individuals, as a de jure form of property. A slave is unable to withdraw unilaterally from such an arrangement and works without remuneration. Many scholars now use the term chattel _________ to refer to this specific sense of legalised, de jure _________. In a broader sense, however, the word _________ may also refer to any situation in which an individual is de facto forced to work against their own will. Scholars also use the more generic terms such as unfree labour or forced labour to refer to such situations. However, and especially under _________ in broader senses of the word, slaves may have some rights and protections according to laws or customs.

Exam Probability: **Low**

3. *Answer choices:*

(see index for correct answer)

- a. Peckerwood
- b. Slavery
- c. Expert Committee on Questions of Population and Racial Policy
- d. Benjamin Prize

Guidance: level 1

:: Slavery ::

_________ , African Holocaust, Holocaust of Enslavement, or Black Holocaust are political neologisms popularized from 1998 onwards and used to describe the history and ongoing effects of atrocities inflicted on African people, particularly when committed by non-Africans and argued as "continued to the present day" through imperialism, colonialism and other forms of oppression. For example, Maulana Karenga puts slavery in the broader context of the _________ , suggesting that its effects exceed mere physical persecution and legal disenfranchisement: the "destruction of human possibility involved redefining African humanity to the world, poisoning past, present and future relations with others who only know us through this stereotyping and thus damaging the truly human relations among peoples".

Exam Probability: **Low**

4. *Answer choices:*

(see index for correct answer)

- a. Haratin
- b. Slave catcher
- c. Holing cane
- d. Capture of the Brillante

Guidance: level 1

INDEX: Correct Answers

Foundations of Psychology

1. a: Mood disorder

2. d: Self-esteem

3. d: Discrimination

4. c: Arousal

5. d: Biofeedback

6. b: Applied psychology

7. d: Law of effect

8. d: Prosocial behavior

9. b: Child care

10. c: Psychopathology

11. c: Dementia

12. a: Consciousness

13. : Stress management

14. : Cerebral hemisphere

15. d: Inference

16. : Apperception

17. a: Anal stage

18. : Heuristic

19. a: Schizophrenia

20. a: Aphasia

21. d: Learning

22. a: William James

23. d: Self-awareness

24. c: Mental health

25. d: Social psychology

26. d: Cognitive neuroscience

27. b: Concept

28. : System

29. : Posttraumatic stress disorder

30. : Hormone

31. : Generalization

32. : Goal setting

33. c: Habituation

34. d: Long-term memory

35. : Sexual harassment

36. b: Corpus callosum

37. c: Description

38. d: Implicit memory

39. c: Personality test

40. a: Experience

41. d: Psychologist

42. d: Nerve

43. d: Factor analysis

44. : Cognitive therapy

45. : Autonomic nervous system

46. b: Clinical psychology

47. b: Nonverbal communication

48. d: Psychoanalytic theory

49. c: High school

50. a: Social change

51. c: Stereotype

52. a: Shyness

53. c: Behavior therapy

54. : Menopause

55. : Crystallized intelligence

56. d: Epilepsy

57. a: Goal

58. : Amphetamine

59. a: Behaviorism

History of Psychology

1. c: Scientific progress

2. d: Research

3. c: Psycholinguistics

4. c: Anxiety

5. a: Incentive

6. b: Civilization and Its Discontents

7. a: Habit

8. a: Principles of Psychology

9. : Penis envy

10. a: Meta-analysis

11. c: Spontaneous recovery

12. : Monism

13. c: Psychometrics

14. a: Humanistic psychology

15. d: Size

16. b: Mathematical psychology

17. a: Discrimination learning

18. a: Occasionalism

19. d: Naturalistic observation

20. d: Averroes

21. a: Critique

22. a: Phenomenon

23. c: Real self

24. d: Countertransference

25. b: Nancy School

26. d: Phallic stage

27. c: Transference

28. a: Gestalt psychology

29. a: Radical behaviorism

30. b: Solipsism

31. b: Secondary source

32. b: Psychophysiology

33. c: Being

34. a: Absolute threshold

35. c: Color vision

36. : Beck Anxiety Inventory

37. b: Explanation

38. c: Archival research

39. d: Epiphenomenalism

40. b: Grief

41. a: Social psychology

42. c: Frequency

43. d: System

44. d: Energy

45. a: Limen

46. c: Introspection

47. b: External validity

48. a: Psychologist

49. d: Individual psychology

50. b: Sleep

51. c: Philosophische Studien

52. d: Sensitivity training

53. a: Main effect

54. b: Person

55. c: Functional fixedness

56. b: Communication

57. a: Structuralism

58. b: Attention

59. a: Causality

Educational Psychology

1. a: Sexual harassment

2. a: Cognitive style

3. d: Direct instruction

4. a: Procedural memory

5. : Problem-based learning

6. b: Classroom management

7. c: Child abuse

8. c: Research question

9. : Construct validity

10. : Procrastination

11. : Self-regulated learning

12. a: Razor

13. d: Hypothetico-deductive model

14. : Critical thinking

15. c: Grounded theory

16. b: Self-determination theory

17. c: Program evaluation

18. : Curriculum-based measurement

19. a: Ecological fallacy

20. a: Legitimate peripheral participation

21. : Standard deviation

22. : Nonprobability sampling

23. d: Reinforcement

24. d: Psychotherapy

25. a: Working memory

26. : Acting white

27. a: Multiculturalism

28. b: Reciprocal determinism

29. c: Brain

30. d: Dual-coding theory

31. : Trial and error

32. b: Encoding

33. b: Theory of multiple intelligences

34. c: Coercion

35. c: Norm-referenced

36. c: Quantitative research

37. d: Mental age

38. a: Alfred Binet

39. b: Specific language impairment

40. a: Autism spectrum

41. d: Inference

42. : Knowledge base

43. c: Rapport

44. a: Memory

45. a: Explicit knowledge

46. c: Perception

47. : Concept learning

48. d: Stanford-Binet

49. a: Nonverbal communication

50. d: Bilingual education

51. b: Short-term memory

52. b: Discovery learning

53. : Survey research

54. : Lecture

55. a: Community of practice

56. a: Placebo

57. : Communication disorder

58. c: Collectivism

59. a: Operationalization

Biopsychology

1. a: Dementia

2. b: Glutamate receptor

3. c: Muscle

4. : Consciousness

5. : Implicit memory

6. : Dendritic spine

7. a: Epilepsy

8. : Central sulcus

9. c: Notochord

10. b: Hallucinogen

11. b: Synapse

12. b: Spinal nerve

13. c: Mescaline

14. a: Language disorder

15. c: Galen

16. b: T cell

17. b: Depolarization

18. b: Atropine

19. d: Aggression

20. d: Sleep

21. a: Agraphia

22. d: Primary motor cortex

23. b: Pheromone

24. c: Card sorting

25. : Putamen

26. a: Learning

27. b: Pituitary gland

28. b: Nervous system

29. a: Tyramine

30. : Sound

31. d: Orbitofrontal cortex

32. : Sildenafil

33. : Astrocyte

34. a: Cranial nerve

35. c: Mouse

36. c: Electroconvulsive therapy

37. b: Image

38. b: Neural tube

39. d: Complex cell

40. : Affective neuroscience

41. b: Stimulant

42. a: Visual agnosia

43. d: Receptive field

44. d: Phencyclidine

45. b: Visual cortex

46. : Nerve

47. d: Persistent vegetative state

48. c: Cerebrum

49. : Opioid

50. c: Proprioception

51. : Inner ear

52. b: Flumazenil

53. c: Addiction

54. a: Paralysis

55. : Coma

56. d: Lewy body

57. c: Hormone

58. : Motor system

59. b: Headache

Developmental Psychology

1. a: Moral development

2. a: Friendship

3. c: Hippocampus

4. d: Postpartum depression

5. d: Parenting style

6. c: Infant

7. c: Dyslexia

8. c: Habit

9. : Naturalistic observation

10. b: Nervous system

11. d: Social cognitive theory

12. c: Long-term memory

13. b: Pregnancy

14. c: Statistics

15. c: Fertility

16. d: Metalinguistic awareness

17. a: Longevity

18. b: Reaction time

19. a: Prosocial behavior

20. a: Empathy

21. : Intelligence

22. d: Electra complex

23. d: Socialization

24. b: Vocabulary

25. b: Intelligence test

26. : Anxiety Disorder

27. b: Mental age

28. c: Prejudice

29. a: Neuron

30. c: Socioeconomic status

31. b: Penis

32. a: Anxiety

33. a: Operant conditioning

34. a: Encoding

35. b: Cognition

36. a: Generativity

37. c: Self-concept

38. b: Gender schema theory

39. b: Psychosexual development

40. a: Hypertension

41. a: Spina bifida

42. b: Anesthesia

43. d: Cystic fibrosis

44. b: Fetal alcohol syndrome

45. b: Neural tube

46. a: Psychotherapy

47. b: Ageism

48. a: Phonics

49. c: Object permanence

50. a: Classical conditioning

51. b: Child abuse

52. b: Autism spectrum

53. : Gender identity

54. c: Gross motor skill

55. b: Systems theory

56. : Body image

57. b: Wisdom

58. b: Peer pressure

59. c: Visual perception

Cognitive Psychology

1. b: Operant conditioning

2. : Functional fixedness

3. d: Brain damage

4. a: Reinforcement

5. b: Intelligence test

6. c: Cognition

7. c: Nerve

8. a: Confabulation

9. a: Visual search

10. : Autism

11. a: Declarative memory

12. d: Spatial memory

13. c: Dichotic listening

14. c: Encoding

15. c: Illusion

16. : Neurotransmitter

17. a: Empathy

18. d: Behavior

19. c: Latent inhibition

20. : Control group

21. b: Visual perception

22. b: McGurk effect

23. : Information Theory

24. a: Long-term potentiation

25. a: Understanding

26. : Hypothesis

27. c: Turing test

28. b: Error

29. d: Word recognition

30. d: Echoic memory

31. : Aggression

32. b: Michael

33. b: Method of loci

34. b: Reminiscence bump

35. c: Placebo

36. a: Premise

37. b: Gene

38. b: Genius

39. b: Spontaneous recovery

40. a: Childhood amnesia

41. : Cognitive neuroscience

42. c: Systematic desensitization

43. : Information

44. d: Introspection

45. c: Misinformation effect

46. c: Communication

47. c: Sensory memory

48. b: Working Memory

49. b: Mental health

50. a: Evaluation

51. a: Memory span

52. a: Temporal lobe

53. : Literacy

54. a: Metaphor

55. a: Feature integration theory

56. : Explanatory style

57. a: Ethics

58. b: Discrimination

59. a: Availability heuristic

Abnormal Psychology

1. d: Gender role

2. c: Taijin kyofusho

3. c: Psychoeducation

4. d: Social support

5. : Psychotherapy

6. b: Wisdom

7. c: Methylphenidate

8. d: Imipramine

9. b: Side effects

10. b: Personality disorder

11. c: Sexual desire

12. : Posttraumatic stress disorder

13. : Brief psychotic disorder

14. : Counseling psychology

15. c: Catharsis

16. b: Methamphetamine

17. : Self-actualization

18. d: Smoking

19. d: Self-esteem

20. c: Flooding

21. c: Child development

22. b: Malingering

23. : Behavior modification

24. : Incest

25. : Stressor

26. d: Longitudinal study

27. c: Bupropion

28. d: Defense mechanism

29. c: Psychiatrist

30. d: Observation

31. b: Mental retardation

32. a: Diagnostic and Statistical Manual of Mental Disorders

33. a: Heroin

34. : Interpersonal psychotherapy

35. : Echolalia

36. : Relapse

37. c: Adjustment disorder

38. b: Adaptive behavior

39. : Reuptake

40. : Oral stage

41. : Phencyclidine

42. d: Neurosis

43. a: Rating scale

44. : Testosterone

45. d: Narcotic

46. c: Self-monitoring

47. b: Encopresis

48. : Habit

49. c: Self-concept

50. d: Adlerian

51. c: Delirium

52. c: Unconditional positive regard

53. c: Behavioral activation

54. d: Contingency management

55. a: Limbic system

56. a: Lysergic acid diethylamide

57. a: Clinical psychology

58. : Generalization

59. b: Dissociative disorder

Social Psychology

1. : Assertiveness

2. d: Genital stage

3. : Family

4. a: Triangular theory of love

5. : Erectile dysfunction

6. a: Phobia

7. d: Beauty

8. a: Same-sex marriage

9. : Critical thinking

10. d: Exhibitionism

11. d: Sexual dysfunction

12. : Social learning theory

13. : Cooperation

14. d: Diffusion of responsibility

15. c: Locus of control

16. c: Domestic violence

17. d: Child abuse

18. : Error

19. a: Homophobia

20. : Detection

21. d: Artificial insemination

22. b: Clinical psychology

23. b: Cognition

24. a: Dating

25. a: Parent

26. : Masturbation

27. : Abstinence

28. c: Racism

29. d: Self-awareness

30. c: Social behavior

31. d: Phallic stage

32. b: Peer pressure

33. d: Emotion

34. a: Prosocial behavior

35. c: Social facilitation

36. b: Glass ceiling

37. : Apperception

38. a: Socialization

39. b: Affirmative action

40. a: Serotonin

41. a: Self-disclosure

42. : Interpersonal attraction

43. : Implicit Association Test

44. a: Stereotype threat

45. c: Sexual identity

46. d: Learning

47. b: Fallopian tube

48. b: Illusory correlation

49. c: Sexual abuse

50. b: Bystander effect

51. a: Infidelity

52. b: Nonverbal communication

53. c: Interpersonal relationship

54. b: Ambivalence

55. a: Fertility

56. b: Androgyny

57. a: Dependent variable

58. : Collectivism

59. d: Case study

Applied Psychology

1. b: Counseling psychology

2. a: Socratic method

3. b: Observation

4. c: Nomothetic

5. d: Case study

6. c: Classical test theory

7. b: Gregory Bateson

8. : Operational

9. : Neurosis

10. d: Gudjonsson suggestibility scale

11. b: California Verbal Learning Test

12. : Trail Making Test

13. d: Organizational justice

14. a: Multiculturalism

15. : Genogram

16. a: Role-playing

17. : Transformational leadership

18. d: Job enrichment

19. d: School psychology

20. d: Guilford-Zimmerman Temperament Survey

21. : Incremental validity

22. a: Opinion poll

23. a: Critical incident stress management

24. c: Aptitude

25. a: Self-concept

26. c: Error

27. d: Probation

28. c: Social exclusion

29. : Conjoint analysis

30. b: 360-degree feedback

31. b: Human resource management

32. a: Army alpha

33. : Incentive program

34. d: Virtual team

35. b: Edinburgh Postnatal Depression Scale

36. : Posttraumatic stress disorder

37. d: Sensation seeking

38. : Educational psychologist

39. d: Community psychology

40. a: Feminist therapy

41. b: Likert scale

42. d: Organizational citizenship behavior

43. b: Forensic

44. d: Classical conditioning

45. d: Albert Ellis

46. b: Ecological validity

47. a: External validity

48. : Perception management

49. c: Social marketing

50. c: Testing effect

51. d: Focus group

52. a: Norm-referenced test

53. : Learning

54. d: Evidence-based practice

55. c: Concurrent validity

56. d: Boston Naming Test

57. b: Self-report

58. a: Personnel psychology

59. d: Workplace bullying

People

1. d: UNITA

2. c: National Movement for Reform and Development

3. b: Slavery

4. : Maafa

CPSIA information can be obtained
at www.ICGtesting.com
Printed in the USA
LVHW062137311019
635718LV00025B/522/P

9 781538 851258